Praise for N

Church historians point to George Whitefield as the central figure in the 18th century awakenings in Great Britain and the American colonies. Many Christians have heard his name, and perhaps know that he was an itinerant evangelist who preached with great emotion. But few today seem to know or understand Whitefield's deep commitment to undergirding his practice of evangelism with a robust theology.

I am grateful for this work by Tim McKnight, based on his PhD dissertation (which I had the privilege of supervising.) McKnight helps us understand Whitefield's historical context, and shows how his evangelistic preaching flowed out of his theological commitments.

As an historian who is passionate about evangelism, I am thrilled to commend this book. It will help the reader not only understand Whitefield better, but also understand theology and the gospel better, all to the glory of the Lord Jesus Christ.

—Dr. Timothy K. Beougher
Associate Dean, Billy Graham School of Missions, Evangelism and Ministry; Billy Graham Professor of Evangelism and Church Growth, The Southern Baptist Theological Seminary, Louisville, KY

As a young seminarian a leader encouraged me to read at least one biography a year the rest of my life. This routine introduced me to a plethora of people used of God in history. George Whitefield rises to the top of all those whose lives I surveyed. He has become one of my favorite evangelists. My friend Tim McKnight has given the church a valuable resource on the life of Whitefield. This volume is both theologically rich and practically accessible. It demonstrates the heart and life of a man used of God while not ignoring he had feet of clay. Read it and be encouraged!

—Dr. Alvin L. Reid,
Senior Professor of Evangelism and Student Ministry/Bailey Smith Chair of Evangelism, Southeastern Baptist Theological Seminary, Wake Forest, NC

In this timely and needed work, Timothy McKnight gives us a three-dimensional portrait of a man whose theology drove his evangelism. May this book inspire scholars and pastors alike to imitate Whitefield's passion for expanding God's kingdom and making much of the name of Jesus Christ.

—Dr. Christian T. George
Associate Professor of Historical Theology,
Curator of the Spurgeon Library
Midwestern Baptist Theological Seminary, Kansas City

When I hear the word "evangelist" my ears automatically perk up and so does my heart rate. It's because I'm an evangelist. I've modeled much of my 30 years in ministry after Billy Graham. After reading *No Better Gospel* I'll be adding George Whitefield to the short list of evangelists I want to imitate. But you don't have to aspire to evangelism to enjoy this book. It is, simply put, a great read! Though academic in his treatment of Whitefield's theology and methodology of preaching, McKnight has managed to write a captivating story about a man who truly helped shape the fabric of a nation in it's nascent form. He winsomely uncovers the powerful influence of a preacher who, before the Declaration of Independence was even penned, had become a mighty tool in God's hands for the conversion of sinners to faith in Christ, while also becoming one of the most well-known Americans right before America actually became a country. This book is not simple history. It's compelling. And entertaining. And enlightening. It would benefit you to read it cover to cover.

—Clayton King
Teaching Pastor, Newspring Church

George Whitefield is one of the key figures in the history of Christianity in America, and in No Better Gospel, Tim McKnight offers a fascinating portrait of this dynamic evangelist. The book provides an interesting historical survey of Whitefield's life and ministry, then an in-depth exploration of his theological views and evangelistic methodology. Pastors and church leaders will particularly enjoy McKnight's study of issues such as Whitefield's views of the evangelistic invitation and his approach to personal evangelism. Given that Whitefield helped lay the foundation for what would eventually become the American Revolution, anyone with an interest in American history will also find this a compelling story.

—Dr. Michael Duduit
Dean, Clamp Divinity School of Anderson University, and
Executive Editor of *Preaching Magazine*

George Whitefield is one of the most significant catalysts behind the Great Awakening of the 18th Century, which was arguably one of the most influential movements of American Christian history. Whitefield was also one of the first celebrity pastors of evangelicalism, who has been viewed and was viewed by his contemporaries, with both uncritical esteem and unrelenting opposition. For these reasons, Whitfield and his ministry are well worth our consideration and reflection. Dr. Timothy McKnight has provided us with an engaging account of Whitfield's doctrine of soteriology and evangelistic methodology, through what I might call "theologically informed biography". McKnight writes with the expertise of a scholar and the heart of an experienced pastor, allowing the reader to journey through the life and thought of one of the great giants of American evangelical Christianity. This book is a great contribution to the church.

—Dr. Matthew Z. Capps
Senior Pastor
Fairview Baptist Church, Apex NC

No Better Gospel

George Whitefield's Theology and Methodology of Evangelism

No Better Gospel

Tim McKnight

Seed Publishing Group, LLC
Timmonsville, South Carolina

No Better Gospel

Copyright © 2017 by Tim McKnight

Published by:
Seed Publishing Group
2570 Double C Farm Ln
Timmonsville, SC 29161
seed–publishing–group.com

Seed Publishing Group is committed to bringing great resources to both individual Christians and the local church (please visit them at www.seed-publishing-group.com). As part of that commitment, they are partners with The Pillar Network for church planting (www.thepillarnetwork.com). $1 from each sale of *No Better Gospel* goes directly to church plants throughout North America. Thank you for purchasing *No Better Gospel,* and thank you for investing in church planting!

To order additional copies of this resource visit
www.seed–publishing–group.com.

Library of Congress Control Number: 2017958802

ISBN–13: 978-0-9985451-0-3

Printed in the United States of America

To Angela,
my love and earthly treasure,
and to
Noah, Micah, Karissa, and MaryAnna,
our gifts from God.

To Mom and Dad,
who consistently point me to Christ.

Abbreviations

SIS   *George Whitefield, Sermons on Important Subjects*

TWRGW   *George Whitefield, The Works of the Rev. George Whitefield*

CONTENTS

Contents

PREFACE

This book is the culmination of a journey with George Whitefield that began seventeen years ago. My Ph.D. supervisor at The Southern Baptist Theological Seminary, Dr. Tim Beougher, introduced me to Whitefield during a conversation regarding dissertation topics. That dissertation would form the foundation of this book.

As with every journey, there are companions who accompany you and help you to arrive at your destination. George Whitefield, my first companion, accompanied me through his sermons, journals, and letters, pointing me to the gospel, convicting me of my need to become a better witness in my actions and words, and warning me of potential pitfalls by allowing me to see his weaknesses.

My wife Angela has been my best traveling companion on this journey. She read every word printed in this book, giving invaluable input and feedback. More importantly she's served as my soul mate and companion in ministry these twenty years of marriage. We journeyed together through my deployment on Operation Noble Eagle and Operation Enduring Freedom shortly after September 11, 2001. We continue to grow together as we serve in ministry at Anderson University and Concord Baptist Church.

My children Noah, Micah, Karissa, and MaryAnna are traveling companions who bring me great joy in the midst of research and writing. I continue to thank God for the blessing they are to Angela and me.

My dean, Dr. Michael Duduit, provided consistent support and encouragement throughout the writing process. He has said, "No", once to me in the five years I have worked with him at Anderson University. Knowing my entrepreneurial spirit, that is a strong statement.

Dr. Bill Curtis graciously asked to publish this work because of his love for preaching the gospel and for George Whitefield. I appreciate his patience and counsel throughout this process. I also am thankful for his commitment to pastoring and church planting.

Dr. Nathan Finn, a new-found companion on this journey, served as an encourager and counselor through this process. I am deeply honored that he agreed to write the foreword to this work, as I possess deep respect for him as a brother in Christ, Christian scholar, and church historian.

Dr. Matt Capps, Pastor Spencer Haygood, and Dr. Ricky Stark provided priceless editorial advice throughout the writing process. Their fingerprints permeate this book.

Finally, my most faithful companion, Jesus Christ, continues to amaze me with His love and grace. I pray that I will be a faithful witness to Him in my actions and words. I pray that this book will bring glory to Him. I pray that it will motivate all who read it to become better stewards of the gospel. We can all be better witnesses, but we will find no better gospel!

FOREWORD

We live in an age when American evangelicalism is theologically fragmented and seemingly in numerical decline. Among the theological debates that tend to divide evangelicals, few are as "hot" as disputes over election, the nature of grace, the intent of the atonement, and the question of perseverance in the faith. Of course, this is not a new debate; Christians have never enjoyed consensus on these issues and entire ecclesial traditions have been formed around particular views of these doctrines. But in the internet age the arguments never cease and anyone with access to a computer can become a polemicist and pamphleteer on behalf of his doctrinal cause. The democratization of information online means that theological disputes, whether thoughtful or not, are always only one click away.

Numerically, evangelical believers comprise a smaller and smaller percentage of the US population. Many observers note the declension of intentional evangelism among believers, despite consistent evidence from researchers that most non-Christians are willing to accept an invitation to church and even hear a personal testimony or gospel presentation. Not too long ago, itinerant evangelists were household names among evangelicals and some, especially Billy Graham, were counted among the most respected figures in America. Today, relatively few believers (and virtually no unbelievers) are aware of the existence of vocational evangelists, and those evangelists who do have name recognition are famous for their partisan politics rather than their commitment to proclaiming the gospel to the lost.

These are two reasons why George Whitefield still matters today. As an ardent *Calvinistic* evangelist, he challenges the old canard that one cannot be a Calvinist and be zealous for the salvation of the lost. Whitefield preached the "doctrines of grace," sometimes resulting in controversy with other believers, but he also cooperated across denominational and theological lines. For Whitefield, the new birth united all authentic Christians, even as he maintained that Calvinism offered the most biblical account of certain aspects of the gospel. Like most of the famous revival preachers from the First Great Awakening, Whitefield saw no conflict between Reformed theology, intentional evangelism, and a longing for spiritual awakening. Some contemporary Calvinists (and many more non-Calvinists) need to be reminded that one can believe that God is sovereign in salvation and also pour himself out in being the means God uses to save those whom he has elected from before the foundation of the world.

As a convictionally Calvinistic *evangelist*, Whitefield reminds us that God calls some individuals to devote their full-time ministries to proclaiming the gospel among the lost. Whitefield preached the gospel to enormous crowds. He preached the gospel in individual homes. He shared the gospel with traveling companions and the orphans whom he provided a home. Like the best evangelists from Christian history, Whitefield was entrepreneurial, but kept his focus on the task at hand—the salvation of the lost. Though he was by no means perfect, he maintained a consistent Christian walk and never brought public scandal upon the name of Christ because of his own sin. Vocational evangelism has fallen on hard times, which is why we need more Whitefields in our own day—men (and women!) who are called and equipped by God to spend a lifetime laboring for the salvation of others.

American evangelicals could use a healthy dose of the spirit of George Whitefield. The good news is that interest seems to be rising. Recent years have witnessed some excellent academic and popular-level studies of the great evangelist, but until now no single work has focused its attention on expounding his theological convictions and demonstrating how they informed his evangelistic methodology. Tim McKnight is one of our very best scholar-practitioners of evangelism, and *No Better Gospel* is the best introduction to Whitefield the theologian-evangelist. By engaging with Whitefield's sermons, journals, and published writings, McKnight not only confirms that Whitefield was both a Calvinist and an evangelist, but he demonstrates how this relationship between theology and practice was not coincidental in Whitefield's life and ministry. Whitefield's Calvinism fueled his evangelism, and his evangelism was one of the fruits of his Calvinism. And God brought revival. He could do it again.

So "take up and read," whether you mostly agree with Whitefield's doctrine or still have your doubts. All of us can learn from Whitefield's model of theologically driven methodology in evangelism—and all of ministry. All of us can learn from Whitefield's passionate commitment to the salvation of souls. All of us can agree that the gospel is still mighty to save and that one day a multitude of believers from every tribe and tongue will gather around the throne (Rev. 7:9-12), regardless of whether Whitefield or Wesley is proven more correct about election and the atonement. And all of us can play our part in spreading the good news of Jesus Christ here, there, and everywhere. Let this book be a tool that equips and emboldens you to do so more faithfully.

—Nathan A. Finn
School of Theology and Missions
Union University

INTRODUCTION

In a recent biography of Whitefield, Thomas Kidd wrote of his fame in the colonies stating, "By 1740 he had become the most famous man in America. (In 1740 George Washington was eight years old, John Adams was four, Thomas Jefferson was not even born. Benjamin Franklin's fame as a printer, which did not extend much beyond Philadelphia, was enhanced by becoming Whitefield's publisher)."[1] Between 1738 and 1770, George Whitefield conducted seven evangelistic tours of the American colonies. His preaching and evangelistic efforts played a pivotal role in the movements of God known as the Evangelical Awakening and the First Great Awakening.[2]

During his itinerant ministry in America, he preached throughout the colonies and towns including New York, Philadelphia, Boston, Charleston, Savannah, Trent Town, Newport, Lewis Town, and Williamsburg. Thousands of Americans, approximately 80 percent of the population, came to hear this English itinerant preach.[3] Referring to Whitefield's tour of the colonies in 1740, Mark Noll writes:

> Before the tour came to an end in late November, he would preach in seven of the American colonies, often two or three times a day, and to crowds regularly into the thousands. It is likely that the total number of his hearers in these ten weeks (with, of course, some attending several times) equaled at least half of the total population of these seven colonies.[4]

In Philadelphia and Boston, Whitefield preached to audiences of ten and fifteen thousand.[5] Before his death on September 30, 1770, the "Great Itinerant" had preached at least eighteen thousand times.[6] Whitefield was so committed to preaching that, as he was dying, he expressed his deep regret of his inability to make a preaching engagement scheduled for the next day.[7]

Both believers and unbelievers commended the life and ministry of George Whitefield. Concerning Whitefield's character, Benjamin Franklin wrote that he "never had the least suspicion of his integrity, but am to this day decidedly of the opinion that he was in all his conduct a perfectly *honest man*; and methinks my testimony in his favour ought to have more weight, as we had no religious connection."[8] Concerning his preaching skills, Luke Tyerman wrote, "The preacher's sonorous voice, his intonations, his actions, his facial expressions, are things which could not be embodied in his published discourses; and yet, to things like these, the discourses were greatly indebted for their astonishing effects. Whitefield was the greatest gospel orator of the age."[9] Although the above accolades help introduce the reader to Whitefield, a biographical sketch of his life can help one better understand the man and his ministry.

Biographical Sketch

George Whitefield was born to Thomas and Elizabeth Whitefield on December 16, 1714 in Gloucester, England. When Whitefield was merely two years of age, his father died suddenly. Elizabeth was left with seven children and the family's inn. When Whitefield turned ten, his mother married an ironmonger named Capel Longden; however, the marriage ended in a bitter divorce, leaving Elizabeth again with seven children and the inn.

At the age of twelve, Whitefield enrolled in St. Mary de Crypt grammar school. In his early years at the school, he began to develop an interest in drama and public speaking. The decline of his mother's business at the inn cut short his first years at school. Concerning Whitefield's decision to quit school, his biographer and friend John Gillies commented, "Before he was fifteen, he persuaded his mother to take him from school, saying, that she could not place him at the university, and more learning would spoil him as a tradesman."[10] Having resigned himself to the idea that he could not attend the university, Whitefield helped his mother by serving guests and cleaning the inn; however, a servitor from Pembroke College at Oxford University interrupted his time away from school.[11] The young student informed Whitefield's mother that attending Oxford was possible for her son. Upon hearing this news, both son and mother agreed that he should finish grammar school and go to Oxford.

Possessed with a deep interest in religion, eighteen-year-old George Whitefield arrived at Oxford. He began to encounter Methodists and, impressed by their examples of piety, longed to be part of their group. In time, he met Charles and John Wesley who invited him to attend their meetings. Shortly after his involvement with the Wesleys and the Methodists, Whitefield fell under deep conviction of sin and was miraculously converted at the age of twenty.

After only a year, in 1736, the Church of England ordained twenty-one-year-old Whitefield a deacon. After preaching for the first time, Whitefield claimed "that a complaint had been made of the bishop, that I drove fifteen mad the first sermon."[12] Following this sermon, his popularity grew to the point that thousands of Englishmen came to hear him that year in Bristol and London. In 1737 six of his sermons were published, Whitefield received many invitations to preach in towns around England; however, he felt the call to be a missionary in Georgia and did not allow his popularity to distract him from this endeavor.

On May 7, 1738, he arrived in Savannah, Georgia. While in Georgia, Whitefield toured the land and met the leaders of the colony. He preached at every opportunity and visited in the homes of residents of Savannah and Frederica. It was during this first visit to Georgia that the young evangelist decided to build an orphanage in that colony.[13]

Whitefield returned to England in 1739 to raise funds for the orphanage and to gain approval for it from the Trustees of Georgia. While in England on January 11, 1739, Whitefield was ordained a priest. After receiving his ordination, he set out to preach throughout England and to obtain contributions for his Orphan House. After being refused access to several churches, George Whitefield preached his first open air sermon to a group of miners in Kingswood, England. He continued to preach in fields throughout the English countryside. During this year in England, it was common for crowds of ten to twenty thousand people to gather in the fields to hear Whitefield preach.[14]

The itinerant, however, did not allow the crowds to take his focus from his work in America. On August 14, 1739, Whitefield commenced his second voyage to the American colonies. During this visit, what is commonly known as the First Great Awakening began. His preaching played a key role in this revival. The evangelist preached in towns and cities throughout the colonies from New York to Savannah. He preached to thousands of people in Philadelphia and Boston. It was unusual for Whitefield to have less than one thousand audience members at any given time that he preached near a colonial town or city. Besides his preaching, he also formed relationships with American clergymen such as Jonathan Edwards, Gilbert Tennent, and William Tennent. Some of these clergy conducted follow up on Whitefield's evangelistic efforts after he left the colonies. Whitefield also began construction on the Orphan House in Georgia. It was, after all, the primary reason he traveled to America.

In March of 1741, upon returning to England, Whitefield encountered a hostile reception by groups whom John Wesley's published criticisms and sermons incited against his Calvinism. In response to Wesley's sermon "Free Grace," which attacked Whitefield's views on the doctrines of grace, Whitefield published a letter that refuted each point of Wesley's argument.[15] Despite this opposition from both friends and foes in England, Whitefield stayed three years in his native land. Toward the end of this visit to England, on November 14, 1741, the evangelist married Elizabeth James; however, he determined not to allow marriage to interrupt his travels or his preaching schedule.

Less than eight months after the loss of their four-month-old-son, John, the Whitefields left for America. During this third trip to the colonies (1745-1748), the evangelist discovered that opposition against him was not confined to England. Critics scorned Whitefield for appealing to people's passions, emphasizing the New Birth, dividing the clergy, and preaching in towns without approval of local clergy. The itinerant wrote responses to his critics and continued to preach to large audiences; however, the third trip witnessed the detrimental effect preaching had upon his health. Upon the suggestion of his doctor, the Whitefields left for Bermuda in 1748.

The orphanage's precarious financial condition cut short the evangelist's fourth visit to the colonies (1751-1752). During Whitefield's fifth trip (1754-1755), he returned to find his orphanage had prospered. Throughout this trip, he generally preached twice a day. Any further specific details of this fifth journey are difficult for scholars to construct due to the lack of letters from Whitefield describing this time of his life.

On his sixth voyage to America (1763-1765), the itinerant's ill health became more apparent than in his previous trips to the colonies. Whitefield suffered from severe asthma and angina. Rather than preaching twice a day, at times, sickness confined him to preaching only twice a week. Concerning the people's reaction to Whitefield's ill health, Arnold Dallimore writes, "The people, however, had heard earlier of his invalided condition, and it is evident that now, seeing him so changed and so weak, they looked upon him as indeed a dying man, and more than ever they held him in affection. Realizing they might have but few further opportunities, they came in still greater earnestness to hear him preach."[16] He did not disappoint them, but preached whenever his strength would allow him to stand.

Shortly before Whitefield was to embark on his seventh voyage to the colonies, his wife Elizabeth died of fever. Concerning his loss, the aging evangelist wrote, "I feel the loss of my right hand daily; but right hands and right eyes must be parted with for Him, who ordereth all things well."[17] True to the devotion to God he exemplified throughout his life, Whitefield did not allow his personal loss to prevent his passage to America.

In November 1769, the evangelist arrived in Charleston. He preached to large congregations there. Whitefield then traveled to Savannah where he attended a dedication ceremony for an addition to the Orphan House. The itinerant then ventured to Philadelphia and preached in the city and surrounding towns. From Philadelphia, Whitefield preached daily in various towns in New England. On the night of September 29, 1770, in Exeter, Massachusetts, George Whitefield preached his last sermon. He died the next day.

Whitefield the Calvinist

Regarding Whitefield's theology, many Christian scholars, church historians, and biographers agree that George Whitefield was a Calvinist.[18] In his biography of

Whitefield, Harry S. Stout writes, "From first to last he was a Calvinist who believed that God chose him for salvation and not the reverse."[19] Describing Whitefield's ministry, Stout states it was characterized by "an all-inclusive ecumenicity that was explicitly 'Calvinist' in theology and opposed to all forms of 'Arminianism.'"[20] He also notes that, in a letter to scholars at Harvard, Whitefield described himself as a Calvinist and stated that he would preach no other doctrines but Calvinism; however, as we will see, George Whitefield believed in evangelism and in calling his hearers to repent and believe in the gospel.[21]

Another biographer of Whitefield, Frank Lambert, identifies him as a Calvinist. He notes that Whitefield wrote a letter replying to critics who claimed he was a newcomer to Calvinism. In the letter, the English evangelist contended that he preached on the doctrine of election even before he left for America in 1739.[22] Regarding the theological content of Whitefield's sermons, Lambert writes, "Although Whitefield preached Calvinist tenets throughout his ministry, his was an evangelical Calvinism, one that emphasized the universal need for preaching."[23] Lambert also cites Whitefield's Calvinism as a reason for his success in the American colonies, asserting, "He was particularly appealing to colonial revivalists. His Calvinism linked him theologically to New England Congregationalists and Middle Colony Presbyterians."[24]

Two of the most comprehensive biographies of Whitefield echo Stout and Lambert's claims identifying Whitefield as a Calvinist. Luke Tyerman, in his two-volume biography of Whitefield, repeatedly designated George Whitefield a Calvinist. Like Lambert, Tyerman mentioned Whitefield's Calvinism as a reason for his warm reception and success in New England. He asserted:

> As to the creed of these miscellaneous religionists, there cannot be a doubt that, speaking generally, it was Calvinistic, and quite in harmony with those views of election and final perseverance which

Whitefield had embraced. In such a colony, Wesley would have been branded as a heretic; whereas Whitefield was warmly welcomed as a friend, whose faith was gloriously orthodox.[25]

Regarding the strong differences in theology between the Wesleys and George Whitefield, Tyerman noted, "Charles Wesley regarded Whitefield's Calvinism with abhorrence; and Whitefield regarded some of Wesley's doctrines as pernicious heresy."[26]

In another two-volume biography of Whitefield, Arnold Dallimore mentioned Whitefield's Calvinism. Regarding the reason for Whitefield's warm reception in Scotland, Dallimore explained, "Ever since his first rise to fame he had appeared a heroic figure in the minds of Gospel-loving people everywhere, and to many in Scotland he seemed very much an embodiment of their ideals: he too was a Calvinist, yet his Calvinism was not mere theory, but, as advocated by *The Marrow*, it was doctrine aglow with evangelistic fire."[27] Describing Whitefield's theological understanding shortly before he was ordained a deacon in 1736, Dallimore asserted:

Certainly the terms "free grace" and "justified by faith only" did not, at this early time, have the immense meaning for him which, as we shall see, he enunciated with clarity and conviction in 1739. Nevertheless, it is evident that he had grasped certain fundamental truths: he knew salvation was a Divine work—the placing of "the life of God in the soul of man"—and that it was an eternal work. These truths were already a foundation upon which he was, from this time forth, to build a steadily increasing understanding and finally a system of theology. This was the beginning of his lifelong adherence to what he called "the doctrines of grace"—the system commonly known as Calvinism.[28]

Besides Dallimore and Tyerman, authors of numerous essays and journal articles on Whitefield note the English evangelist's Calvinism. Church historian Mark Noll comments that "Unlike later American revivalists, Whitefield was a Calvinist."[29] In an essay entitled "John Calvin and George Whitefield," D. M. Lloyd-Jones noted, "George Whitefield was a follower of the teaching of Calvin. He was a truly Reformed man in his doctrine, whereas Wesley was Arminian."[30] Addressing Whitefield's Reformed theology, J. I. Packer identifies Whitefield as "an Anglican Calvinist of the Puritan type."[31]

The above examples are only a few of the plethora of printed works that describe George Whitefield as a Calvinist. I know of only one work on Whitefield that does not affirm his adherence to Calvinism. Stuart C. Henry, in his biography entitled *George Whitefield, Wayfaring Witness*, denied Whitefield was a Calvinist because the evangelist stated that he had not read Calvin; however, this biographer also quoted Whitefield's admission that he "embraced the 'calvinistical scheme, not because *Calvin*, but Jesus Christ'" had taught it to him. In the same chapter Henry denied Whitefield's Calvinism, he mentioned Whitefield's belief in human depravity, predestination, and unconditional election.[32] With the exception of Henry, every Christian scholar, church historian, and biographer I encountered in his research identified Whitefield as a Calvinist. I know of no scholar besides Henry who has denied the English itinerant's Calvinism.

Whitefield the Evangelist

Christian scholars, church historians, and biographers also agree that George Whitefield was a passionate evangelist. Numerous testimonies throughout church history praise this itinerant preacher's zeal for evangelism.[33] In a sermon preached on the occasion of Whitefield's death, John Wesley queried:

> Have we read or heard of any person since the apostles, who testified the gospel of the grace of God, through so widely extended space, through so large a part of the habitable world? Have we read

or heard of any person, who called so many thousands, so many myriads of sinners to repentance? Above all, have we read or heard of any, who has been a blessed instrument in his hand of *bringing so many sinners form darkness to light, and from the power of Satan unto God?*[34]

Biographers of Whitefield present accolades regarding his evangelistic efforts. Luke Tyerman wrote, "George Whitefield was pre-eminently the outdoor preacher, evangelist extraordinaire who pioneered open-air preaching;--the most popular evangelist of the age;--a roving revivalist,--who, with unequalled eloquence and power, spent above thirty years testifying to enormous crowds, in Great Britain and America, the gospel of the grace of God."[35] J. C. Ryle claimed that Whitefield "seemed to live only for two objects—the glory of God and the salvation of souls."[36] In his history of preaching, Edwin Charles Dargan asserted, "The history of preaching since the apostles does not contain a greater or worthier name than that of George Whitefield (1714-1770)."[37] Arnold Dallimore contended that "Whitefield was superbly equipped for the work to which God had called him—'the work of an evangelist.'... God has had His great and good men in all ages, but there can be little doubt Whitefield deserves the primacy often accorded him: 'The greatest evangelist since Paul.'"[38] D. M. Lloyd-Jones said of Whitefield, "Here is the greatest evangelist England had ever produced and he was a Calvinist."[39]

Although a great preponderance of evidence affirms that Whitefield was indisputably a Calvinist and an evangelist, few authors have attempted to explore the relationship between Whitefield's Calvinistic theology and his evangelistic methodology. Those works that have mentioned this association present only brief treatments regarding the topic. J. I. Packer presents an indirect discussion of the issue in the last five pages of his essay entitled "The Spirit with the Word."[40] In a five-page essay examining the relationship between Calvinism and evangelism, Packer mentions Whitefield twice as an example that "Calvinists can really be evangelists."[41] D. M. Lloyd-Jones, in his essay on Calvin and Whitefield, devoted a single paragraph to contend that Whitefield's Calvinism was compatible with and motivated his evangelistic zeal. Stuart C. Henry devoted eleven pages of his biography of Whitefield to examine whether the evangelist's presentation of a universal invitation to accept the gospel was consistent with his professed Calvinism.[42] Henry is the *only* author this writer encountered who contended, "The chronic dilemma of the Calvinist who seeks to justify the validity of his preaching to a humanity that can respond only to the voice of God, Whitefield solved uniquely: he professed Calvinism, lived by an Arminian faith, and preached them both."[43]

My Journey with Whitefield

An introduction into the longstanding debate regarding the compatibility between Calvinism and evangelism led me to my interest in George Whitefield. As a young Ph.D. student, I encountered John Wesley's sermon entitled "Free Grace." Within this message, Wesley contended against Calvinism in general and the doctrine of predestination in particular. He asserted that Calvinism removes the validity of and motivation for preaching the gospel. Wesley wrote:

> But if this be so, then is all preaching in vain. It is needless to them that are elected; for they, whether with preaching or without, will infallibly be saved. Therefore, the end of preaching—to save souls—is void with regard to them; and it is useless to them that are not elected, for they cannot possibly be saved: They, whether with preaching or without, will infallibly be damned. The end of preaching is therefore void with regard to them likewise; so that

in either case our preaching is vain, as your hearing is also in vain.[44]

Shortly after reading this sermon, I discovered Whitefield's response to Wesley. Regarding the above quote, Whitefield replied:

> Hath not God, who hath appointed salvation for a certain number, appointed also the preaching of the word, as a means to bring them to it? Does any one hold election in any other sense? And if so, how is preaching needless to them who are elected; when the gospel is designed by God himself, to be the power of God unto their eternal salvation? And since we know not who are elect, and who reprobate, we are to preach promiscuously to all. For, the word may be useful, even to non-elect, in restraining them from much wickedness and sin.[45]

I became curious regarding Whitefield's theology and methodology of evangelism. My curiosity prompted two questions: What was Whitefield's theology and methodology of evangelism? What was the relationship between the two? These two essential questions led to other inquiries: Was he really a Calvinist and a passionate evangelist? Were the English evangelist's sermons both Calvinistic in theology and evangelistic in their presentations of the gospel? Did he profess Calvinism, yet preach like an Arminian?

My attempts to answer the above questions revealed the necessity of obtaining an understanding of the eighteenth-century historical and theological context of England and the American colonies. This pursuit led to the discovery of Peter Toon's book entitled *The Emergence of Hyper-Calvinism in English Nonconformity, 1689-1765* and an introduction to the debate between Calvinism and hyper-Calvinism which occurred during the beginning and the end of the eighteenth century.[46] Two of the primary issues raised in this contention were whether preachers should extend a universal invitation to the gospel and whether it was obligatory for non-elect hearers to respond affirmatively to such invitations.[47] Study of this eighteenth-century interchange prompted me to ask a number of questions regarding Whitefield: Did he believe ministers should extend universal invitations to the gospel? How did he invite people to respond to the gospel in his preaching? Did Whitefield believe and did he communicate in his preaching the idea that all of his hearers were responsible to repent and believe in Christ? How did Whitefield view offers of salvation in evangelistic preaching?

I searched for any sources that would answer the above questions through an analysis of the relationship between Whitefield's theology and methodology of evangelism. I found, as mentioned previously, that no other Christian scholar, church historian, or biographer had examined thoroughly the connection between the English itinerant's theology and methodology of evangelism. The absence of literary work regarding this issue prompted me to make such an analysis the focus of this book.

One must limit the scope of the question, due to the numerous historical, theological, and methodological issues surrounding George Whitefield and the eighteenth-century context of the Great Awakening. A failure to do so would result in a study too broad for the scope of this work.

This book does not attempt to present an exhaustive analysis of every aspect of George Whitefield's theology. He never attempted to produce a systematic theology nor claimed to be a systematic theologian; however, even a surface reading of the English evangelist's sermons reveals he took great interest in doctrine. Whitefield concentrated most of his thought, preaching, and writing upon the doctrines of grace and the doctrine of the new birth; therefore, the question regarding his theology of evangelism will discuss the evidence of these doctrines in his life and preaching.

Similarly, there is a plethora of aspects of George Whitefield's methodology that one may address in a discussion of his ministry. Some historians focus on Whitefield's use of the press in promoting his preaching and the First Great Awakening.[48] Another author emphasizes Whitefield's oratory skills and use of drama in the pulpit.[49] One could even conduct a word count study of Whitefield's sermons to determine the prevalence of various words or concepts in his preaching.[50]

Forging Ahead

In this book, I analyze and describe Whitefield's Calvinistic theology and his evangelistic methodology, and explore the relationship between the two. In the introduction, I present a brief biographical sketch, establish Whitefield's reputation as a Calvinist evangelist, offer some questions regarding Whitefield from my own journey, and clarify the limitations to the scope of this work.

In Chapter 1, I lay some contextual groundwork by investigating the historical and theological milieu of eighteenth-century England and the American colonies. In this regard, several items merit some consideration, including: (1) the state of the church in England and the colonies and the significant groups and beliefs affecting the period; (2) a discussion of church membership, especially as the Thirty-Nine Articles of the Anglican churches and the Half-Way Covenant in New England Congregational churches bore on the matter; (3) and an examination of the eighteenth-century controversy over Calvinism and Hyper-Calvinism, a matter encompassing such issues as whether a Calvinist can or should extend a universal invitation to embrace the gospel, whether means should be used in evangelism, and whether sinners who are not elect are still accountable to respond to the gospel.

In Chapter 2, I explore Whitefield's theology of evangelism by sifting through his *Works*, *Journals*, and sermons and (1) offering an assessment of the influence the Thirty-Nine Articles had in his theology; (2) setting out Whitefield's own views regarding total depravity, unconditional election, limited atonement, irresistible grace, and perseverance of the saints; and (3) delineating his views on new birth, justification, sanctification, and the content of the gospel message.

In Chapter 3, I inquire into Whitefield's methodology of evangelism, again by digging into his *Works*, *Journals*, and sermons. How did he give instructions to his listeners, and how did he treat the cross in such invitations? What direction and counsel did he give inquirers? How did he use letter writing for personal evangelism and follow-up? What place did societies, and ministry evangelism, and cooperation with other ministers hold in his evangelistic method?

In the conclusion, I submit for your consideration a concise but deliberate treatment of the relationship between Whitefield's Calvinistic theology and evangelistic methodology. Then, to close, I unpack the practical significance of his particular theological evangelism (or, we might also say, his evangelistic theology) for Our Time.

CHAPTER ONE

George Whitefield's Historical and Theological Context

George Whitefield's evangelistic efforts in England and the American colonies did not occur in a vacuum. To understand fully the theological and methodological aspects of his evangelistic ministry, one must first grasp the theological, ecclesiological, and historical context of eighteenth-century England and America that surrounded that ministry. While the scope of this book does not permit an exhaustive treatment of these factors, a summary of some of the significant individuals, topics, and events related to the theology, ecclesiology, and history of the eighteenth century is helpful in placing the First Great Awakening and George Whitefield's ministry in context.

State of the Church in England

Numerous writers from a wide range of disciplines acknowledge that the Church of England experienced significant decline during the early middle period of the eighteenth century. Alfred Plummer wrote that "the history of the English Church during the eighteenth century is the history of a steady and grievous decline."[51] Another church historian asserted, "The early days of the century witnessed a declension in religion in public morality scarcely to be matched in the history of the nation."[52]

The observations of these historians coincide with the descriptions made by eighteenth-century contemporaries regarding the state of the church and society. The French philosopher Voltaire made numerous comments regarding the Church's decline in England. He relished in announcing that Christianity was dying in England. Voltaire also commented that "there was only just enough religion left in England to distinguish Tories who had little from Whigs who had less."[53] The English philosopher David Hartley delineated six factors that led to the decline of the Church of England in the eighteenth century. He cited:

> First, the great growth of atheism and infidelity, particularly amongst the governing part of these states.
>
> Secondly, the open and abandoned lewdness, to which great numbers of both sexes, especially in the high ranks of life, have given themselves up.
>
> Thirdly, the sordid avowed self-interest, which is almost the sole motive of action in those who are concerned in the administration of public.
>
> Fourthly, the licentiousness and contempt of every kind of authority, divine, and human, which is so notorious in inferiors of all ranks.
>
> Fifthly, the great worldly-mindedness of the clergy, and their gross neglects of the discharge of their proper functions.
>
> Sixthly, the carelessness and infatuation of parents and magistrates with respect to the education of youth, and the consequent early corruption of the rising generation.[54]

These disturbing observations came not only from individuals outside the Church of England, but from her own clergymen. Church historians repeatedly refer to the former Bishop of Bristol Joseph Butler's comments regarding the state of the English Church and society as an accurate description of the clergy's understanding of the situation. In the advertisement to his work written in 1736, Butler wrote:

It is come, I know not how to be taken for granted, by many persons, that Christianity is not so much as a subject of inquiry; but that it is, now at length, discovered to be fictitious. Accordingly, they treat it, as if, in the present age, this were an agreed point among all people of discernment; and nothing remained, but to set it up as a principal subject of mirth and ridicule, as it were by way of reprisals, for its having long interrupted the pleasures of the world.[55]

Such evidence regarding the decline of the English Church and society in the early eighteenth century raises the question, "What factors and events led to such decline?"

Church and State

One factor that contributed to the decline of the Church of England and the English Church was the close relationship that existed between the government and the Church of England during the eighteenth century. The Church of England was essentially the State Church.[56] On the intermingling of the Church of England and the State, Alfred Plummer commented, "But the affairs of Church and State were so closely intertwined that every leading statesman had an immense influence on the Church, and, either from choice or necessity, many of the clergy, and most of the bishops, were politicians."[57]

The fact that the Court appointed the bishops of the Church of England is an axiomatic indicator of the close relationship between Church and State.[58] As members of English Parliament's House of Lords, bishops possessed the power to influence the government through their votes. Gerald Cragg wrote, "The appointment of bishops was one of the few ways in which the balance of power could be affected, and it became a matter of prime concern to select men of proven party loyalty. In making appointments, political considerations outweighed all others."[59] The gentry often appointed relatives or close friends to bishoprics, because they knew these appointments would prove politically loyal; therefore, they did not appoint bishops solely based upon their spiritual maturity, theological integrity, or piety.

This intermingling of Church and State created a ripe atmosphere for factions both within and without the Church of England. A brief delineation of a few of the various factions helps paint a clearer political, ecclesiastical, and historical picture of Whitefield's eighteenth-century milieu.

The Tories and the High Church party. The Tories and their counterparts in the Church of England, the High Churchmen, are the first parties we will examine. Who were the Tories? Alfred Plummer stated, "The Tories, strongest in the country, were for the exclusive privileges of the English Church and for divine right. The nation as a whole, had more sympathy with the Tories than with the Whigs. It was quite determined as to two points: (1) to defend the Established Church, and (2) to exclude any Roman Catholic from the throne."[60] They stood firmly against any attempt to withdraw power from the king or the established church. Tories opposed any effort to grant Nonconformists or Dissenters freedom.

The High Churchmen were Anglican clergymen, Tories, who advocated the unity of the Christian monarchy and Christian Parliament that would exercise their power in and through the Church of England. The increasing number of Dissenters shocked the members of this party. They attributed the decline in attendance at services and the Eucharist throughout Anglican churches to the Act of Toleration that granted Dissenters their freedom of worship. The High Churchmen opposed other Anglican ministers who were tolerant toward the Dissenters. This group of Tories advocated the censorship of books that damaged the faith of the people or led them to disrespect the clergy. They sought to defend the Church of England against decline and "to return to the concept of a national Church in a Christian realm, the clergy exercising spiritual discipline over the whole nation, supported by the laity acting through Parliament."[61]

The Whigs and the Low Church party. The Whigs came largely from towns and cities. The middle class, including merchants and businessmen, formed most of this political party's composition. They believed in "religious toleration and the right of the people to elect and control the King."[62] This political party advocated extending more rights and freedoms to the Dissenters or Nonconformists; however, Whigs also realized that they must attempt to maintain support in the Church of England to secure the bishops' seats in the House of Lords.[63] In the spirit of such toleration, the members advocated freedom of the press and an openness to the interaction of various viewpoints within society, the Church, and government.

The Low Churchmen were Whig clergymen within the Church of England who proposed more toleration both within and outside of the Church. These more tolerant clergymen possessed control over the Church of England in the eighteenth century.[64] The Latitudinarians made up most of the Low Churchmen's composition.[65] The High Churchmen particularly opposed the Latitudinarians because of the "sympathy for the novel and horribly fashionable skepticism" this group of Low Churchmen adopted from the wave of rationalism that crashed upon eighteenth-century England.[66] During the early years, until their seizure of power around 1715, the Low Churchmen bitterly contested their High Church brethren in the Church of England.[67]

Dissenters/Nonconformists. Although the Dissenters/Nonconformists were a religious group established because of religious differences, they are significant to this discussion because of the contentious political struggle which occurred during the eighteenth century regarding the issue of granting them freedom and toleration. The Nonconformists were largely middle class and sympathetic to the Whigs.

The Act of Uniformity (1662) augmented Dissenters' conflicts with the Church of England. This Act stated that only clergy who had received episcopal ordinations could preside over the churches. It also stipulated that all clergy must swear not to oppose the authority of the Church of England or the State. In addition, the Act mandated that all clergy accept and support the Prayer Book. The Dissenters could not conform to the stipulations presented by the Act of Uniformity; therefore, they separated from the Church of England.[68]

The Act of Uniformity was one of many legislative measures designed to limit the freedom of the Dissenters. Regarding legal action against Nonconformists, Gerald Cragg wrote:

> The Act of Uniformity was merely one part of a wider programme for suppressing the nonconformists. The Corporation Act (1661) had already debarred them from holding municipal office; the Five Mile Act (1664) was directed against ministers, and the Conventicle Acts (1664 and 1670) against people who attended their services of worship. Collectively this legislation forms the Clarendon Code, named after Charles's great Chancellor, but the responsibility of fashioning this engine of repression rests with the ardently Anglican House of Commons.[69]

With the growth of the Whig Party and the Low Churchmen, Dissenters began to experience more freedom. The Toleration Act (1690) granted Nonconformists more freedom of worship. Ministers who registered their places of worship and agreed with the Thirty-Nine Articles were free to preach and build chapels for worship. Although this Act granted Dissenters more freedom, it did not repeal the previous pieces of legislation that prohibited the same freedoms; however, it did terminate the enforcement of those restrictive statutes.

Though one might assume that the increase in freedom led to an increase in population of Dissenters in the early eighteenth century, this group actually decreased in number. Explaining this decline, Roy Porter wrote:

> Dissenters faced the dilemma of being neither persecuted nor privileged....Old Dissent lost is spur to zeal and minded its own business, and the grandchildren of revolutionary Puritans became quietists, inward-looking and even lukewarm, as worldly in their own prim way as Anglicans. Early in the century there were about 179,000 Presbyterians, 59,000 Independents (or Congregationalists), 58,000 Baptists and 38,000 Quakers. Many sidled over to conformity or just became indifferent. The tally of Dissenters may have fallen by up to 40 percent between 1700 and 1740.[70]

Naturally, this decline did not bode well for the condition of the Dissenting churches before the First Great Awakening and the ministry of George Whitefield.

What do we know about the various Dissenting denominations? Many Nonconformist denominations contributed to the religious landscape of the era. The Presbyterians were a significant group during this epoch in English history. They emphasized Puritan Calvinism and practiced a Reformed view of church discipline. Richard Baxter was one of the Puritans who influenced this denomination.

The Congregationalists stressed the doctrine of the "gathered Church." John Owen was one of the founding leaders of this denomination. They stressed the importance of the laity and allowed lay persons to form churches and draw up covenants before calling a pastor. The churches made decisions through meetings of and votes by the members. The Congregationalists emphasized the importance of members professing faith. Gordon Rupp noted, "Congregationalists differed from the Presbyterians, and perhaps from the early Separatists, in demanding not only a profession of faith from candidates of membership or for admission to Holy Communion, but an account of Christian experience."[71] Although they emphasized the importance of such examinations, lapses in this practice led to the numbers of unregenerate members who became true converts as a result of the First Great Awakening.[72]

The Baptists were another group of Dissenters in England during the eighteenth century. The two main groups were the Particular Baptists and the General Baptists. Particular Baptists adhered to a Calvinistic theology, while General Baptists rejected particular redemption and adopted a more Arminian theology. Both groups organized churches into associations or assemblies. They did not adopt creeds, but did draft a number of confessions of faith.[73] Although the Particular Baptists emphasized the importance of education, many Baptist pastors received no formal training.

Although other religious groups were present in eighteenth-century England, those were some of the more significant denominations at the time. They also help illustrate the close relationship between Church and State that existed in eighteenth-century England. The intermingling of political and ecclesiological affairs created numerous factions among ministers within the Church of England, among Dissenters, and between Anglican clergymen and Nonconformist ministers. Describing the extent of these arguments and contentions, E. J. Poole-Connor wrote:

> Churchmen began to gird against Dissenters; Dissenters to grow pugnacious against Churchmen; High-Churchmen under Atterbury quarreled with Low-Churchmen under Wake; Non-jurors attacked both; the Orange and Stuart factions renewed their antagonisms; others added their quota of independent assaults. A free-for-all battle began to be joined.[74]

The disputes resulting from this disunity and political strife drew the attention of both Anglican and Dissenting clergy away from more critical spiritual issues with English society. The close relationship between Church and State, particularly the political appointments and political functions of bishops, also contributed to the evident decline in the quality of Anglican clergymen during the eighteenth century.

State of the Clergy

Although some faithful Anglican clergymen conducted ministry during the eighteenth century, overall a decline in the quality of ministers from the Church of England characterized this period of English history. Mark Noll asserted that "even objective evaluators have recognized that confident religious life, persuasive preaching of the gospel and effective Christian pastoring were in relatively short supply during the first decades of the eighteenth century."[75]

While assessments from historians of the caliber of Noll are invaluable, the most credible comments regarding the state of clergy in this era come from their peers. One cleric, Archdeacon Blackburne wrote:

> The collective body of the clergy, excepting a very inconsiderable number, consists of men whose lives and occupations are most foreign to their profession—courtiers, politicians, lawyers, merchants, usurers, civil magistrates, sportsmen, musicians, stewards of country squires, tools of men in power, and even companions of rakes and infidels, not to mention the ignorant herd of poor curates to whom the instruction of common people is committed, who are accordingly, in religious matters, the most ignorant common people who are in any Protestant, not to say in any Christian society upon the face of the earth.[76]

In his call for clerical reform entitled *Discourse of the Pastoral Care* (1712), Archbishop Gilbert Burnet grieved over the condition of priests during the early eighteenth century. Regarding many priests' ignorance of the Scriptures, he bemoaned that they "cannot make it appear that they have read the Scriptures or any one good book since they were ordained; so that the small measure of knowledge upon which they got into holy orders not being improved, is in a way to be quite lost; and then they think it is a great hardship if they are told they must know the Scriptures and the body of divinity better, before they can be trusted with the care of souls."[77] This archbishop also lamented the negative effects of the intermingling between the clergy and politics. He asserted:

> Politics and party eat out among us not only study and learning, but at which is the only thing that is more valuable, a true sense of religion, a sincere zeal in advancing that for which the Son of GOD both lived and died, and to which those who are received into holy orders have vowed to dedicate their lives and labors....But a remiss unthinking course of life, with little or no application to study, and the bare performing of that, which if not done, would draw censures when complained of, without ever pursuing the duties of the pastoral care in any suitable degree, is but too common, as well as too evident.[78]

In short, he grieved over the fact that his brothers in ministry concerned themselves more with politics than they did with personal piety or their respective ministries.

Many bishops of the time allowed their political responsibilities to overshadow their pastoral duties. To have an impact in the House of Lords, it was necessary for the bishops to be present to cast their votes. The patrons who appointed them to their bishoprics depended upon their political allegiance and activity. Bishops who were absent from London lost their influence and connection with the political process. Norman Sykes wrote, "Residence in London for the greater part of the year was indeed essential if the episcopate was to maintain an interest and concern in public affairs. In an age of slow travel and slower circulation of news, propinquity to the capital was indispensable for bishops desiring to participate in the business of state."[79]

Such absenteeism of bishops from their dioceses detrimentally affected the Church of England, both clergy and congregations. While the bishops were in London for extended periods, they remained absent from their areas of ministerial responsibility. Some bishops never entered their sees throughout their tenure.[80] They neglected pastoral duties within their respective sees and could not adequately supervise the ministers under them from London. A few bishops were pluralists who obtained political appointments to multiple bishoprics, making it impossible for them to provide adequate pastoral coverage to the members of their dioceses.

The absence of the bishops also prevented them from presiding over ordination councils. It was common for bishops to issue Letters Dismissory that allowed another bishop to ordain candidates based upon their recommendation within their letter. Often bishops who issued such letters never even examined the candidate in any way at all.[81] They ordained some candidates without any firm evidence that they had an understanding of theology, let alone a degree in the subject.[82] Regarding this crisis, Sykes commented:

> Around the administration of the rite of ordination there gathered a further crop of difficulties, associated particularly with the grant of testimonials and the bestowal of titles, which increased the embarrassment of the episcopate. A general agreement existed that the aggregate of ordinations was too great, and considerably in excess of the practical possibilities of regular employment, but the establishment of a due and proportionate relation

between the number of persons admitted to Holy Orders and the benefices available for their preferment was a task entirely beyond the execution of the bench.[83]

In other words, in many cases, political expediency became more of a factor in ordination than the candidate's knowledge of theology or spiritual piety.

The immense wealth of the Church of England drew numerous candidates for ordination. Denied the possibility of obtaining wealth and status from the gentry, sons of lesser gentry looked toward the ministry as an avenue for attaining such benefits. The leniency of the ordination process, coupled with the fact that bishoprics were political appointments, allowed candidates to enter the ministry who concerned themselves more with greed and obtaining affluence than with piety or a pursuit of personal holiness. Most of the clergy could capably prepare sermons and defenses against attackers of the Church; however, their personal lives, although not publicly scandalous, did not reflect a desire to live above reproach. On this matter, John Overton asserted that their "speculation was not carried into practice. The doctrine was accepted, but the life was not lived."[84] Gerald Cragg argued that "the standards of the clergy were not conspicuously higher than those of their society. They had a leavening, not a transforming effect, but at least the Church did not stand aloof from the life of the age."[85]

Rationalism and the Church of England

Another factor that weakened the Church of England during the early eighteenth century was an attack by rationalists. This group of philosophers elevated reason above faith in their pursuit of understanding. They contended that belief was primarily the result of rational proof, and could solve numerous theological problems. These thinkers also elevated reason above revelation. They proposed that human beings are able to come to faith through reasonable observation of nature. They called such an application of reason natural religion.

The primary proponent of rationalist thinking in England was John Locke. Two of his works, *An Essay Concerning Human Understanding* (1690) and *The Reasonableness of Christianity* (1695), delineate this rationalist's understanding of the relationship between various matters of faith and reason. Locke argued that reason judges whether a particular revelation is valid, true, and accurate. He wrote:

> Reason is natural revelation, whereby the eternal Father of light, the fountain of all knowledge, communicates to mankind that portion of truth which he has laid within the reach of their natural faculties: revelation is natural reason enlarged by a new set of discoveries communicated by God immediately, which reason vouches the truth of, by the testimony and proofs it gives that they come from God.[86]

This rationalist believed that revelation was subordinate to reason. In another example of Locke's understanding of the relationship between revelation and reason, he asserted that no revelation may "shake or overrule plain knowledge; or rationally prevail with any man to admit it for true, in a direct contradiction to the clear evidence of his own understanding."[87]

Besides denigrating the role of revelation when compared to reason, Locke also countered the ideas of human depravity and the inability of human beings to come to God based upon their own ability and effort. He believed that human beings possess a divine spark that enables them to come to a relationship with an understanding of God through the application of reason alone. In his discussion of the fate of persons who never hear of Christ, Locke wrote:

God had, by the light of reason, revealed to all mankind, who would make use of that light, that he was good and merciful. The same spark of the divine nature and knowledge in man, which making him a man, showed him the law he was under, as a man; showed him also the way of atoning the merciful, kind, compassionate Author and Father of him and his being, when he transgressed that law. He that made use of this candle of the Lord, so far as to find what was his duty, could not miss to find also the way to reconciliation and forgiveness, when he had failed of his duty; though, if he used not his reason this way, if he put out or neglected this light, he might, perhaps, see neither.[88]

Rather than focusing upon the doctrine of original sin and the resulting guilt that all humankind shares, Locke contended that men possessed an innate ability to find God through natural application of their reason. He maintained that humans are not totally depraved from birth; rather, they are like blank slates on which no writing has yet occurred. There is no sin in them from birth that separates them from God; however, they must use their rational skills to seek Him. Rather than focusing on Christ's death on the cross being a satisfaction of God's wrath over man's guilt and sin and faith in such an atonement as the foundation of saving faith, Locke contended that the confession that Jesus Christ was the Messiah is the only foundation of faith. He proposed that individuals who reasonably assent to this belief and who follow Christ's moral teachings are Christians.

Such rationalist ideas influenced clergymen within the Church of England.[89] This rationalistic philosophy also laid the foundation for other beliefs and world views—such as Deism and Latitudinarianism--that directly challenged the doctrines traditionally held by the Church of England.

The Deists. In their history of the Church of England in the eighteenth century, Charles Abbey and John Overton declared:

> Of the many controversies which were rife during the first half of the eighteenth century, none raised a question of greater importance than that which lay at the root of the Deistical controversy. That question was, in a word, this—How has God revealed Himself—how is He still revealing Himself to man? Is the so-called written Word the only means—is it the chief means—is it even a means at all, by which the Creator makes His will known to His creatures?[90]

The Deists presented a number of controversial and unbiblical answers to these questions.

Alfred Plummer presented an excellent description of Deists, stating, "On the whole, what they contended *for* was Natural Religion, and what they contended *against* was Supernatural Religion."[91] Deists refuted the idea that God is personally involved in the everyday events of the world and of humankind. They believed that God created the universe, established various natural laws, and left the universe to function from those laws of nature rather than from His daily intervention in natural affairs. Deists contended that revelation is not necessary for one to obtain a relationship with or knowledge of God. Influenced by Locke's rationalism, they claimed that mere rational observation and reflection of God's creation leads to knowledge of God. In relation to revelation, Deists considered the Bible both unnecessary and unreliable. No revelation possessed the same power and force as natural revelation through the created universe.

Matthew Tindal and Thomas Woolston were two Deists of this era who promoted their views through written media. In his work *Christianity as Old as the Creation, or the Gospel, a Republication of the Religion of Nature*, Tindal asserted that nature, not the gospel of Scripture, is the highest revelation of God. Attacking the validity and authority of Scripture, this Deist wrote, "There's no book, but you may own its infallibility, and yet be entirely governed by your reason, if you, as often as you find any thing not agreeable to your reason, torture it, to make it speak what is so."[92] Tindal argued further that God's intention is for the happiness of humankind. The gospel must not be true because God's condemnation of humans would fly contrary to His pursuit of their happiness.

Thomas Woolston chipped away further at Christian doctrine in his work *Six Discourses on the Miracles of Our Saviour and Defences of His Discourses 1727-1730*. In these six discourses, Woolston refuted the claim that Christ's miracles attest to His messianic identity. He argued that the miracles of Christ are not to be read literally, but allegorically. Woolston further claimed that such signs and wonders "are none of the proper miracles of the Messiah, nor are they so much as a good proof of Jesus' divine authority to found and introduce a religion in to the world."[93] This Deist asserted that such miracle accounts in the gospels are unreliable and inaccurate. Woolston contended that the physical resurrection of Christ was a farce. He declared:

> Who knows not, that many errors in philosophy, and as many frauds in religion have been sometimes accidentally, sometimes designedly espoused and palm'd upon mankind, who in the process of time become so wedded to them thro' prejudice and interest, that they will not give themselves leave to enquire into the rise and foundation of them. False miracles have been common things among Christians; and as the resurrection of Jesus is their grand and fundamental one, so it is not at all difficult to account for the rise, propagation and continuance of the belief in it.[94]

Clergymen from both the Church of England and Dissenting congregations met such attacks with vehement responses. One of the strongest refutations of Deism was Bishop Joseph Butler's treatise entitled *The Analogy of Religion to the Constitution and Course of Nature,* in which he attacked the Deists' presuppositions and presumptions. He questioned whether individuals can know if their application of reason is accurate in situations when there may be a reality that is supernatural rather than natural. Butler contended that "there is no presumption at all from analogy, that the *whole* course of things, or divine government naturally unknown to us, and *everything* in it, is like to anything in that which is known; and therefore no peculiar presumption against any thing in the former, upon account of its being unlike to any thing in the latter."[95] Butler expounded that the inability of individuals to comprehend or find a cognitive reference for the unknown reality of miracles does not negate their reliability, tangibility, or truth.

Butler's argument is representative of the many sermons, pamphlets, and treatises Anglican and Dissenting clergymen wrote against the Deists.[96] English ministers expended much time and energy defending their doctrines against this attack. The sudden demise of Deism in the middle of the eighteenth century testifies to the strength of these refutations. Although these pastors successfully defended their churches against Deism, the debate distracted much of their attention from their pastoral responsibilities. Regarding such a distraction, Abbey and Overton lamented:

> There was something much more attractive to a clergyman in immortalizing his name by annihilating and enemy of Faith, than in the ordinary routine of parochial work. Bishops, too, had no time to see that the clergy did their duty. The claims of remote diocese had to be postponed to the more pressing requirements of the defence of Christian mysteries.[97]

Thus, the controversy over Deism further weakened the state of the Church of England.

The Latitudinarians. In addition to contributing to attacks from outside the Church of England, like Deism, rationalism also weakened the Anglican Church from within in the form of a group of ministers known as the Latitudinarians. This group maintained control over the Church of England throughout most of the eighteenth century. They emphasized reason and natural theology. They believed in the ability of the individual to demonstrate and realize God's existence through the mere application of reason. As a reflection of this focus on human ability, the Latitudinarians were Arminian in their theology. In the spirit of rationalism, they emphasized the use of reason in the interpretation of Scripture and de-emphasized the role of revelation.

These Anglicans also advocated tolerance toward other Christian groups such as the Dissenters. Although they held strongly to certain doctrines of the Church of England, such as the teachings related to the Sacrament, they exhibited a willingness and tendency to forsake doctrinal integrity for the sake of unity. Describing this tendency Abbey and Overton wrote, "In their praiseworthy appreciation of all that tends to unity they are inclined to disparage the meaning and spiritual significance of all differences that hinder it."[98]

These ministers were open to including members into the Church of England who adhered to false doctrines. They contended that some humans are unable to apprehend fully correct doctrine. Because these fallible people have limited capacity to comprehend the full meaning of such doctrines, Latitudinarians contended that they should accept these mistaken men into the Church of England based on the little knowledge of doctrine they possessed, no matter how inaccurate. Alfred Plummer decried that Latitudinarians opened the Church of England to "those who wish to shirk all definiteness, in order that they may have the benefit of belonging to, and perhaps being paid ministers in, a particular Church, without being in any way bound as regards belief, or teaching, or practice."[99] Due to such openness, the Church of England allowed Arians and Socinians to become members of its clergy.[100] However, even Latitudinarians had limits to their tolerance.

One group which Latitudinarians vehemently opposed was people they labeled "enthusiasts." A definition from the era defines "enthusiasm" as the "mistaken persuasion in any person that he is a peculiar favorite with God; and that he receives supernatural marks thereof."[101] Particularly, the Latitudinarians considered it "enthusiasm" for an individual to refer to some inner testimony or inner workings of the Holy Spirit as an evidence of conversion. One Latitudinarian bishop, Archbishop John Tillotson, contended in typical form that the Holy Spirit did not operate through inner feelings or an inner witness. Tillotson maintained that the Holy Spirit operates upon the mind of man through reason in imparting saving faith to him. Regarding the faith of Abraham, Tillotson asserted that it "was the result of the wisest reasoning."[102]

Rather than emphasizing the inner workings of the Holy Spirit as evidence of conversion, Latitudinarians like Tillotson stressed morality and ethics as evidences of salvation. They believed it was more important for believers to be moral than it was for them to be doctrinally sound. Gerald Cragg contended that the Latitudinarian form of Christianity "presented doctrine in general, not in concrete, terms, and it was concerned with values, not with facts."[103] It was sufficient to these clergymen that Englishmen be baptized into the Church of England, attend religious services, partake of the sacraments, and live moral lives. They considered any requirement of knowledge of an inner testimony of the Holy Spirit as a prerequisite to salvation or church membership as a dangerous attack by "enthusiasts" upon the Church of England.[104]

Church Membership in the Church of England

The Thirty-Nine Articles of the Church of England formed the confessional beliefs of that body during the eighteenth century.[105] Article Twenty-Seven delineated the Church of England's understanding of baptism and its relationship with church membership.[106]

From their reading of this Article, the ministers of the Church of England did not consider baptism merely as a public profession of an individual's faith in Christ. They asserted that baptism was a means of grace whereby individuals become members of the Body of Christ, the Church. Anglican clergymen considered it irrelevant whether an individual's baptism occurred in adulthood or in infancy; baptism in either stage made that individual a member of Christ's Body and the Church of England.

Bishop Gilbert Burnet's *An Exposition of the Thirty-Nine Articles of the Church of England* (1699) sheds light upon the eighteenth-century Anglican ministers' understanding of Article Twenty-Seven and the relationship between baptism, salvation, and church membership. Regarding the baptism of infants, Burnet wrote:

> The office of baptizing infants is in the same words with that for persons of riper age; because infants being in the power of their parents, who are of age, are considered as in them, and as binding themselves by the vows that they make in their name. Therefore the office carries on the supposition of an internal regeneration; and in that helpless state the infant is offered up and dedicated to God; and provided, that when he comes to age he takes those vows on himself, and lives like a person so in covenant with God, then he shall find the full effects of baptism; and if he dies in that state of incapacity, he being dedicated to God is certainly accepted of by him; and by being put in the second Adam, all the

bad effects of his having descended from the first Adam are quite taken away.[107]

Burnet further explained:

> Therefore our Article puts the efficacy of baptism, in order to the forgiveness of our sins, and to our adoption and salvation, upon the virtue of prayer to God; that is, upon those vows and other acts of devotion that accompany them: so that when the seriousness of the mind accompanies the regularity of action, then both the outward and inward effects of baptism are attained by it; and we are not only "baptized into one body," but are also "saved by baptism."[108]

Burnet's comments represented the view of most Anglican ministers regarding baptism, salvation, and church membership. They held that children presented by their parents for baptism become members of the Church of England and Christians. The clergymen emphasized that church members must adhere to their vows of compliance to the Church and her Articles and live moral lives. Remember, the Church placed much emphasis upon the outward acts of church members and de-emphasized any inward testimony of the Holy Spirit confirming one's salvation. One could be baptized as an infant, attend worship services, receive the sacraments, and still not have any concept of the new birth described in Scripture and preached by Whitefield; however, the Church considered these individuals members in right standing. The result of such an interpretation of Article Twenty-Seven was a noticeable presence of unregenerate members within the Church of England.

George Whitefield noted the presence of such lost church members in his preaching and correspondence.[109] In a description of a sermon he preached in the church of his baptism, the English evangelist wrote, "After the solemnity was over, I gave a word of exhortation from the font; and it being the place where I myself not long since had been baptized, it gave me an opportunity of reflecting on my own frequent breaches of my baptismal vow, and proving the necessity of the new birth from the Office of our Church."[110] Whitefield lamented being barred from many Anglican churches because it prevented him from preaching "to those poor baptized heathens that they might be saved."[111] It is clear from his preaching and from Burnet's exposition of Article Twenty-Seven that the issue of unregenerate church members was a problem in the early eighteenth century, a factor in the decline of the Church of England at that time.

English Society Prepared for Revival

What supporting factors were connected with and contributed to the Great Awakening in eighteenth-century England?

Not everything related to the state of the church in the eighteenth century was negative. Gordon Rupp asserted, "The notion of a Church sick, languishing, and corrupt, only saved at the last moment by the irruption[sic] of the Evangelical Revival ignores that the revival itself had its roots, and that it would have been impossible apart from the several converging movements of renewal which had already begun."[112] One of the first movements Rupp presented as a contributing factor to the revival is the establishment of religious societies.

Religious societies began decades before the Evangelical Revival. The first societies were founded in 1670, long before the births of George Whitefield or John Wesley. A German named Anthony Horneck founded the first religious societies in England for the purposes of encouraging piety among their members and Christian reform in English society. The societies involved persons from every area of society, from ministers to plumbers. Describing the clientele of the societies, Rupp wrote, "They were young men, literate and only able to anticipate moderate livelihood, but they were also intelligent and articulate Christian laymen, dissatisfied for whatever reason with their spiritual condition, and now given an instrument for their own discipline and enabled to make their own contribution in an active way, to the life of the Church."[113] By the beginning of the eighteenth century, there were nearly 100 societies in London and Westminster alone.[114]

Horneck established rules for the societies that were intended to help members grow spiritually. He required that the participants of the society be members of the Church of England. He also directed that a minister from the Church of England would preside over the meetings. The societies gave members' dues to charity.

The beginning of the eighteenth century, shortly after the foundation of the societies, was a time in which vice and poverty permeated English society. One church historian described the problems stating:

> It was a callous and insensitive age, where people enjoyed public executions, and where a visit to watch the antics of the demented in Bedlam was as great an attraction as the lions in the Tower of London....there were masses of ignorant and depraved human beings in foetid tenements, cripples, beggars, and destitute children running wild, such as may still be seen in some parts of Asia, but here on the doorstep of the Church and in a nation which had the Christian gospel for a thousand years.[115]

Foreigners who visited England noted the baseness of the English and their propensity to violence. The people of eighteenth-century England loved a good fight. They gambled on prize fights, cock fights, and dog fights. One of the favorite activities of the people involved "beating cockerels to death with clubs and throwing dead dogs and cats at one another on certain festival days."[116] Public executions were a spectator event in which the crowd oftentimes threw dung and rotten eggs at the condemned or the executioners. One of the cruelest forms of capital punishment involved the executioner's disemboweling the condemned and burning his bowels before him as the dying person watched.[117]

In response to these conditions, Christians established societies that sought to alleviate poverty and improve the morality of the English people. In 1698 Thomas Bray founded the Society for the Promotion of Christian Knowledge (SPCK). This organization endeavored to establish charity schools and to spread the gospel. Before the Sunday schools that followed the Evangelical Revival were established, societies like the SPCK built charity schools throughout England. In 1704 there were fifty-four schools in London attended by 2,131 children. By 1714 this number increased to 1,000 schools that graduated more than 2,000 apprentices.[118] Prominent ministers preached charity sermons to help raise financial support for the schools.

The schools taught impoverished children how to read and write. The Bible, catechisms, and the Book of Common Prayer were among the textbooks used in the charity schools. By using these texts, Christians believed they prevented the ignorance of Scripture and taught the children basic moral values that were absent in the surrounding society. The charity schools contributed to the increase in literacy that occurred during the eighteenth century.

In addition, Christian philanthropic societies also initiated the founding of hospitals. In response to the problem of abandoned infants prevalent throughout England, Thomas Coram and leaders of the SPCK founded a hospital for illegitimate children called the Foundling Hospital. Mothers waited in line to turn their impoverished or illegitimate children over to the hospital. Describing the scene of the hospital's opening, Derek Jarrett wrote, "The doors were besieged by crowds of women with babies in their arms and it took only four hours to fill up the hospital."[119] The Foundling Hospital was but one of the many hospitals that philanthropic individuals and societies established in eighteenth-century England.

Although it is unclear to what extent they influenced the Evangelical Revival, it is clear that there are connections between the awakening and such supporting factors. The religious societies played a pivotal role during the Evangelical Awakening.[120] George Whitefield preached his first messages of the Evangelical Revival to religious societies. He was close in age with the young men in the societies and held a rapport with them. He wrote letters to societies and revisited them as he traveled. Most importantly, the societies offered Whitefield a place to direct new converts for discipleship. Because of the valuable role the societies played in discipling new converts during the Evangelical Revival, Rupp writes, "Certainly the cell, the *koinonia*, the society was the heart of the Revival."[121]

Additionally, there was a connection between the charity schools and the Evangelical Revival. The schools helped the literacy rates climb during the eighteenth century. Roy Porter claimed, "Almost all males from the middle class and above were literate, but a little more than half of the population of labouring men (women were proportionally less literate)."[122] In a representative study of literacy in the diocese of Gloucester, Lawrence Stone maintained that, in the year 1725, 100 percent of professionals, 72 percent of yeomen and husbandmen, 87 percent of tradesmen and artisans, and 48 percent of laborers and servants were literate. Regarding literacy in eighteenth century England, Stone asserted, "Fairly extensive literacy was here to stay, and the restrictions imposed could do little more than hinder its growth. The result was that in the eighteenth century the political nation embraced a wide public who read the pamphlets, ballads, and provincial newspapers."[123] Because many members of the population were taught to read, Whitefield could disseminate his journals, sermons, and pamphlets throughout the population of England. The people enjoyed reading anything they could purchase. They especially liked to read sermons. This increase in literacy and reading came at just the time Whitefield was beginning his itinerant ministry.

These positive, supporting activities, among others, prepared the way for the First Great Awakening and the Evangelical Revival in England.

State of the Church of England: Conclusion

Several factors led to the decline of the Church of England in the early eighteenth century. The close relationship between Church and State resulted in politically appointed bishops who were not always spiritually qualified to serve in their offices. Political controversy between Low Churchmen, High Churchmen, Anglicans, and Dissenters distracted the attention of clergymen away from their congregations. The political involvement of clergymen also contributed to absenteeism and weaker standards of ordination for Anglican ministers. Rationalism and Deism attacked the doctrines of the Church of England, drawing away their focus further from their congregations. Rationalism also led to the formation of the Latitudinarians, their Arminianism, their de-emphasis of doctrine, and their inclusion of Arians and Socinians into the Church of England.[124] In addition, the prevalent interpretation of the Church of England's Article regarding baptism allowed for the presence of numerous unregenerate members within the churches. Such negative characteristics laid a foundation for the First Great Awakening and the Evangelical Revival by gaining the attention of revivalists like George Whitefield who preached against such errors.

To be sure, not all aspects of the English Church's life in the early eighteenth century were negative. The establishment of societies began a focus on personal piety among believers and laid the groundwork of the First Great Awakening and the Evangelical Revival. The establishment of charity schools and Sunday Schools contributed to an increase in literacy rates among Englishmen. This rise in literacy in turn made the numerous sermons, pamphlets, and essays of the revivals available to a wider reading public. These positive contributions helped pave the path for Whitefield and the coming revivals.

The American Colonies' Historical and Theological Context

To understand fully George Whitefield's ministry in the American colonies, one must also grasp the historical and theological context surrounding that ministry.[125] Through God's providence, numerous factors in the colonies, preceding Whitefield's arrival, prepared the colonists for the movement of the Holy Spirit known as the First Great Awakening, opening the colonies to Whitefield's preaching and evangelistic ministry.

State of Church Membership in Colonial America

One of the historical and theological factors that helped prepare the colonies for the evangelistic preaching of George Whitefield and other revivalists was the debate over regenerate church membership that occurred in New England in the early 1700's. According to the Cambridge Platform of 1648, those persons who studied religion, repented and professed faith, obeyed God's Word, and avoided scandals could be considered regenerate church members.[126] Only church members could have their children baptized according to this Platform. The problem with the Platform was that several members showed no sign of regeneration, yet they participated in the Lord's Supper.

Synods from Massachusetts and Connecticut agreed to compromise over the Platform of 1648. This position was known as the Half-Way Covenant. Concerning the Covenant, Edwin Scott Gaustad explains, "Only visible saints, the regenerate under the covenant of grace, were fully within the church covenant. Members of this other group constituted an inferior class of church membership; they could neither partake of the Lord's Supper nor vote in church affairs."[127]

It was the prohibition of unregenerate church members from the Lord's Supper that Solomon Stoddard, the grandfather of Jonathan Edwards, opposed. He wrote:

> No scandalous person may be admitted to Baptism, neither may any Scandalous person be admitted to the Lord's Supper; but those that are not scandalous may partake of it though they are not Regenerate. . . . It is lawful for Unregenerate men to celebrate the Memory of the death of Christ, which is a great encouragement and comfort unto them: and so they do in this Ordinance: It is lawful for Unregenerate men to give Solemn Testimony to the virtues of the death of Christ, and show it forth; and so they do in this Ordinance, I Cor. 11, 26.[128]

Stoddard opened the Lord's Supper to everyone in his congregation. This practice and viewpoint regarding unregenerate church members spread throughout other churches in New England.

The practice had numerous detrimental effects upon New England's churches. There could be no practice of church discipline, because some unregenerate members would not expose another member to the authority of the church. Of the issues of church discipline and the immorality of lost church members, Joseph Tracy lamented, "The difference between the church and the world was vanishing away. Church discipline was neglected and the growing laxness of morals was invading the churches."[129] Describing the conduct of some church members prior to the 1734 revival at Northampton, Jonathan Edwards stated, "Licentiousness for some years greatly prevailed among the youth of the town; they were many of them very much addicted to night-walking, and frequenting the tavern, and lewd practices, wherein some, by their example, exceedingly corrupted others."[130] Church members in the colonies possessed a similar understanding of membership as their cousins in the Church of England. If one was baptized in the church, attended services, partook of the ordinances, and avoided scandalous activity in the community, he could bear the title Christian while simultaneously participating in activities such as drinking and gambling.

State of the Clergy in Colonial America

Another result of these compromises over the requirement of regenerate church membership was the presence of unregenerate clergy in the churches. Concerning this problem, Joseph Tracy wrote:

> It is easy to see, that this system favored the entrance of unconverted men into the ministry. If one was fit to be a member of the church; if he was actually a member in good standing; if he was living as God requires such men to live, and pressing forward, in the use of the appointed means, after whatever spiritual good he had not yet attained; if conversion is such a still and unobservable matter, that neither the candidate nor anyone else can judge whether he has yet passed that point or not; and if his mental qualifications are found sufficient; why should he be excluded from ministry?[131]

Solomon Stoddard's words advocating an openness to unregenerate clergy helped perpetuate this practice in colonial churches. Contending for the propriety of unregenerate clergymen to administer the ordinances of baptism and the Lord's Supper, Stoddard asserted:

> If a man do know himself to be Unregenerate, yet it is lawful for him to administer Baptism and the Lord's Supper. The blessing of this Ordinance does not depend upon the Piety of him that doth admin-

ister it. Christ knew Judas to be Unregenerate, yet he let him as well as the rest of the Disciples to administer Baptism: John 4.2. *Jesus baptised not but his Disciples*. . . . men that are destitute of Grace are not prohibited in the word of God, to administer the Ordinances of God, if such may Preach, surely they may administer Sacraments. Paul speaks of Preaching as a greater work than administering Baptism, I. Cor. 1. 17. And we may argue that it is greater than administering the Lord's Supper.[132]

George Whitefield's comments in his journals and his sermons indicate the presence and problem of unconverted ministers in colonial churches. On the matter, the itinerant claimed, "Many, nay most that preach, I fear, do not experimentally know Christ; yet I cannot see much worldly advantage to tempt them to take up the sacred function."[133] Whitefield preached to ministers, encouraging them to consider whether they had experienced true conversion. In his description of one of these occasions, the English itinerant recounted:

I insisted much in my discourse upon the doctrine of the new birth, and also the necessity of a minister being converted, before he could preach Christ aright. The Word came with great power, and a strong impression was made upon the people in all parts of the assembly. Many ministers were present. I did not spare them. Most of them thanked me for my plain dealing. One of them, however, was offended; and so would more of his stamp, if I were to continue longer in New England. Unconverted ministers are the bane of the Christian Church. I honour the memory of that great and good man, Mr. Stoddard; but I think he is much to be blamed for endeavouring to prove that unconverted men may be admitted into the ministry. How he has handled the controversy, I know not; but I believe no solid argument can be brought to defend such a doctrine.[134]

The presence of unregenerate pastors in congregations made churches susceptible to more of such theological fallacies.

In addition to the problem of unregenerate ministers, the rationalism that led to the formation of the Latitudinarians and their skeptical Arminianism began to cross the Atlantic and threaten colonial churches. Regarding this problem, Alan Heimert and Perry Miller wrote:

> For the old orthodoxy was being reinforced (and having its implications disclosed) by imported notions of "natural religion," and taking the form of a suggestion (not yet a proclaimed doctrine) that men, by use of their rational capacities alone, could come to know God's will, and, knowing, choose to fulfill it, and thus count themselves among the saved....One of the more obvious expressions of the new mood was the defection of New Englanders to the Church of England, which, since the days of Archbishop Laud, had been identified with Arminianism.[135]

Some ministers in the colonies began to emphasize the ability of human beings to prepare themselves for and cooperate in salvation. These clergymen comforted such persons who underwent such preparation with the assurance that they would eventually be converted. The focus was largely on outward acts rather than an inward change of the heart. These Arminians also emphasized the human's ability to come to God through one's application of reason. As we will see, such theological thinking shocked and disturbed men like Jonathan Edwards.

Colonial Revivals and Contextual Factors

Although churches in New England and other American colonies contained unregenerate ministers, God utilized a number of regenerate pastors in breaking out sparks of revival that would prepare the colonies for the First Great Awakening. One of those pastors, Jonathan Edwards, experienced a revival in his congregation in Northampton in 1734. Edwards dealt with the effects of the unregenerate pastors and church members. He also contended against the introduction of Arminianism into colonial churches. In his account of the awakening at Northampton, Edwards wrote, "About this time began the great noise, in this part of the country, about Arminianism, which seemed to appear with a very threatening aspect upon the interest of religion here."[136] The sermons through which God brought the awakening contained Calvinistic doctrines opposed to this Arminianism. Many of his messages focused on the relationship between election and the regeneration of the individual. Edwards also mentioned the visible proofs that evidenced regeneration. God worked an amazing awakening within Edwards' congregation and among other churches throughout New England. Sadly, Edwin Gaustad noted, "The revival halted with an abruptness not unlike that with which it had begun, while through it all man could only behold and wonder."[137]

The revival that occurred in the Middle Colonies, in 1720, under the ministry of Theodore J. Frelinghuysen was another awakening that prepared the way for George Whitefield's evangelistic ministry. This movement of the Holy Spirit took place among Dutch Reformed farmers in New Jersey. Frelinghuysen traveled throughout the colony, preaching in meeting houses, homes, and even barns. Concerning the impact of this itinerant's ministry, Arnold Dallimore wrote, "With the passing of the months and the years he saw large numbers of people converted; among them were many of the unchurched and several notorious sinners, but among them also were several deacons and elders and church members who earlier had been his severest opposers."[138]

Another awakening that preceded Whitefield's evangelistic efforts in America was the revival among

Presbyterians in the Middle Colonies. William and Gilbert Tennent, a father and son, both preached sermons based on the doctrines of original sin, repentance, the necessity of conversion, and divine judgment. They helped wake a sleeping denomination from its spiritual apathy. John Rowland, another Presbyterian, also contributed to this revival. He, like Frelinghuysen, preached in barns when denied the use of meeting houses. God used his messages on divine judgment to bring people under the convicting power of the Holy Spirit.

Besides the awakenings, the newspaper accounts of the response to George Whitefield's preaching in England were another factor that prepared the colonists for his arrival.[139] Although the awakenings in the colonies had largely subsided, they were still fresh in the minds of the leaders who led them and the people who experienced them. These colonists read newspaper accounts of the revival that was taking place in England as a result of the Holy Spirit working through Whitefield's preaching. From the news accounts, the American revivalists knew it was only a matter of time until the English evangelist would travel to the colonies. These clergy had advance notice to plan for Whitefield's arrival in their area. In recounting the English revival and granting American clergy notice of his coming to America, these publications insured that Whitefield would have numerous invitations to preach when he arrived.

Geography and demographics were two other contextual factors that affected the English itinerant's evangelistic efforts in the colonies. The colonies in the northeastern part of America were more densely populated than those areas further south. The towns in these northern colonies were also closer together. Referring to parts of Georgia, Tyerman noted, "Many immense tracts of country could scarcely be said to have any population whatever; and yet there was an almost countless number of Indian tribes, differing but little from each other in their usages and manners, and forming a striking picture of human antiquity."[140] When homes or towns were spread further apart, organizing crowds in time to hear Whitefield was harder. Because of the dense population in the northern colonies, crowds there were able to assemble quickly.

Conclusion: American Historical and Theological Context

Each of the these historical and theological factors affected George Whitefield's ministry in the American colonies. The controversy over regenerate church membership led to an influx of more unregenerate people into the church. It was the efforts of revivalists to reach the unregenerate church members that led to the awakenings that occurred prior to the English itinerant's arrival. Many of these same revivalists longed for Whitefield to come to the colonies after reading of his evangelistic successes in England. These Americans worked together with the Englishman to reap the harvest of souls the Holy Spirit provided during the First Great Awakening. The Holy Spirit orchestrated these many factors to prepare the colonies for this revival.

Calvinism, Hyper-Calvinism, and the Modern Question

An often-neglected aspect of the eighteenth-century theological and historical context in England and the American colonies is the debate that occurred during that era regarding Hyper-Calvinism and the Modern Question. Yet, my research revealed no attempt by a Christian scholar to discuss how George Whitefield's theology and methodology of evangelism relate to this controversy. Considering that the debate began before Whitefield's ministry and continued after his death, it is important to examine its highlights to gain an understanding of how Whitefield's evangelistic ministry fits within the context of the contention. The limited scope of this book prevents a full treatment of this subject; however, we can highlight major concepts and events within the controversy.[141] Then, in chapters on Whitefield's theology and methodology, we will explore the English itinerant's own viewpoint regarding aspects of the argument.

Debate in the Early Eighteenth Century

The rationalism that attacked the English Church in the early eighteenth century not only led to Deism, Arianism, Socinianism, and the rational Arminianism of the Latitudinarians, but also helped produce Hyper-Calvinism. As Calvinists received such attacks and observed the movement of clergymen toward rationalism and Arminianism, they began to formulate a defense for their theology. Regarding their process of producing such a defense, Peter Toon stated that these theologians "were in danger either of absorbing the rationalism, or of rejecting it completely, or of doing both."[142] Hyper-Calvinism developed as a result of a number of these Reformed clergymen's attempts to apply reason and logic to defend their doctrines.

The eighteenth-century emergence of Hyper-Calvinism and the resulting debate surrounding the issue began with the publication of two books written by a Congregational minister named John Hussey. These two works, *The Glory of Christ Unveil'd or the Excellency of Christ Vindicated* (1706) and *God's Operations of Grace but No Offers of His Grace* (1707), introduced the idea that the Reformed doctrines of unconditional election and irresistible grace prevent one from offering a universal invitation to the gospel. Hussey arrived at this position partly as a result of his adoption and development of a logical defense of supralapsarianism; however, his understanding of irresistible grace formed the primary foundation for his opposition toward universal invitations.[143] Claiming such invitations are an affront to the Spirit's work in effectually calling the elect, Hussey maintained, "In the Gospel we have directly God's gift of the Spirit, or the Holy Spirit, by and through Christ, which no offer of the Spirit can equal, for it is an effectual conveyance, and so not an offer, for that is ineffectual."[144]

This English hyper-Calvinist also asserted that Calvinists who claim they believe in particular redemption, yet offer universal invitations to the gospel, are inconsistent and unbiblical. He contended that "men may easily see that without general offers of grace they preach consistent enough with general redemption doctrines, though without general redemption doctrines they cannot preach consistent with general offers of grace."[145]

The "Modern Question" Debate

Thirty years after Hussey published *God's Operations of Grace but No Offers of Grace*, a English clergyman named Matthias Maurice contributed to the debate between Calvinism and hyper-Calvinism with his pamphlet entitled *A Modern Question Mostly Answer'd*. In this work, Maurice asked whether persons who are unconverted possess a duty and responsibility to respond affirmatively to the gospel. He contended that all persons are responsible to accept the good news of salvation. Thus began the debate over what became known as the "Modern Question."

Men like John Brine (1703-1765) and John Gill (1697-1771) disagreed with Matthias Maurice. They asserted that unconverted people are not accountable to respond to the gospel positively; therefore, they should not receive offers of grace. Both men maintained that non-elect individuals are unable to respond to the gospel. Although they are still condemned for their sin, their inability excuses them from any duty to respond affirmatively to gospel preaching. Based on this understanding, Brine contended, "*Offers* of grace as I conceive, are not made to those who are not under grace, nor interested in the Covenant of Grace, which many are not, to whom the Gospel is preached."[146] Similarly, in a tract written in response to an opponent, John Gill argued, "What this author's ideas of God are, I know not, but this I say, it is not consistent with our ideas of God, that he should send ministers to offer salvation to man, to whom he himself never intended to give it, which ministers have not power to bestow, nor the men to receive."[147]

Particular Baptists like Brine and Gill disagreed with George Whitefield's practice of offering universal invitations to the gospel. In his excellent work on Andrew Fulller and Particular Baptists in eighteenth-century England, Peter J. Morden explained that "against the background of High Calvinism, Whitefield's adherence to true Calvinistic principles was considered deeply suspect, and Particular Baptists spoke dismissively about his 'Arminian dialect.'"[148] While Brine and Gill wrote against offers of grace and the concept of a universal invitation to the gospel, Whitefield was traveling throughout England preaching the gospel to large crowds.[149] And there is no evidence to hand that the debate between the Calvinists and hyper-Calvinists distracted the English itinerant from this purpose. Whitefield's focus was to preach the gospel to as many people in as many places as possible.

Although Whitefield was not directly involved in the debate between Calvinism and hyper-Calvinism, the First Great Awakening and Evangelical Awakening of which he was a leader had a profound impact upon the contention. In particular, these revivals influenced the fathers of the modern missionary movement and the Baptist Missionary Society, including the theologian of the movement, Andrew Fuller. Regarding the connection between the awakenings and this missions movement, Richard Lovett stated, "The London Missionary Society, like the other great religious and philanthropic organizations which sprang into existence at the close of the eighteenth and the beginning of the nineteenth century, is a child of the evangelical revival in England originated by Whitefield and the Wesleys."[150]

Fuller began to question the hyper-Calvinism of his fellow Particular Baptists, their rejection of offers of grace or universal invitations to the gospel, and their contention that unconverted persons are not under obligation to respond affirmatively to the gospel.[151] In his essay entitled *The Gospel Worthy of All Acceptation, or the Duty of Sinners to Believe in Jesus Christ,* Fuller argued that unconverted persons have a duty to believe in Christ because:

> 1) Unconverted sinners are commanded in Scripture to believe in Christ. 2) Men are bound to believe what God reveals. 3) The gospel, though not law, requires obedience, including the necessity of exercising saving faith. 4) Unbelief is ascribed to men's depravity, and is itself a heinous Sin. 5) God has threatened and inflicted the most awful punishments on sinners, for their not believing in Jesus Christ. 6) Other spiritual exercises, inseparably connected with faith in Christ, are represented as the duty of men in general.[152]

He asserted that, because all men are responsible to believe in Christ, it is obligatory for all Christians and Christian clergymen to present universal invitations or offers of salvation. Fuller's theology became the impetus for the modern missionary movement at the end of the eighteenth century.

Although Fuller opposed the hyper-Calvinists, it would be a mistake to surmise that his theology was a modification or moderation of Calvinism. Fuller's own descriptions of his theology do not support such a conclusion. He stated that he espoused "strict Calvinism to be my own system."[153] In his definition of such Calvinism, Fuller explained that it included five articles which were "denominated the five points. These are predestination, particular redemption, total depravity, effectual calling, and the certain perseverance of the saints."¹⁵⁴

One should also not suspect that Fuller did not believe all five points of Calvinism. Some historians, like William R. Estep, believe Fuller possessed a modified view of particular redemption; however, his response to a hyper-Calvinist who claimed one could not present offers of grace to persons for whom Christ did not die, reveals that Fuller believed in particular redemption. Describing his beliefs regarding the relationship between offers of grace and particular redemption, Fuller commented, "With respect to substitution, from what I have read of Calvin, he appears to have considered the death of Christ as affording an offer of salvation to sinners without distinction; and the peculiar respect which bore to the elect as consisting in the sovereignty of its application, or in God's imparting faith and salvation through it, to them, rather than to others, as it was his design to do."¹⁵⁵ Fuller did not agree with hyper-Calvinists critics who contended that, because one extended offers of salvation and universal invitations to the gospel, one was inconsistent or a "half-hearted" Calvinist. This missionary-minded minister believed that evangelists who made such offers were merely exercising the same evangelical Calvinism that was evident in the Puritans and in leaders of the First Great Awakening like Jonathan Edwards and George Whitefield.

Fuller's theology, commonly known as "Fullerism," was an impetus to the modern missionary movement which sent men like William Carey across the globe to preach the gospel. This theology also led to a waning of hyper-Calvinism during the late eighteenth century and early nineteenth century. His work presented a strong apologetic against the hyper-Calvinists' claim that it was inconsistent with Calvinism to present offers or a universal invitation to the gospel.

Conclusion: Calvinism, Hyper-Calvinism, and the "Modern Question"

The eighteenth-century debate between Calvinism and hyper-Calvinism chronologically surrounded the evangelistic ministry of George Whitefield. While men contended over whether one should present offers of grace, Whitefield preached the gospel in the fields of England and America. While John Gill and John Brine asserted that unconverted persons had no duty to accept the gospel, the English itinerant preached to large audiences in meeting houses. Throughout his ministry, however, there is no evidence that George Whitefield formally entered a discussion whose subject pertained directly to the type of ministry to which the itinerant dedicated his life—evangelism.

Whitefield's apparent absence in this debate prompts several questions. What did George Whitefield believe regarding the subject of presenting offers to the gospel or universal invitations? Like hyper-Calvinists, did he preach doctrines about salvation, yet not make offers of salvation to his hearers? Did he believe that his hearers were responsible or possessed a duty to accept the gospel? Would he agree with Fuller's contention that making universal offers or invitations to the gospel was consistent for five-point Calvinists? Would he also share Fuller's claim that one who believes in particular redemption can still present universal invitations to the gospel? Would Whitefield not agree with either Fuller or the hyper-Calvinists? Did he possess a viewpoint regarding such issues that differed from both sides in the debate? The following chapters on George Whitefield's theology and methodology of evangelism will answer these and a number of other questions regarding the itinerant's beliefs and ministry.

CHAPTER TWO

George Whitefield's Theology of Evangelism

A few biographers of Whitefield question his competence as a theologian. In his biography of the evangelist, Stuart C. Henry asserted, "Strictly speaking, Whitefield was not even a theologian, not so much because he did not produce a theology–as he did not–but because he did not address himself formally to the problems of speculative thought, nor attempt to systematize his dogma in any organized form."[156]

In his biography of Whitefield entitled *The Divine Dramatist: George Whitefield and the Rise of Modern Evangelicalism*, Harry S. Stout claims that Whitefield focused more on personal experience than on theology in his preaching. He contends, "Throughout, he showed no interest in theology. Instead of doctrine, he explored the feelings of the New Birth and through his exploration invited hearers to experience it for themselves."[157] Noticing the context in which Stout's comment is made, one might interpret his statement as merely pertaining to one of Whitefield's sermons entitled "The Nature and Necessity of Our Regeneration or New Birth in Christ Jesus"; however, further perusal of the biography reveals that, while Stout may refer to this sermon in particular, he also is referring to Whitefield's preaching and evangelistic ministry in general.[158] The general intent of Stout's comment is evident in another description of Whitefield's preaching where he writes, "But when performed live, with all the body language and pathos of a great actor, the lines receded into the passion and the hearer was locked into a dramatic world from which there was no easy exit. Doctrines, uses, proofs, and applications all receded into the background as the passions took over."[159] Stout asserts that Whitefield was more concerned about dramatic flair in his preaching than he was in theology or in communicating the gospel. However, examining Whitefield's sermons, letters, and journal entries reveals that both Henry and Stout are mistaken about his emphasis on theology. The evangelist's sermons are filled throughout with doctrines that he believed were crucial to matters of salvation. His journals and works also indicate a sincere concern for theology in his evangelistic ministry. A most recent biographer of Whitefield, Thomas S. Kidd, is more accurate when he writes, "But Whitefield was not shallow, even for his time. Instead, he was a learned and theologically precise gospel preacher."[160]

So, what exactly was Whitefield's theology of evangelism?[161] It will help to examine the primary sources of authority upon which the itinerant based his theology of evangelism, and to review Whitefield's comments regarding Calvinism. We will then be able to examine the connection between the doctrines of grace and Whitefield's theology of evangelism. And, further, we will be better situated to present the itinerant's theological understanding of the Great Commission and preaching universal invitations to the gospel.

Sources of Authority

Any analysis of George Whitefield's theology of evangelism should present the sources of authority forming the basis for such a theological position. For the moment, I want to describe two of the primary sources of authority to which Whitefield referred in the formation of his theology of evangelism. They are, in order of the emphasis he placed upon them, the Scriptures and the Thirty-Nine Articles.

Whitefield on the Authority of Scripture

To understand Whitefield's theology of evangelism, it is first imperative to comprehend his views regarding the authority of Scripture. How did he view the relationship between God's Word and other sources of authority? Did he believe that Scripture was the ultimate source of authority? These questions are important avenues of investigation when considering Whitefield's understanding of Scripture.

Throughout his ministry, George Whitefield asserted that Scripture is the believer's ultimate source of authority over every other source of authority and in every aspect of life. In a time when rationalists questioned the veracity and accuracy of Scripture, Whitefield emphasized its authority and infallibility.[162] Speaking against the practice of elevating oneself as an authority over God's Word, he declared:

> If we once get above our Bibles, and cease making the written word of God our sole rule both as to faith and practice, we shall soon lie open to all manner of delusion, and be in great danger of making shipwreck of faith and a good conscience. Our blessed Lord, though he had the Spirit of God without measure, yet always was governed by, and fought the devil with, "It is written."[163]

Whitefield also communicated this emphasis on the authority of Scripture in the many letters he wrote to both believers and unbelievers. In a letter written during the early stages of his evangelistic ministry, he stated, "The Scriptures (as I take it) are to be the only rule of action. And the examples of our blessed Lord and his apostles, the grand patterns whereby we are to form the conduct of our lives."[164] This conviction regarding the authority of God's

Word formed the foundation of Whitefield's preaching and ministry.[165]

While he was a minister in the Church of England, George Whitefield acknowledged that the authority of Scripture overshadowed the authority of the Thirty-Nine Articles. He maintained that Scripture was to judge both the Articles and the Church of England. His support of the Church and her Articles was contingent upon their agreement with Scripture. In a statement revealing his view of the relationship between biblical authority and the Articles, Whitefield noted, "I judge of the state of a Church, not from the practice of its members, but its primitive and public constitutions; and so long as I think the Articles of the Church of England agreeable to Scripture, I am resolved to preach them without either bigotry or party zeal."[166]

In addition to presenting Scripture as the judge over the Articles, Whitefield also advocated that Scripture test the validity of believers' experiences. He understood his critics' concern that he and other preachers of the First Great Awakening made experiences and arbitrary inner feelings their sources of authority.[167] He encouraged believers to evaluate their experiences through the lens of Scripture. In a warning to his hearers, Whitefield admonished:

> And though it is the quintessence of enthusiasm, to pretend to be guided by the Spirit without the written word; yet it is every Christian's bounden duty to be guided by the Spirit in conjunction with the written word of God. Watch, therefore, I pray you, O believers, the motions of God's blessed Spirit in your souls, and always try the suggestions or impressions that you may at any time feel, by the unerring rule of God's most holy word: and if they are not found to be agreeable to that, reject them as diabolical and delusive.[168]

The itinerant believed strongly that Scripture was to form the foundation for every experience of the believer.

For Whitefield, Scripture was not only the judge of the believers' experiences, but contained the very revelation of Christ that led to their salvation. In his sermon entitled "The Potter and the Clay," the English evangelist asserted that "all divine revelation from the beginning to the end, all centre in these two points, to shew us how we are fallen, and to begin, carry on, and complete a glorious and blessed change in our souls."[169] He exhorted his hearers to embrace the truths of the gospel found in Scripture as their only hope for salvation.[170] Whitefield believed strongly that the Bible was the good news of the gospel, the source of his message, and the only hope for his listeners. In addition to relying upon Scripture as the source of his gospel message, Whitefield also referred to biblical passages to defend various doctrines and ideas related to his ministry. When faced with criticism and opposition regarding his open-air preaching, Whitefield referred the critics to field preachers in Scripture.[171] He pointed to Scripture to support the existence of hell. In his sermon entitled "The Eternity of Hell Torments," he points his audience to biblical evidence from Daniel, Isaiah, Jude, and Revelation supporting the existence of hell and the eternal punishment of the damned.[172] Whitefield also cited passages from John and Acts to contend "that the Holy Ghost is truly and properly God, as well as the Father and the Son."[173]

Throughout his evangelistic ministry, Whitefield emphasized the authority of Scripture. Scripture overshadowed all other sources of authority, including the Thirty-Nine Articles of the Church of England.

Whitefield and the Thirty-Nine Articles

Numerous biographers of Whitefield and students of the First Great Awakening attest to his adherence to the doctrines contained within the Thirty-Nine Articles of the Church of England. Arnold Dallimore asserted that the English evangelist agreed with the Articles, especially those sections pertaining to predestination and election.[174] On the relationship between Whitefield's preaching and the Articles, Dallimore wrote:

> But Whitefield thought this movement as particularly within the Church of England. He believed that the doctrines he taught were simply those of her Articles and, having convinced himself (whether rightly or wrongly) that his open-air and itinerant proceedings were not contrary to her laws, he sought to induce other members of the clergy to believe the same things and perform the same work.[175]

D. M. Lloyd-Jones contended:

> Whitefield remained more loyal to the Thirty-Nine Articles of the Church of England than did John Wesley. Those Articles have a Calvinistic emphasis, and Whitefield adhered to that, whereas John Wesley departed from that and therefore was mainly responsible for the division.[176]

Those claims prompt some questions: What did Whitefield write about the Articles? Did he mention the Articles in his preaching? Did he refer to the Articles to support the doctrines contained in his sermons? Did he view the Articles' treatment of doctrine favorably?

From the time of his ordination, Whitefield expressed his support of the Thirty-Nine Articles.[177] Having examined of the Articles prior to his ordination, Whitefield wrote, "In the meanwhile, having before made some observations upon the thirty-nine Articles, and proved them by Scripture, I strictly examined myself by the qualifications required for a minister in St. Paul's Epistle to Timothy, and also by every question that I knew was to be publicly put to me at the time of my ordination."[178] Because Whitefield believed the Articles passed the test of his ultimate source of authority, the Scriptures, he did not hesitate to preach the doctrines contained within these confessions of faith. The following examples indicate the influence of the Articles upon Whitefield's soteriology, preaching, and evangelistic ministry.

One of the criticisms raised against Whitefield, by the Bishop of London, was related to the itinerant's contention that believers can be mindful of the Holy Spirit indwelling them. In response to such opposition, Whitefield wrote, "My constant way of preaching is, first, to prove my propositions by Scripture and then to illustrate them by the articles and collects of the church of England."[179] Whitefield then included a copy of a sermon entitled "The Indwelling of the Spirit, the Common Privilege of All Believers" for the bishop's perusal.[180] In this sermon, Whitefield lamented the failure of ministers within the Church of England to preach in accordance with the Articles. He attributed the false teaching of his opponents regarding the Holy Spirit to this infidelity. Whitefield declared:

> But here is the misfortune; many of us are not led by, and therefore no wonder that we cannot talk feelingly of, the Holy Ghost; we subscribe to our Articles, and make them serve for a key to church-preferment, and then preach contrary to those very Articles to which we have subscribed. Far be it from me to charge all the clergy with this hateful hypocrisy; no, blessed be God, there are some left among us who dare maintain the doctrines of the Reformation, and preach the truth as it is in Jesus: but, I speak the truth in Christ, I lie not; the generality of the clergy are fallen from our Articles, and do not speak agreeably to them, or to the form of sound words delivered in the scriptures; woe be unto such blind leaders of the blind! How can you escape the damnation of hell?[181]

Whitefield also utilized the Articles to support various aspects of the doctrine of total depravity in his preaching. Regarding the effect of sin upon man's ability to come to God, he quoted one of the Articles, stating, "Our own free-will, if improved, may restrain us from the commission of many evils and put us in the way of conversion: but, after exerting our utmost efforts, (and we are bound in duty to exert them) we shall find the words of our own church article to be true, that 'man since the fall hath no power to turn to God.'"[182] After citing references to numerous supporting passages from Scripture, Whitefield quoted Article IX to support his contention that all humans are affected by original sin because sin was imputed from Adam to his posterity.[183] In another sermon, Whitefield quoted the same Article, claiming "it is obvious, on the contrary, that we are all equally included under the guilt and consequences of our first parent's sin, even as others; and, to use the language of our own church-article, 'bring into the world with us, a corruption, which renders us liable to God's wrath, and eternal damnation.'"[184]

Whitefield's adherence to the Thirty-Nine Articles is also apparent in numerous references in his preaching, journals, and correspondence to the relationship between faith and works. He quoted Article XII in a response to the Bishop of London's criticism of his preaching on justification by faith alone. In response to the Bishop's comment that good works are a necessary condition of justification, Whitefield responded:

> Had your Lordship insisted on your clergy's preaching up good works as a *necessary fruit* and consequence, instead of a necessary condition of our being justified, your Lordship would have used your authority aright. For we are commanded to show forth or declare to others, that we have a true faith by our works. And the 12th article of our church says, that "good works *follow* after justification;" and how then, my Lord, are they a necessary condition of our justification? No, my Lord, salvation (if the gospel be true) is the free gift of God through Jesus Christ.[185]

The English itinerant held strongly to the position that good works follow salvation and are not a condition for salvation.[186]

The most poignant examples of George Whitefield's loyalty to the Thirty-Nine Articles are his letters responding to John Wesley's preaching against various doctrines pertaining to Calvinism.[187] Whitefield lovingly rebuked Wesley for opposing various Articles of the Church of England.[188] In response to Wesley's claim that the doctrine of predestination "tends to destroy the comforts of religion," Whitefield referred to Article XVII to show that predestination was a source of comfort to believers rather than a cause of distress.[189] In another of Whitefield's letters to Wesley, he cited one of the Articles in writing against his friend's adherence to the concept of sinless perfection. He wrote:

> I cannot see wherein the heterodoxy of the article of our church doth consist, which says, "That this corruption remains even in the regenerate"; and if that after conversion we cannot sin in thought, word or deed, I do not know why our Lord taught us to pray to our heavenly Father, "Forgive us our trespasses". I am sorry, honoured Sir, to hear by many letters, that you seem to own a sinless perfection in this life attainable.[190]

The above quotes from Whitefield clearly indicate his loyalty and adherence to the doctrines contained in the Thirty-Nine Articles. His comments indicate the influence of the Articles upon his theology and soteriology, and substantiate statements from biographers of Whitefield asserting his loyalty to the Articles.

Whitefield and Calvinism

One reason this evangelist's loyalty to the Articles of the Church of England is significant is the Calvinistic tone of this confession of faith.[191] Whitefield acknowledged, embraced, and referred to the Calvinistic theology contained in the Articles. His warmness to their Reformed character is evident in a response he wrote to Thomas Church's criticism that the English itinerant's preaching "revived the old *Calvinistical disputes* concerning predestination." Whitefield stated:

> But if this be my shame, I glory in it. For what is this but reviving the essential articles of the Church of England, which undoubtedly are Calvinistical, and which, by your own confession, have happily slept for so many years? This is too true. But however you may count this a happiness, yet in my opinion it is one of the greatest judgements that has befallen our nation. And if it had not been for the remnant of free-grace, dissenting ministers, (styled by the author of the observations, dissenting teachers) and the little flock of the Methodist preachers, that the Lord Jesus has raised up and preserved amongst us, many of the essential doctrines of the articles of the Church of England might have, as you term it, happily slept many years more.[192]

In his letters, sermons, and journals, George Whitefield identified himself with Calvinism and described the principles in his theology and preaching as "calvinistical." At times, the he openly and bluntly referred to himself as a Calvinist. In response to accusations he was a Moravian, the itinerant asserted he was a "staunch Calvinist."[193] He closed a letter to the president of Harvard, stating, "Gentlemen, I profess myself a Calvinist as to principle, and preach no other doctrines than those which your pious ancestors, and the founders of Harvard College, preached long before I was born."[194] It is interesting that, in both of these examples, Whitefield strongly identified his Calvinistic theology in response to attacks against his personal theology. Perhaps, Whitefield spoke in such strong terms to bring clarity to these disputes regarding his personal theological beliefs.

Although Whitefield identified himself as a Calvinist, he was more committed to Christ and the Scriptures than to any theological system. The itinerant repeatedly asserted that his adoption of Calvinism was preceded by his study of the Scriptures and not vice versa. He described his theology to Benjamin Colman stating, "I embrace the calvinistical scheme, not because Calvin, but Jesus Christ, I think has taught it to me."[195] During his second visit to the American colonies, Whitefield wrote a letter to John Wesley stating:

> I cannot bear the thoughts of opposing you: but how can I avoid it, if you go about (as your brother C_____ once said) to drive John Calvin out of Bristol. Alas, I never read any thing that Calvin wrote; my doctrines I had from Christ and his apostles; I was taught them of God; and as God was pleased to send me out first; and to enlighten me first, so I think he still continues to do it.[196]

These citations point to a concern in Whitefield to emphasize Christ and the Scriptures over Calvinism.

Such concern for the supremacy of Christ over an identification with Calvinism or any other theological system is evident in the itinerant's comments regarding disputes over Calvinism. While he unapologetically identified himself a Calvinist, Whitefield also stressed the importance of preaching Christ and showing love and a spirit of unity towards believers who were not Calvinists. Following the words to Benjamin Colman cited above, Whitefield stated, "I go on preaching the cross and power of the Redeemer, and desire to say as little as possible about others, lest thereby I should divert people's minds from the simplicity of the gospel."[197] His concern was that his audiences hear and understand the gospel of Jesus Christ and not become confused over a focus upon Calvin. In a letter written to a man disturbed by John Wesley's attacks against Calvinism, George Whitefield admonished:

But what is Calvin, or what is Luther? Let us look above names and parties; let Jesus, the ever-loving, the ever-lovely Jesus, be our all in all.—So that he be preached, and his divine image stamped more and more upon people's souls, I care not who is uppermost. I know my place, (Lord Jesus enable me to keep it!) even to be the servant of all. I want not to have a people called after my name, and therefore I act as I do. The cause is Christ's, and he will take care of it.[198]

Whitefield attempted to avoid disputes over Calvinism and encouraged like-minded believers to do the same, encouraging them to show love towards one another regardless of theological differences. He asked one of his audiences:

Has he wrought in thee a love to his people, not people that are Calvinists only; not people that hold universal redemption only? O be careful as to that. O what nonsense is that, for people to hold universal redemption, and yet not love all mankind. What nonsense is it to hold election, and not "as the elect of GOD to put on bowels of mercy, kindness, humbleness of mind, meekness, and long-suffering." As the woman said, I have a house will hold a hundred, a heart ten thousand.[199]

He advocated that Calvinists treat their opponents with humility and gentleness, writing to a man who was like-minded theologically:

I pray you, for Christ's sake, to take heed lest your spirit should be embittered, when you are speaking or writing for God. This will give your adversaries advantage over you, and make people think your passion is the effect of your principles. Since I have been in England this time, Calvin's example has been very much pressed upon me. You know how Luther abused him. As we are of Calvinistical principles, I trust we shall in this respect imitate

Calvin's practice, and show all meekness to those who may oppose.[200]

In a letter written to John Willison, Whitefield wrote, "Though I am a strenuous defender of the righteousness of Christ, and utterly detest Arminian principles, yet I know that God gave me the Holy Ghost, before I was clear in either as to head-knowledge: and therefore, dear Sir, I am the more moderate to people who are not clear, supposing I see the divine image stamped upon their hearts."[201]

The display of such moderation is evident in his dispute with his close friend John Wesley. Although he was diametrically opposed to Wesley's theological views regarding sinless perfection and election, Whitefield gently admonished his friend and attempted to avoid entering a dispute with him. His concern to avoid distractions caused by such confrontations and his desire to focus upon the preaching of the gospel are clear in his words written to Wesley in the early moments of their theological debate:

> The doctrine of *election*, and the *final perseverance* of those that are truly in Christ, I am ten thousand times more convinced of, if possible, than when I saw you last.—You think otherwise: why then should we dispute, when there is no probability of convincing? Will it not in the end destroy brotherly love, and insensibly take from us that cordial union and sweetness of soul, which I pray God may always subsist between us? How glad would the enemies of the Lord be to see us divided? How many would rejoice, should I join and make a party against you? And in one word, how would the cause of our common Master every way suffer by our raging disputes about particular points of doctrines? *Honoured Sir*, let us offer salvation freely to all by the blood of Jesus, and whatever light God has communicated to us, let us freely communicate to others.[202]

Important

Rather than focus on differences in theology, Whitefield wanted to find common ground with his friend in the preaching of the gospel of Jesus Christ.[203]

Doctrines of Grace

The doctrines of grace formed the foundation of Whitefield's theology of evangelism and the primary content of his gospel preaching.[204] Of these doctrines, the English evangelist wrote, "You know how strongly I assert all the doctrines of grace as contained in the Westminster Confession of Faith, and in the doctrinal Articles of the Church of England. I trust, I shall adhere to these as long as I live; because I verily believe they are the truths of GOD, and because I have felt the power of them in my heart."[205] On preaching the doctrines of grace, he told one of his audiences, "I do not want, that Arminian husks should go down with you; ye are king's sons and daughters, and have a more refined taste; you must have the doctrines of grace, and blessed be God that you dwell in a country where the sincere word is so plainly preached."[206] To opponents who attacked him for preaching the doctrines of grace, Whitefield responded, "And now, are you not ashamed of yourselves, who speak against the doctrines of grace, especially that doctrine of being justified by faith alone, as though it led to licentiousness?"[207]

Such remarks point to the critical role these doctrines occupied in Whitefield's theology of evangelism and in his evangelistic ministry. But what, more precisely, was his understanding of the doctrines of grace and their relationship with his theology of evangelism?

Total Depravity

In his theology of evangelism, Whitefield understood the very bleak condition of humanity apart from the saving work of Jesus Christ. He believed that all by nature are depraved and fallen. His sermon entitled "The Potter

Sermon

and the Clay" contains some of Whitefield's clearest and most detailed depictions of the extent of human depravity, affording numerous examples of his convictions on the matter.[208] For example, Whitefield stated that, apart from Christ, humans "are altogether equally become abominable in God's sight, all equally fallen short of the glory of God, and consequently all alike so many pieces of marred clay."[209] He described all as "notoriously ungodly" in their fallen condition.[210]

Whitefield not only believed that all are depraved, but contended that every aspect of the individual is fallen and offensive to God. He argued that human beings' minds are fallen and unable to reason their way to a saving knowledge of Christ. Speaking of the persecution of believers by "men of reason," he declared:

Yep!

unable

> And however his servants and followers may now be looked upon as fools and madmen; yet there will come a time, when those who despise, and set themselves to oppose divine revelation, will find, that what they now call reason, is only reason depraved, and as utterly incapable of itself, to guide us unto the way of peace, or show the way of salvation, as the men of Sodom were to find Lot's door, after they were struck with blindness by the angels who came to lead him out of the city. The horrid and dreadful mistakes which the most refined reasoners in the heathen world ran into, both as to the object as well as manner of divine worship, have sufficiently demonstrated the weakness and depravity of human reason: nor do our modern boasters afford us any better proofs of the greatness of its strength, since the best improvement they generally make of it, is only to reason themselves into downright wilful infidelity, and thereby reason themselves out of eternal salvation.[211]

He maintained that humanity's affections are also fallen. In his fallen state, no one loves God, holiness, or righteousness. Whitefield lamented:

> We love what we should hate, and hate what we should love; we fear what we should hope for, and hope for what we should fear; nay, to such an ungovernable height do our affections sometimes rise, that though our judgments are convinced to the contrary, yet we will gratify our passions, though it be at the expense of our present and eternal welfare.[212]

He espoused not only does fallen humanity not love God, but also feels no need of Him. Possessing a relationship with God is not a priority in the unbeliever's life.[213]

In addition to the affections, Whitefield also believed that the human will is depraved. He maintained that, in Eden, Adam's and Eve's will was to honor their Maker; however, after the Fall, they turned their wills against Him. Whitefield opposed the idea that fallen humans can have any free will or ability to obey God prior to the Holy Spirit awakening them. He asserted that the unregenerate sinner "hath a will as directly contrary to the will of God, as light is contrary to darkness, or heaven to hell."[214] And so he preached:

> Indeed, our deists tell us, that man now has a free will to do good, to love God, and to repent when he will: but indeed, there is no free will in any of you, but to sin; nay, your free will leads you so far, that you would, if possible, pull God from his throne. This may, perhaps, offend the Pharisees; but (it is the truth in Christ which I speak, I lie not) every man by his own natural will hates God......[215]

He preached that sinners, in their depraved state, are at enmity with God. He claimed that "the carnal mind, the mind of the unconverted natural man, nay, the mind of the regenerate, so far as any part of him remain unrenewed, is enmity, not only an enemy, but enmity 'itself, against God; so that it is not subject to the law of God, neither indeed can it be.'"216 Whitefield contended that such enmity spread to all humanity because of original sin, concluding, "And this same enmity rules and prevails in every man that is naturally engendered of the offspring of Adam.... I mean the enmity of man's wicked and deceitful heart. He that cannot set his seal to this, knows nothing yet, in a saving manner, of the holy scriptures or the power of God."217

This sampling from Whitefield's preaching indicates that he adhered to the doctrine of total depravity. He maintained that human beings are entirely corrupted by the Fall and are enmity with God. And this corruption, which began with Adam, he believed spread to humankind—the doctrine of original sin.

Original Sin. George Whitefield emphasized the doctrine of original sin in his theology of evangelism. He contended that this truth was a critical element of the gospel, because of its firm foundation in Scripture. On the matter, Whitefield stated:

> I know indeed, it is now no uncommon thing amongst us to deny the doctrine of original sin, as well as the divinity of Jesus Christ; but it is incumbent on those who deny it, first to disprove the authority of the holy scriptures: if thou canst prove, thou unbeliever, that the book, which we call The Bible, does not contain the lively oracles of God; if thou canst show, that holy men of old, did not write this book, as they were inwardly moved by the Holy Ghost, then will we give up the doctrine of original sin; but unless thou canst do this, we must insist upon it, that we are all conceived and born in sin; if for no other, yet for this one reason, because that God, who cannot lie, has told us so.218

Whitefield unapologetically held to and preached this doctrine.

Explaining original sin to audiences, Whitefield indicated his belief that Adam and Eve had free will in the Garden of Eden before they fell from grace. Prior to the Fall, Whitefield explained, "God made man upright, and with full power to stand if he would. He was just, therefore in suffering him to be tempted. If he fell, he had no one to blame except himself."[219] He asserted that, because of their free will, it was possible for both Adam and Eve to fulfill the covenant of works that God made with them; however, they both chose to rebel against God and ate of the forbidden fruit. Their violation of the covenant placed them at enmity with God which, Whitefield argued, was evident in the couple's attempts to flee and hide from God.[220] And what did it get them? Whitefield declared, "Let us take a short view of the miserable circumstances our first parents were now in: They were legally and spiritually dead, children of wrath, and heirs of hell."[221]

According to Whitefield, when Adam and Eve sinned, they were acting as representatives for all of humanity. He maintained that "Adam was our representative, so we were to stand or fall in him; and as he was our federal head, his falling involved all our race under the power of death, for death came into the world by sin; and we all became liable to the eternal punishment due from God, for man's disobedience to the divine command."[222] So what did it all get for us? Whitefield argued, "you, and I, and all their posterity, (whom they represented,) fell in them."[223]

Whitefield held that God imputed Adam's sin and its effects to all of humanity because Adam and Eve served as our representatives.[224] He mentioned this doctrine of imputed sin in his sermons and in his written response to Wesley's sermon "Free Grace." In this message, Wesley asked the question, "How uncomfortable a thought is this, that thousands and millions of men, without any preceding offence or fault of theirs, were unchangeably doomed to everlasting burnings?" Whitefield responded:

How then are they doomed without any preceding fault? Surely Mr. Wesley will own God's justice in imputing Adam's sin to his posterity; and also, that after Adam fell, and his posterity in him, God might justly have passed them all by, without sending his own Son to be a saviour for any one. Unless you heartily agree to both these points, you do not believe original sin aright.[225]

In his sermon "Of Justification By Christ," Whitefield contended that the doctrine of imputed sin is based upon strong biblical support, stating that:

we are all chargeable with original sin, or the sin of our first parents. Which, though a proposition that may be denied by a self-justifying infidel, who "will not come to Christ that he may have life;" yet can never be denied by any one who believes that St *Paul's* epistles were written by divine inspiration; where we are told, that "in *Adam* all died;" that is, *Adam's* sin was imputed to all: and lest we should forget to make a particular application, it is added, in another place, "that there is none that doeth good, (that is, by nature) no, not one: that we are all gone out of the way, (of original righteousness) and are by nature the children of wrath."[226]

Whitefield preached that, because of the imputation of Adam's sin, humanity stands utterly guilty and corrupt. All humans are born with a sinful nature and possess within themselves nothing that is inherently good. Whitefield taught his audiences that this sinful nature places within humanity a hatred towards God and causes individuals to hide from, rather than seek, God. Acting upon this enmity towards God, human beings participate in sinful behavior. The effects of original sin corrupt the entire individual, including his understanding, reason, and will.

The English evangelist also maintained that, left to his own sinful nature, the inclination of natural man is to sin and serve himself. Even when attempting to perform

moral acts, humans are motivated by their own self-inter-
ests rather than by a love for God. Whitefield stated that
the critical question was "does your obedience proceed
from love to God, to Christ? If not, may God convince you
of your miserable state before you go hence!"[227] Apart
from experiencing renewal in Christ, men continue to
serve themselves rather than Christ.

In addition to a sinful nature that chooses to serve
self and rebel against God, Whitefield contended that
death and hell are also results of original sin. He asserted
that original sin brings spiritual death to all and creates
within all a moral inability to see, understand, or follow
God.[228] Additionally, physical death results from original
sin. Whitefield pointed to the death of infants as evidence
of physical death resulting from the imputation of Adam's sin to all humanity.[229] And he warned his audiences against ignoring the reality of death and hell resulting
from original sin, preaching:

> Alas! how many does Satan lead captive at his will,
> by flattering them, that they shall not surely die;
> that hell-torments will not be eternal; that God is
> all mercy; that he therefore will not punish a few
> years' sin with an eternity of misery? But *Eve* found
> God as good as his word; and so will all they who
> go on in sin, under a false hope that they shall not
> surely die.[230]

Whitefield emphasized that individuals must come
under the conviction of the Holy Spirit regarding not only
their actual sins, but also the reality of original sin and
their inherent sinful nature and enmity against God. He
claimed that such conviction of original sin is necessary
for one to become a believer. In his sermon "The Method
of Grace," Whitefield contended:

> But further: you may be convinced of your actual
> sins, so as to be made to tremble, and yet you may
> be strangers to Jesus Christ, you may have no true
> work of grace upon your hearts. Before ever, there-

fore, you can speak peace to your hearts, conviction must go deeper; you must not only be convinced of your actual transgressions against the law of God, but likewise of the foundation of all transgressions. And what is that? I mean original sin, that original corruption each of us brings into the world with us, which renders us liable to God's wrath and damnation.[231]

His belief that such conviction of original sin was critical to an individual's conversion compelled the English evangelist to emphasize this doctrine in his preaching. He summarized his concern for this truth saying:

> I have been more particular in treating of this point, because it is the very foundation of the Christian religion: For I am verily persuaded, that it is nothing but a want of being well grounded in the doctrine of original sin, and of the helpless, nay, I may say, damnable condition, each of us comes into the world in, that makes so many infidels oppose, and so many who call themselves Christians, so very lukewarm in their love and affections to Jesus Christ. It is this, and I could almost say, this only, that makes infidelity abound among us so much as it does.[232]

In a letter to the Bishop of Gloucester, Whitefield called the doctrine of original sin a doctrine "upon which the doctrine of the new birth is entirely founded."[233] Thus, it is evident that the doctrine of original sin occupied an essential position in George Whitefield's theology of evangelism.

Moral inability. Whitefield believed that sinners have no power to awaken themselves to their sinful condition, but require the Holy Spirit to convict them. He held that humans are spiritually dead and possess no ability or inclination to grant themselves spiritual life, contending "that there is no ability or inclination in the heart of a natural man, so much as to do any thing spiritual; he is stupid and dead."[234] On this point, Whitefield declared:

> Stop there now, pause awhile; and whilst thou art gazing upon the corpse of Lazarus, give me leave to tell thee with great plainness, but greater love, that this dead, bound, entombed, stinking carcass, is but a faint representation of thy poor soul in its natural state: for, whether thou believest it or not, thy spirit which thou bearest about with thee, sepulchred in flesh and blood, is as literally dead to God, and as truly dead in trespasses and sins, as the body of Lazarus was in the cave. . . . And what is still more affecting, thou art as unable to raise thyself out of this loathsome, dead state, to a life of righteousness and true holiness, as ever Lazarus was to raise himself from the cave in which he lay so long.[235]

Without question, Whitefield maintained that the deadness of all by nature is reflected in their moral inability to come to Christ based upon their own power.

By moral inability, he did not intend an inability to commit morally good acts. The evangelist acknowledged that people may perform acts of charity and morality; however, he contended that their sinful nature taints every moral action, making the deeds unacceptable to God because they fall short of His holiness. Whitefield argued:

> But before you can speak peace to your heart, you must be brought to see that God may damn you for the best prayer you ever put up; you must be brought to see that all your duties—all your righteousness—as the prophet elegantly expresses it—put them all together, are so far from recommending you to God, are so far from being any motive and inducement to God to have mercy on your poor soul, that he will see them to be filthy rags, a menstruous cloth—that God hates them, and cannot away with them, if you bring them to him in order to recommend you to his favour.[236]

He further asserted that the natural man's attempts to gain favor with God through religious activity are also tainted by sin.[237]

Coupled with this moral inability is a lack of desire for Christ or for the things of God. Whitefield argued strongly against the idea that humans by nature possess any free will or moral ability to seek or choose God. On the contrary, he held that their natural will is to sin against God rather than to serve Him. In a letter written early in his ministry, Whitefield said of free will, "Man is nothing: he hath a free will to go to hell, but none to go to heaven, till God worketh in him to will and to do after his good pleasure."[238] *Great quote*

The evangelist also maintained that the will to sin and the inability to seek God's pleasure are related to the enmity existing between God and fallen men. Until the sinner's nature is supernaturally changed, he or she will continue to possess an inability to have fellowship with God. Whitefield stressed "that before a man can be said to walk with God, the prevailing power of this heart-enmity must be destroyed: for persons do not use to walk and keep company together, who entertain an irreconcilable enmity and hatred against one another."[239] Such enmity is incompatible with any will or moral ability to seek salvation in Christ.

Whitefield espoused that, in addition to creating enmity with God, the sinner's nature also produces an inability to obtain an accurate understanding of spiritual matters. He contended that they are spiritually blind, declaring "that they are not only darkened, but become darkness itself, . . . they are alienated from the light and life of God, and thereby naturally as incapable to judge of divine and spiritual things, comparatively speaking, as a man born blind is incapacitated to distinguish the various colours of the rainbow."[240]

Whitefield anticipated that some of his hearers may question God's fairness in condemning such blind and morally incapacitated individuals for their sin. In response to such thinking, he reminded his audiences that all by nature still possess a duty to obey God's commands.[241] In addition, the unregenerate also possess a willful disobedience and enmity towards God because of their inherent sinful nature. He contended that God is just in punishing such, explaining "God compels no man to sin. . . . The devil and our own hearts tempt, but they cannot force us to consent without the concurrence of our own will. So that our damnation is of ourselves, as will evidently appear at the great day, notwithstanding all men's present impudent replies against God."[242] According to the itinerant, it is sinners' own sins and guilt that condemn them.

Conclusion. Such is the desperate condition of all by nature according to Whitefield's theology of evangelism. Their depravity corrupts every aspect of their persons. They have Adam's sin imputed to them and are born in original sin. Fallen humans possess no inherent ability to gain fellowship or communion with God. Their enmity creates a hatred within them towards God. Apart from God revealing this hopeless condition to them through the saving work of the Holy Spirit, they naturally possess no succor.[243]

Unconditional Election[244]

Regarding the doctrine of election, in his book *American Evangelism*, Darius Salter declared, "Election that demands the arbitrary coddling of some at the expense (predetermined damnation of others) is the Calvinistic *faux de pas* ("false step"). This debilitating error often leads to a misrepresentation of the mind of God."[245]

George Whitefield did not share such a perspective regarding the doctrine of unconditional election. He wrote to John Wesley that this doctrine "is children's bread, and ought not in my opinion to be with-held from them, supposing it is always mentioned with proper cautions against the abuse."[246] Whitefield believed that the doctrine of election is essential in revealing to humans their moral inability and need for electing grace.[247]

What role, then, did the doctrine of election play in Whitefield's theology of evangelism? Interestingly, his letters to his friend John Wesley are some of the most helpful resources for obtaining both men's opposing views of this doctrine.[248] Key topics they address in their correspondence provide a helpful framework for exploring Whitefield's view of the doctrine of election.

God's sovereignty in election. Whitefield held that, because of original sin through the imputation of Adam's sin, humanity is dead in sin and morally incapable of choosing God. He asserted that all would be damned had not God sovereignly chosen to elect some to be given to the Son for their salvation. He contended that salvation is not based upon any merit in or choice by anyone, but is entirely dependent upon the sovereign will of God. It is unconditional.

Against proponents of unconditional election, Wesley preached that it was inconsistent that God would mercifully elect some, yet leave others to perish. He stated, "They infer from the text, 'I will have mercy on whom I will have mercy,' (Romans 9:15), that God is love only to some men, viz., the elect, and that he hath mercy for those only; flatly contrary to the whole tenor of Scripture, as is that express declaration in particular, 'The Lord is loving unto every man; and his mercy is over all his works.' (Psalm 145:9)"[249] In response to this assertion by Wesley, Whitefield asserted:

> For God is no respecter of persons, upon the account of any outward condition or circumstance in life whatever; nor does the doctrine of election in the least suppose him to be so. But as the sovereign Lord of all, who is debtor to none, he has a right to do what he will with his own, and to dispense favours to what objects he sees fit, merely at his plea-

sure. And his supreme right herein, is clearly and strongly asserted in those passages of scripture, where he says, "I will have mercy on whom I will have mercy, and have compassion on whom I will have compassion," Rom. ix. 15, Exod. Xxxiii. 19.[250]

Whitefield argued that, because God has created all, He has the right and power to do what He will with them. He likened men as to clay in the hands of a Divine Potter. Speaking as if from God's vantage point, Whitefield stated, "'Behold, as clay is in the hands of the potter, lying at his disposal, either to be destroyed, or formed into another vessel, so are ye in my hands, O house of Israel: I may either reject, and thereby ruin you, or I may revisit and revive you according to my own sovereign good-will and pleasure, and who shall say unto me, what dost thou?'"[251] Unlike Wesley, Whitefield did not see God's electing some men to be saved and allowing others to perish as unjust; rather, he viewed election as evidence of God's sovereign free grace. Because humans have no merit within themselves to appeal to God, only His grace and great love would motivate Him to choose to save some of them.[252] In addition, the idea that God elects sinners even while they actively rebel against him further amazed the English itinerant.[253] Whitefield summarized his understanding of free grace in the opening words of his sermon, "The Conversion of Zaccheus," stating, "Salvation, every where, through the whole scripture, is said to be the free gift of God, through Jesus Christ our Lord. Not only free, because God is a sovereign agent, and therefore may withhold it from, or confer it on, whom he pleases; but free because there is nothing to be found in man, that can any way induce God to be merciful unto him."[254]

Citing the fact that God, not man, is the initiator of election was, he contended, another evidence of election being unconditional and dependent upon God's sovereign will. He maintained that God chose the elect before the foundation of the world, and that God the Father made a covenant of redemption with Christ the Son in which He elected some of humanity to be given to the Son for their salvation. Whitefield referred to this covenant saying, "God the Father and God the Son had entered into a covenant concerning the salvation of the elect from all eternity, wherein God the Father promised, that, if the Son would offer his soul a sacrifice for sin, he should see his seed."[255] God, "from all eternity," took the initiative in choosing the elect and in entering into the covenant with His Son. Humans were not present nor involved in this decision of election. It was entirely the act of the sovereign God.

In further support, Whitefield presented examples from Scripture as evidence of God being the sovereign initiator in election and of the fact that sinners would not choose Christ unless He first chose them. Regarding Christ, Whitefield stated that He "speaks particularly of and to his own school, his little college of apostles: 'Thine they were and thou gavest them to me; I have chosen you, but ye have not chosen me.'"[256] He presented Adam as another biblical support for God's initiative in election, asking:

> Pray who called first, did Adam call after Christ, or did Christ call after him; or do you think there is any difference between us and Adam, or that we have got better hearts than Adam had; do you think we are wiser and better now? Adam run away from God, and so should we to this very day, unless Jesus Christ had called us to himself.[257]

He contended that the story of Christ and Zaccheus also testifies to God's sovereignly choosing the elect,[258] as does the story of Ananias and Paul.[259]

Throughout his ministry, Whitefield possessed a theology of evangelism that emphasized God's sovereignty in election. He contended that God justly elects whomever he wishes, not based upon human merit, but based upon His sovereign will. The itinerant emphasized the fact that God is the sovereign initiator of election and must first choose sinners before they will choose Him. He also argued that election is a testimony to God's sovereign free grace rather than to man's free will.

Election and foreknowledge. In his sermon "Free Grace," John Wesley claimed that proponents of unconditional election "infer, that our being predestinated, or elect, no way depends on the foreknowledge of God."[260] Whitefield's response to Wesley's statement yields a clear understanding of his own view regarding the connection between foreknowledge and unconditional election:

> For if foreknowledge signifies approbation, as it does in several parts of Scripture, then we confess that predestination and election do depend on God's foreknowledge. But if by God's foreknowledge, you understand God's foreseeing some good works done by his creatures as the foundation or reason of choosing them, and therefore electing them, then we say, that in this sense, predestination does not any way depend on God's foreknowledge.[261]

George Whitefield opposed the Arminian view of foreknowledge which contended that God based election upon his prior knowledge of an individual's decision to either accept or reject Him. According to this view, those persons He saw would accept Him became members of the elect, while individuals He knew would deny Him were not chosen. The itinerant contended that such a view of foreknowledge causes election to be conditional upon the sinner's merits and choice to receive Christ, rather than solely relying upon God's free grace and sovereign will.

Against this view of election and foreknowledge, Whitefield wrote, "What was there in you and in me, dear Mr. O____ , that should move God to chuse [sic] us before others? Was there any fitness foreseen in us, except a fitness for damnation? I believe not. No, God chose us from eternity, he called us in time, and I am persuaded will keep us from falling finally, till time shall be no more."[262] As mentioned previously, Whitefield held that all by nature are spiritually dead and morally unable to gain fellowship, salvation, or communion with God. Whitefield scoffed at the idea that an individual could choose Christ in such a condition. He contended that "we can no more turn our hearts than we can turn the world upside-down; it is the Redeemer, by his Spirit, must take away the heart of stone, and by the influence of the Holy Spirit give us a heart of flesh."[263] Because God must do the choosing, changing, and calling for such individuals to come to Him, Whitefield deemed it unbiblical and nonsensical to say that election would be conditional upon the foreknowledge of such a spiritually-dead person's decision.

Election and assurance. Besides opposing Wesley's view of foreknowledge, Whitefield also contended that his friend's position on conditional election grants no security or assurance for believers. Responding to a section of "Free Grace" in which Wesley claimed that unconditional election "tends to destroy the comforts of religion," Whitefield contended that the doctrine of unconditional election is for the believer:

> an anchor of hope, both sure and steadfast, when he walks in darkness and sees no light; as certainly he may, even after he hath received the witness of the Spirit, whatever you or others may unadvisedly assert to the contrary. Then, to have respect to God's everlasting covenant, and to throw himself upon the free distinguishing love of that God, who changeth not, will make him lift up the hands that hang down, and strengthen the feeble knees. But, without the belief of the doctrine of election, and the immutability of the free love of God, I cannot see how it is possible that any should have a comfortable assurance of eternal salvation.[264]

In contrast, he stated that Wesley's view of conditional election "has a natural tendency to keep the soul in darkness for ever; because the creature thereby is taught, that his being kept in the state of salvation, is owing to his own free will. And what a sandy foundation is that for a poor creature to build his hopes of perseverance upon?"[265]

If election he argued is conditional, the eternal security or assurance of salvation of the individual must also be conditional. If a person's election is based upon his choice to accept Christ, then his rejection of Christ could jeopardize his security as a believer. Such a state of affairs could cause the person to question from day to day whether he is maintaining his status as one of the elect. Because it places the professed believer in such a tenuous position, Whitefield maintained that conditional, not unconditional, election "tends to destroy the comforts of religion."[266]

On the other hand, he contended that unconditional election causes the believer to say with Paul, "'For I am persuaded, that neither death nor life, nor angels, nor principalities nor powers, nor things present, nor things to come, nor height nor depth, nor any other creature, shall be able to separate me from the love of God which is in Christ Jesus my Lord.'"[267]

Election and reprobation.[268]   The doctrine of reprobation was another issue in the debate over election between Whitefield and Wesley. In response to Wesley's assertion that it is unjust for God to condemn men "without any preceding offence or fault of theirs," Whitefield responded that his friend "must acknowledge the doctrine of election and reprobation to be highly just and reasonable. For if God might justly impute Adam's sin to all, and afterwards have passed by all, then he might justly pass by *some.*"[269]

Regarding whether or not God's action in election is related to the cause of men's reprobation, Wesley argued further, "Whatever be the cause of their perishing, it cannot be his will, if the oracles of God are true; for they declare, 'He is not willing that any should perish, but that all should come to repentance.'"[270] Wesley contended that election cannot be unconditional if it is against God's will that some men face condemnation. He held that passages of Scripture, such as the one cited above, indicate that sinners' salvation or condemnation must be based on the condition of the exercise of their free will in either denying or accepting Jesus Christ rather than upon God electing unconditionally.

George Whitefield claimed that Wesley's interpretation of 2 Peter 3:9 and other similar passages was faulty. He stated that if such passages are "taken in their strictest sense, then no one will be damned."[271] He contended that these passages, rightly interpreted, suggest that "God taketh no pleasure in the death of sinners, so as to delight simply in their death, but he delights to magnify his justice, by inflicting punishment which their iniquities have deserved."[272] Whitefield depicted God as a judge who, while possessing compassion for the condemned criminal, must uphold justice and punish wrongdoing.

Whitefield believed that the two doctrines—election and reprobation--are inseparable. In fact, he contended that "without a doubt, the doctrine of election and reprobation must stand or fall together."[273]

Election and evangelistic preaching. In his sermon "Free Grace," John Wesley contended that unconditional election makes gospel preaching unnecessary. He claimed:

> It is needless to them that are elected; for they, whether with preaching or without, will infallibly be saved. Therefore, the end of preaching–to save souls–is void with regard to them; and it is useless to them that are not elected, for they cannot possibly be saved: they, whether with preaching or without, will infallibly be damned.[274]

Wesley contended that, because it is clear in Scripture that believers must preach the gospel, unconditional election must be false by invalidating the need for such preaching.

Whitefield's response to Wesley was, in essence, that such line of reasoning was nonsensical. God intends, he argued, the preaching of the gospel as a means to draw the elect to Himself, and contended further, "And since we know not who are elect, and who reprobate, we are to preach promiscuously to all. For the word may be useful, even to the non-elect, in restraining them from much wickedness and sin."[275] Whitefield's position was that God mandates the preaching of the gospel, and the preacher does not know who is elect or not elect; therefore, the evangelist must be faithful in preaching the gospel freely.

Conclusion. Whitefield's belief in the doctrine of unconditional election comprised another aspect of his theology of evangelism. He held firmly that God is the sovereign initiator and agent in choosing to save some. This decision is not based on the foreknowledge of an exercise of free will on anyone's part; rather, it is based upon God's will in exercising free grace or unmerited favor upon rebellious sinners who are at enmity with Him. The itinerant maintained that God was just in condemning the reprobate whom He did not choose. Whitefield also contended that gospel preaching was in no way made null and void by the doctrine of unconditional election.

Particular Redemption

The issue of universal redemption was another point of contention between George Whitefield and John Wesley. Their debate sheds light upon the view of redemption that Whitefield held within his theology of evangelism. Wesley believed in universal redemption, a theological position that teaches that Christ's death on the cross was for all whether they be among the elect or among those persons condemned to hell.[276] He affirmed that particular redemption stands contrary to Scripture and to God's will that all be saved. Whitefield, on the other hand, held that Christ did not die on the cross for all. He contended that Jesus died for a particular group of people—the elect. What, then, was Whitefield's belief in particular redemption?

Covenant of grace. Remember, Whitefield believed that God the Father entered into a covenant with God the Son to save an elect group of sinners from damnation. This covenant, he held, related to redemption as well as election. Whitefield wrote Wesley regarding this covenant:

> But blessed be God, our Lord knew for whom he died. There was an eternal compact between the Father and the Son. A certain number was then given to him, as the purchase and reward of his obedience and death. For these he prayed, *John* xvii, and not for the world. For these, and these only, he is now interceding, and with their salvation he will be fully satisfied.[277]

Whitefield also referred to this covenant of particular grace in his preaching. In his sermon "The Good Shepherd," he declared that "Christ purchased those whom he calls his own; he redeemed them with his own blood, so that they are not only his by eternal election, but also by actual redemption in time; and they were given to him by the Father, upon the condition that he should redeem them by this heart's blood."[278] He alluded to this covenant when he preached:

> Now, this should endear God to us, to think that from all the ages of eternity, God had thoughts of you; God intended the Lord Jesus Christ to save your souls and mine: hence it is, that God, to endear *Jeremiah* to him, tells him, I have loved thee with an everlasting love. Hence it is, that the Lord Jesus, when he calls his elect people up to heaven, says, "Come, ye blessed of my Father;" what follows? "receive the kingdom prepared for you;" how long? "from the foundation of the world." All that we receive in time, all the streams that come to our souls, are but so many streams flowing from that inexhaustible fountain, God's electing, God's sovereign, God's distinguishing, God's everlasting love;

and therefore the righteousness of Jesus Christ may properly be called an everlasting righteousness, because God intended it from everlasting.[279]

It is evident, from Whitefield's preaching and correspondence with Wesley, that the itinerant understood that this covenant of grace held the Father's act of election and the Son's act of redemption very closely together. Because he believed the actions were part of the same covenant, he would not accommodate Wesley's contention that Christ died for non-elect individuals. According to Whitefield, such unregenerate persons were not part of God's act in election; therefore, they could not be persons for whom Christ died. They are not recipients of the covenant of grace.

Universalism and universal redemption. Whitefield also took exception to Wesley's claim that Christ died for the elect and for those persons condemned to hell. He acknowledged the passages Wesley cited that speak of Christ being the Savior of "all men;" however, his interpretations of this phrase differed from Wesley.[280] The itinerant unpacked his understanding of how Christ is the Savior of "all men" in his preaching. In the sermon "The Beloved of God," Whitefield stated:

> God's mercy is sure, and over all his works; and in one sense, our Lord Jesus Christ is the Saviour of all men, that is, of all sorts of men. Even the wicked are beholden to Jesus Christ, whom they despise, for every worldly comfort they enjoy. In this sense we should learn to love as our Lord, we are told, loved the young man when he saw he had been a harmless and good liver.—But we must go more to what we call Calvinism, what I call Scriptural truth. The love which Jesus Christ bore for the young man, quite differed from that love with which he loved Martha, Mary, and their brother.[281]

The itinerant maintained that Christ possesses a special love toward the elect that is not shared with unregenerate men. Although he acknowledged that Christ is the Savior of "all sorts of men," Whitefield did not believe that Christ died for those who would perish in hell.

He believed that suggesting that Christ died for the reprobate was a travesty upon the blood of Christ. Against such a suggestion from Wesley, Whitefield replied, "I would hint farther, that you unjustly charge the doctrine of reprobation with blasphemy, whereas the doctrine of universal redemption, as you set it forth, is really the highest reproach upon the dignity of the Son of God and the merit of his blood. Consider whether it be not rather blasphemy to say as you do, page 20, 'Christ not only died for those that are saved, but also for those that perish.'"[282]

He argued that Wesley's view of universal redemption, when carried to its logical conclusion, leads to universalism. Because Christ was the righteous substitute for the elect, his work purchased their salvation.[283] If, as Wesley claimed, Christ died for those persons in hell, then His substitutionary atonement would also pay for their salvation. Whitefield's use of this rationale is clear in his response to Wesley regarding the issue. He stated:

> You cannot make good the assertion, "That Christ died for them that perish," without holding (as *Peter Boehler*, one of the *Moravian* brethren, in order to make out universal redemption, lately frankly confessed in a letter) "That all the damned souls would hereafter be brought out of hell." I cannot think *Mr Wesley* is thus minded. And yet without this can be proved, universal redemption, taken in a literal sense, falls entirely to the ground. For how can all be universally redeemed, if all are not finally saved?[284]

Whitefield held that Wesley could not avoid universalism in advocating universal redemption.

Conclusion. George Whitefield's theology of evangelism incorporated the doctrine of particular redemption. He believed that a covenant of grace occurred in which God the Father presented the elect to Christ the Son who would redeem them with His shed blood on the cross. While Whitefield believed Christ is the Savior of "all sorts of men," he did not believe that Jesus died for the reprobate. In fact, he argued that such a position of universal redemption may only logically lead to universalism. He also believed that universal redemption made a mockery of the blood of Christ.

Effectual Calling

George Whitefield maintained that, because humans possess a moral inability to seek God or to change themselves, it is necessary that the Holy Spirit change their inclination to sin and dispose their wills to God. He called the process of the Holy Spirit changing sinners' volitions "effectual calling." But how did he understand this doctrine?

A sovereign call. As in his understanding of unconditional election, the English evangelist emphasized the sovereignty of God in the effectual call of the Holy Spirit.[285] Whitefield stressed that, apart from this work of the Holy Spirit upon their lives, human beings are helpless to change themselves. He asserted that sinners will continue in darkness and sin unless the Holy Spirit grants them an awareness of their plight. Regarding his own conversion experience, the itinerant wrote, "I can trace my conversion through its several steps, but cannot find one step I first took towards God . . . Had not God called after me, and by his spirit said unto me, as unto Adam, 'Where art thou? Into what dreadful condition hast thou plunged thyself?' I should have fled from him (if possible) forever."[286] As in election, God the Holy Spirit must take the initiative in calling and drawing souls to Christ. He must "speak also as effectually to these spiritually dead souls, whom Satan for many years hath so fast bound by sensual pleasures, that they are not so much able to lift up their eyes or hearts to heaven."[287]

A particular call. In addition to being a call based upon the sovereignty of God and not upon man's effort, the call of the Holy Spirit is one that is granted only to a particular group of people–the elect. While Whitefield held that one must preach a universal call to the gospel, he stated that it is the particular call of the Holy Spirit to elect individuals that is effectual for salvation.[288]

Whitefield held that the three Persons of the Trinity were involved in the covenant of grace regarding the elect. God the Father chose the elect and gave them to the Son for their redemption. Then the Holy Spirit's role in the covenant is to sanctify these chosen individuals. Speaking of the Trinity's involvement in the covenant of grace, Whitefield stated:

> . . . they who once held a consultation to create, are all equally concerned in making preparations for, and effectually bringing about the redemption of man. The Father creates, the Son redeems, and the Holy Ghost sanctifies all the elect people of God. Being loved from eternity, they are effectually called in time, they are chosen out of the world, . . . by a free, voluntary, unconstrained oblation, they devote themselves, spirit, soul, and body, to the entire service of Him, who hath loved, and given himself for them.[289]

Because the three Persons of the Trinity are unified regarding the covenant of grace, the effectual call of the Holy Spirit is only extended to the elect whom the Father has chosen and whom the Son redeemed. In another statement regarding the particular nature of effectual calling, Whitefield asserted that "none but those that are beloved by him with an everlasting love, are brought to believe in him."[290]

Conviction and call. George Whitefield preached that, in the process of effectual calling, the Holy Spirit awakens elect individuals and convicts them of their fallen sinful state. He asserted that a pattern is evident regarding the manner in which the Holy Spirit convicts unbelievers of their sinful condition and works out their conversion. In his message "The Holy Spirit Convincing the World of Sin, Righteousness, and Judgment," the evangelist stated, "This is the method the Spirit of God generally takes in dealing with sinners; he first convinces them of some heinous actual sin, and at the same time brings all their other sins into remembrance, and as it were sets in battle-array before them: 'When he is come, he will reprove the world of sin.'"[291]

Whitefield expressed that, once the Holy Spirit convicted the individual of particular sins, He would then grant the person a painful comprehension of original sin. During this stage of conviction, the sinner begins to ponder the source of his particular sins. According to the itinerant, the Holy Spirit then reveals to the unbeliever "that he has no good thing in him by nature; then he sees that he is altogether gone out of the way, that he is altogether become abominable, and the poor creature is made to lie down at the foot of the throne of God, and to acknowledge that God would be just to damn him, just to cut him off, though he never had committed one actual sin in his life."[292] Whitefield taught that this understanding of original sin goes beyond intellectual assent and involves the Spirit granting a deep conviction within the heart of the sinner regarding spiritual deadness and the just punishment of his eternal damnation.

He further maintained that, after the unbeliever is made aware of the truth of original sin, the Holy Spirit then convicts the sinner of his sinful efforts to justify himself by his own works. Whitefield asserted that the Spirit leads the individual to comprehend that his best efforts to achieve right standing with God are corrupted by his sinful nature and are totally incapable of saving him. He declared to his hearers:

We all naturally are Legalists, thinking to be justified by the works of the law. When somewhat awakened by the terrors of the Lord, we immediately, like
the Pharisees of old, go about to establish our own
righteousness, and think we shall find acceptance
with God, if we seek it with tears: finding ourselves
damned by nature and our actual sins, we then
think to recommend ourselves to God by our duties,
and hope, by our doings of one kind or another, to
inherit eternal life. But, whenever the Comforter
comes into the heart, it convinces the soul of these
false rests, and makes the sinner to see that all his
righteousnesses are but as filthy rags; and that, for
the most pompous services, he deserves no better a
doom than that of the unprofitable servant, "to be
thrown into outer darkness, where is weeping, and
wailing, and gnashing of teeth."293

The itinerant held that the Holy Spirit reveals to sinners
that any reliance upon their own works for salvation would
result in their damnation.

According to Whitefield, once the unbeliever is convicted of the sinfulness of his efforts toward self-justification, the Holy Spirit then convicts the individual of his unbelief–his lack of faith. The evangelist held that true faith
involves more than intellectual assent or religious activity.
An individual could take communion or go to church, yet
not be a true believer. He advised that saving faith is a
gift of God that works a radical change in the heart of the
sinner. Whitefield claimed that, in this pattern of conviction, the Holy Spirit tests the unbeliever and reveals to him
that he lacks saving faith. The itinerant contended that the
Spirit also reveals to the sinner that, because of his sinful
nature, he is incapable of exercising saving faith in his own
power.294 The result of the Spirit's conviction of unbelief,
he held, then leaves the individual with the understanding
that he has no recourse but to throw himself upon the mercies of God.

The will and the call. Whitefield maintained that, in addition to the Holy Spirit convicting lost individuals of sin, effectual calling also involves the Spirit enabling them to come to Christ. The Holy Spirit changes the individuals' natural will and makes them willing to follow Christ and, until the Holy Spirit attends the preaching of the gospel in making the individual willing to come to Christ, sinners will continue in their spiritual deadness and inability.

Remarks from two of Whitefield's messages shed light upon his view of the Spirit's work in effectually changing the sinner's will. He acknowledged the preaching of the gospel alone did not guarantee his hearers would come to Christ. The Holy Spirit must effectually draw them, make them willing, and grant to them faith in Jesus.[295] Speaking of Christ's call to Zaccheus, Whitefield declared:

> But what saith the scripture? "I will make a willing people in the day of my power." With this outward call, there went an efficacious power from God, which sweetly overruled his natural will: and therefore, verse 6, "He made haste, and came down, and received him joyfully;" not only into his house, but also into his heart.
>
> Thus it is the great God brings home his children. He calls them by name, by his word or providence; he speaks to them also by his Spirit. Hereby they are enabled to open their hearts, and are made willing to receive the King of glory.[296]

Because he believed that effectual calling involved the Holy Spirit making sinners willing to come to Christ, Whitefield also maintained that evangelists must pray that the Spirit would effectually empower the preached gospel. Two examples of such prayers are found in his sermons about blind Bartimeus and about the conversion of the apostle Paul.[297] The itinerant evangelist depended upon the effectual call of the Holy Spirit to make elect individuals willing to believe the preached gospel.

Conclusion. The doctrine of effectual calling comprised part of George Whitefield's theology of evangelism. He held that the Holy Spirit takes the initiative in sovereignly calling spiritually dead men to life. This call is a particular call that the Holy Spirit only extends to the elect. In calling the elect, the Holy Spirit participates in the covenant of grace. Whitefield asserted that, during the process of His effectual call, the Holy Spirit convicts the elect of particular sins, of original sin, and of their efforts at self-justification. The call is effectual because it changes their natural will to live in sin and makes them willing to follow Christ.

Perseverance of the Saints

Another doctrine included in George Whitefield's theology of evangelism, one related to unconditional election, was the doctrine of the perseverance of the saints. He believed that, because salvation is entirely dependent upon the choice and power of God, the believer can be confident that God will preserve His elect during their lives on earth and throughout eternity. Several aspects of Whitefield's understanding of the doctrine of the perseverance of the saints bear consideration.

God's sovereign keeping. Whitefield maintained that, just as He sovereignly chooses the elect and grants them redemption through the blood of Christ, God sovereignly protects these objects of His grace and preserves their salvation. In his letter to Wesley, Whitefield stated, "I should utterly sink under a dread of my impending trials, was I not firmly persuaded that God has chosen me in Christ from before the foundation of the world, and that now being effectually called, he will suffer none to pluck me out of his almighty hand."[298]

God's sovereignty and immutability, he contended, guarantee the believer's security. Thus Whitefield preached, "All his attributes are engaged for your preservation, and all things shall work together for your good, who love God, and, by being thus married to the Lord Jesus, give an evident proof that you are called according to his purpose."[299] He preached that believers are kept in "a garrison" of security by God's power.[300] Because no one can oppose God's sovereignty and power, and because of the fact that He does not change regarding His choice in electing, the believer may possess assurance.

Christ's redemption and love. In addition to being kept by God's sovereign power, Whitefield asserted that believers are held secure by Christ's redemption and love. Because Christ cannot fail in redeeming the elect, believers are secure in their salvation. In this regard, Whitefield asserted:

> For He hath sealed you to the day of redemption, and hath given you the earnest of your future inheritance. His eyes and heart shall therefore be upon you continually: and in spite of all opposition from men or devils, the top-stone of this spiritual building shall be brought forth, and you shall shout Grace, grace unto it: your bodies shall be fashioned like unto the Redeemer's glorious body, and your souls, in which (O infinite condescension!) he now delights to dwell, shall be filled with all the fullness of God.[301]

The infinitely righteous blood of Christ secures the salvation of the elect.

In addition to Christ's redemption providing assurance for the elect, Whitefield also maintained that His love for the elect holds them fast. The evangelist assured believers that "death itself shall not separate a true believer from the love of God, which is in Christ Jesus his Lord; for he will never cease loving his bride, till he has loved her to heaven, and presented her before his Father, without spot or wrinkle, or any such thing. Nay, his love will, as it were, but be beginning, through the endless ages of eterni-

ty."[302] He contended that Christ's love for the elect holds
and keeps them to the end.

Sin and persecution. Whitefield contended,
then, that persecution, Satan, and the believer's own sin
cannot place his salvation in jeopardy. God may discipline
believers when they sin; however, He will not take His love
or salvation away from them. He exhorted his believing
hearers:

> Indeed, some people tell us, that a person may be in
> Christ to-day, and go to the devil to-morrow: but,
> blessed be God, ye have not so learned Christ! . .
> . Though God's people may fall foully; and though
> many are full of doubts and fears, and say, "One day
> I shall fall by the hands of Saul;" however ye may
> say in your haste, "All men are liars;" however your
> poor souls may be harassed, yet no wicked devil,
> nor your own depraved heart, shall be able to sep-
> arate you from the love of God: God has loved you,
> God has fixed his heart upon you, and, having loved
> his own, he loves them unto the end.[303]

This steadfastness of Christ's love and forgiveness was a
great encouragement to Whitefield.

Additionally, he claimed, Christ is also with the believer in the midst of persecution. God will uphold His believers when they suffer at the hands of evil men. So, he
encouraged his hearers, "Christ obliges himself to love you
here; he will not, indeed he never will leave you, he will
protect you from the malice of the Pharisees of this generation, he will provide for you in all difficulties, he will live
with you here, and at last he will take you to himself, to
live with you for ever."[304] Believers like Whitefield could
minister and evangelize with the freedom of knowing that
Christ would preserve them here and in the hereafter.

Conclusion. The doctrine of the perseverance of
the saints occupied a significant place in George Whitefield's theology of evangelism. He found this truth to be a
comfort in his own life and sought to communicate such

comfort to his believing hearers. Whitefield believed that God sovereignly keeps the believer secure in life and in death. God will not allow one of His chosen believers to be taken from His hand. The itinerant also emphasized the fact that Christ's redemption and eternal love hold believers fast. Neither the believer's own sin nor persecution can separate him from Jesus' presence. The Lord keeps him and upholds him in all situations.

New Birth and Regeneration

The doctrine of the new birth, or regeneration, was a significant element of George Whitefield's theology of evangelism. Thomas Kidd writes, "Although the doctrine of the new birth was not new, Whitefield was the most important popularizer of the concept in Anglo-American history, at least until Billy Graham's revivals of the twentieth century."[305] As mentioned previously, Whitefield believed that it is necessary for sinners to become new creations because original sin leaves them radically depraved, dead in their sins, at enmity with God, and damned to Hell. Sinners, by nature, must experience a transformation of every aspect of their being; their wills, affections, understanding, minds, and hearts. The itinerant applied several terms to this process.

The regeneration, conversion, and the ordo salutis.[306] Any discussion of George Whitefield's view of the new birth must include a presentation of the nomenclature he used to refer to this aspect of his theology of evangelism. Whitefield acknowledged that people use numerous terms to refer to the moral change that the Holy Spirit works in transforming sinners into new creatures. Of this transformation he said:

> This moral change is what some call repentance, some conversion, some regeneration; choose what name you please, I only pray God that we all may have the thing. The scriptures call it holiness, sanc-

tification, the new creature, and our Lord calls it a "new birth, or being born again, or born from above." These are not barely figurative expressions, or the flights of eastern language, nor do they barely denote a relative change of state conferred on all those who are admitted into Christ's church by baptism; but they denote a real, moral change of heart and life, a real participation of divine life in the soul of man.[307]

Whitefield used three terms to refer to this work of God in man. He called it either "new birth," "regeneration," or "repentance."[308] He used the terms "new birth" and "regeneration" synonymously in describing the changing of sinners' natures that the Holy Spirit works in the lives of the elect. In his sermon, "On Regeneration," Whitefield used the two terms interchangeably by referring to "the doctrine of our regeneration, or new birth in Jesus Christ."[309] He also referred to the opposites of both terms synonymously.[310] The itinerant also used the words "regeneration" and "repentance" synonymously in one of his sermons, stating, "A man that has truly repented, is truly regenerated: it is a different word for one and the same thing; the motley mixture of the beast and devil is gone: there is, as it were, a new creation wrought in your hearts."[311]

Although Whitefield does not portray conversion as being synonymous with regeneration, one might logically deduce from his synonymic use of the terms "repentance" and "regeneration" that he held such a position.[312] If he did, it would call to question whether Whitefield's understanding of the *ordo salutis* varied from the Reformed tradition. Because the itinerant did not present a formal treatment regarding his understanding of the order of salvation, a close examination of his letters, journals, and sermons helps establish his position on the matter, and reveals that Whitefield's understanding is consistent with the Reformed tradition.[313]

At this point, J. I . Packer's comments regarding Whitefield's understanding of conversion might shed light upon the eighteenth-century evangelist's remarks touching the relationship between repentance and regeneration. Packer writes:

> Whitefield followed the Puritans in presenting the conversion process in a two-sided way, as Augustinians typically do. When speaking psychologically and evangelistically, he depicted the realizing of one's sin and need, the praying and seeking to which this must lead, and the decision-making that faith and repentance involve, as a person's own acts, which we must ask for the Holy Spirit's help to perform. When speaking theologically and doxologically, however, he interpreted the entire process as one which the Holy Spirit works from first to last, in which each of our steps Godward is taken only because the Holy Spirit is moving us forward by his secret action within us.[314]

This two-sided approach in explaining aspects of conversion and the *ordo salutis* is evident in Whitefield's comments regarding repentance.

In one sense, the itinerant describes repentance as an act which God performs in the individual. Whitefield stated, "Repentance, my brethren, in the first place, as to its nature, is the carnal and corrupt disposition of men being changed into a renewed and sanctified disposition."[315] He spoke of repentance being "wrought" in people's souls by the work of the Holy Spirit.[316] The itinerant preacher also prayed that God would grant his hearers such repentance. He beseeched God, "Shew them, O Father, wherein they have offended thee; make them to see their own vileness, and that they are lost and undone without true repentance; and O give them that repentance, we beseech of thee, that they may turn from sin unto thee, the living and true God."[317] In all of these examples, Whitefield speaks of repentance as a change that God accomplishes in the sinners's heart, who will not turn from sins and turn toward God if his nature is not first changed and a new will to turn is granted to him. In this sense, the itinerant speaks of repentance as an act of God within sinners prior to their action.

In another sense, Whitefield describes repentance as an action sinners perform in turning from sin and throwing themselves upon the mercy of Christ. This aspect of repentance is evident where he prays that God will "give them that repentance, . . . that they may turn from sin unto thee, the living and true God."[318] In the same sermon, Whitefield described repentance as an individual's grieving over, hating, and forsaking sin.[319] He summarized these aspects of repentance, stating that repentance involves an individual resolving to resist Satan and sin and casting himself upon Christ for his salvation.[320] The itinerant also described repentance as a turning to God and walking in the things of the gospel.[321] In all of these examples, Whitefield referred to repentance as an action carried out by the individual; however, the Holy Spirit must first grant the individual a heart of repentance that is willing to forsake sin and turn to God.

George Whitefield related the act of repentance, the individual forsaking sin and turning to God, to the process of conversion. In his sermon "Repentance and Conversion," Whitefield asserted, "Repentance and conversion are nearly the same. The expression in the text is complex, and seems to include both what goes before and follows 'turning to God.'"[322] In maintaining that such repentance, an abandonment of sin and pursuit of God, is related to the process of conversion, Whitefield remained consistent with the traditional Reformed understanding of the *ordo salutis*.[323]

One might argue that Whitefield's understanding that, in a sense, repentance and regeneration are different words for the same action represents a departure from the Reformed tradition; however, we must not overlook the context within which the evangelist suggested such a relationship.

Whitefield used both words to refer to "a new creation wrought in your hearts." He suggested further that sinners' actions in repentance are based on such a change of heart that disposes their wills toward repentance. Although some may attempt to challenge his judgment in using the term "repentance" to refer to such a change of heart, Whitefield's understanding of this change being directly connected with and prior to man's repentant actions in conversion is consistent with the Reformed tradition.[324]

With the exception of his comment in "Repentance and Conversion," Whitefield referred to the inner change of nature wrought by the Holy Spirit as the "new birth" or "regeneration." The itinerant defined this new birth as "receiving a principle of new life, imparted to our hearts by the Holy Ghost, changing you, giving you new thoughts, new words, new actions, new views, so that old things pass away, and all things become new in our souls."[325] He called it the "Spirit's divine influences" upon the heart of the individual.[326] Notice, in this short definition, the itinerant does not mention an act of repentance or exercising a belief in Christ as seen in conversion. His definition referred to the work of the Spirit which grants "new life" that leads to such actions; however, such repentance and faith are also gifts of the Spirit.

Religious activity and the new birth. In his preaching regarding the new birth, George Whitefield admonished his hearers not to take confidence in outward religious activities such as baptism, church membership, or moral acts. While the itinerant did not enter into a debate regarding the mode of baptism or the merits of the baptism of infants, he did assert that baptism alone is not sufficient for an individual's salvation.[327] Whitefield also opposed the belief in baptismal regeneration which was prominent among numerous eighteenth-century Anglican clergy.[328] In two of his pamphlets, he referred to baptismal regeneration as the "Diana of the *present clergy*."[329] The itinerant asserted that a baptism with water is not sufficient for one's salvation nor is it an instrument of regeneration.[330]

Whitefield contended that one must experience the inward baptism of the Holy Spirit which changes the heart, resulting in new birth or regeneration. "He is a true Christian," he maintained, "who is one inwardly, whose baptism is that of the heart, in the spirit, and not merely in the water, whose praise is not of man, but of God. . . so our souls, though still the same as to essence, yet are so purged, purified, and cleansed from their natural dross, filth, and leprosy, by the blessed influences of the Holy Spirit, that they may be properly said to be made anew."[331] He declared further, "I do believe baptism to be an ordinance of Christ, but at the same time no candid person can be angry for my asserting, that there are numbers that have been baptized when grown up, or when very young, that are not regenerated by God's Spirit, who will all go to one place, and that place is where there will be no water to quench that dreadful fire that will parch them with thirst."[332] Whitefield repeatedly exhorted his hearers that their only security must be found in the Holy Spirit baptism of the new birth.

The itinerant also claimed that church membership would not suffice for one's salvation. He contended that building one's hopes for salvation upon church membership is depending upon a "sorry and rotten foundation."[333] He maintained:

> . . . there are more unbelievers within the pale than without the pale of the church; .
>
> . . all are not possessors that are professors, all have not got the thing promised, all are not partakers of the promise, that talk and bless God they have got the promised Saviour; I may have him in my mouth and upon my tongue, without having the thing promised, or the blessed promise in my heart.[334]

Church membership alone could not provide an individual a relationship with God.

Morality and religious activity were also inadequate to secure one's salvation. Whitefield opposed persons who claimed that Christianity consisted of outward religious performances or acts of morality. On this matter, the evangelist declared:

> Christianity includes morality, as grace does reason; but if we are only mere moralists, if we are not inwardly wrought upon, and changed by the powerful operations of the Holy Spirit, and our moral actions proceed from a principle of a new nature, however we may call ourselves Christians, we shall be found naked at the great day, and in the number of those who have neither Christ's righteousness imputed to them for their justification in the sight, nor holiness enough in their souls as the consequence of that, in order to make them meet for the enjoyment of God.[335]

He emphasized further that participating in the "duties of religion," such as church attendance, prayer, communion, and all other religious activities are insufficient to grant one rest or peace with God. One must be a Christian inwardly, possessing a heart that has been changed by the regenerating work of the Holy Spirit, before one may claim membership in Christ's Church.[336]

Inward feelings. George Whitefield maintained that individuals can feel an inward change when the Holy Spirit grants their souls new birth. He contended:

> For there is a spiritual, as well as a corporeal feeling; and though this is not communicated to us in a sensible manner, as outward objects affect our senses, yet it is as real as any sensible or visible sensation, and may be as truly felt and discerned by the soul, as any impression from without can be felt by the body. All who are born again of God, know I lie not.[337]

The itinerant believed that believers may sense a change in their lives that caused their wills to turn towards God and away from sin. Without such a change, they would not want the things of God; rather, their wills would lead them to rebel continually against him. Such a change of will would motivate them to repentance and faith.

Conclusion. The doctrine of the new birth was another significant element of George Whitefield's theology of evangelism. He asserted that the Holy Spirit must work a transformation in every aspect of sinners' beings before they will desire to come to Christ. Although in one sermon Whitefield refers to this change as repentance, he predominately referred to this work of the Holy Spirit as "new birth" or "regeneration." This action of the Holy Spirit occurs prior to sinners' actions of repentance and belief during conversion; however, as we will see, these acts in conversion are also gifts of the Holy Spirit. The itinerant warned his hearers that they must not depend on baptism, church membership, or moral activity to save them. Only an inward change would place them on the path to salvation by disposing their wills towards Christ. Whitefield also believed that the regenerate experience inward feelings which testify to this change of their natures.

Conversion[338]

George Whitefield spoke of two aspects of conversion. In one aspect, he spoke of conversion was an act of God in granting the sinner the gifts of repentance and belief. The other aspect of conversion was the individual's conscious response to the conviction of the Holy Spirit in turning from sin and placing faith in Christ. What, then, were some of the various factors involved in Whitefield's understanding of conversion?

An act of God. Whitefield, remember, believed sinners naturally will not come to God unless their hearts are first changed by the Holy Spirit; therefore, conversion is closely related to the Holy Spirit's work of regeneration. The itinerant emphasized that no one will repent and believe until the Holy Spirit places the desire to do so within the hearts. Whitefield asserted that God grants the gifts of repentance and faith to the elect, he claimed, as a result of the covenant of grace between the Father, Son, and Holy Spirit. Thus "God, as a reward of Christ's sufferings, promised to give the elect faith and repentance, in order to bring them to eternal life: and both these, and every thing else necessary for their everlasting happiness, are infallibly secured to them in this promise; as Mr. Boston, an excellent Scots divine, clearly shews, in a book entitled, 'A view of the covenant of grace.'"[339]

Whitefield contended that the faith the believer exercises at conversion is a gift of God. Divine faith is not wrought in the heart by moral persuasion (though moral suasion is very often made use of as a means to convey it), he argued, emphasizing that "faith is the peculiar gift of God."[340] He contended that natural men cannot work up this faith on their own using their own fallen abilities, he held; it must be given to them by God. Because they had no hope of formulating such faith within themselves, Whitefield encouraged his hearers to "Beg of God to give you faith; and if the Lord give you that, you will by it receive Christ, with his righteousness, and his all."[341] God acts by instilling such faith necessary for conversion in the sinner's heart.

The itinerant also contended that God must act in granting an individual repentance before the individual will turn from his/her sin and turn to Christ. Repentance is "wrought" in the heart of the believer through the work of the Holy Spirit during regeneration.[342] The evangelist prayed for God to grant his hearers repentance so that they would turn from their sin.[343] He emphasized that repentance involved the Holy Spirit changing sinners' hearts of stone and granting them hearts of flesh that desire to repent.[344]

An act of humans. While the itinerant emphasized that repentance and faith are works of God in the hearts of sinners during conversion, he stressed that people must also act during conversion by repenting and believing through the power of God's grace. Whitefield stated that by "heartily repenting of all our sins, and cordially believing the everlasting gospel, we receive the Lord Jesus Christ for righteousness and life, resting our souls on the value of his atonement, and the efficacy of his grace."[345] In other words, there were conscious actions taken by his hearers in response to conscious conviction from the Holy Spirit.

Whitefield believed that the individual's conscious awareness of this conviction from the Holy Spirit is the first step in conversion. Describing such conviction, he stated that it is "not a little flight now and then, or a qualm of conscience; the devil and natural conscience may do this; but when it is wrought in thy heart by the Spirit of God, it goes to the bottom, the arrow sticks fast, and a poor soul sometimes endeavours to pray, endeavours to pull it out, but in vain."[346] He maintained that, during this time of conviction, the Holy Spirit brings to the individual's consciousness conviction over particular sins, original sin, self efforts at salvation, and unbelief.[347] Further, he held, that the Spirit then brings individuals to the point of sorrow and helplessness regarding their sins and enmity against God.[348] Whitefield claimed that, after the sinner reaches this point of despair, the Holy Spirit "begins more immediately to act in the quality of a Comforter, and convinces the soul so powerfully of the reality and all-sufficiency of Christ's righteousness, that the soul is immediately set a hungering and thirsting after it."[349] The individual's conviction over sin and the realization of his need for Christ lead him to act in repentance and belief.

How did Whitefield describe repentance in its individual acts and what light does that shed on his understanding of this crucial aspect of conversion? The evangelist stated that individuals repent when they "leave all thy [their] sinful lusts and pleasures; renounce, forsake, and abhor, thy [their] old sinful course of life, and serve God in holiness and righteousness all the remaining part of life."[350] He stated that repentance involves "a resignation of ourselves to God, and a thorough renunciation of all worldly and corrupt affections."[351] Whitefield believed sinners must come to a point in repentance where they are so convicted of their sin, unworthiness, and lack of righteousness that they feel their "very repentance needed to be repented of."[352] They turn from their own attempts at righteousness and "come as poor, lost, undone sinners, to the Lord Jesus Christ; to be washed in his blood; to be clothed in his glorious imputed righteousness."[353] Repentance involves individuals' forsaking sin, Satan, and their old selves and turning to Christ for their salvation.[354]

Accompanying repentance in conversion, Whitefield held that individuals also exercise faith. And he was clear what he believed faith is and is not. In his view, faith is not "a dead speculative faith, a faith in the head."[355] In fact, he warned that such faith as that could not save an individual. Whitefield, instead, asserted that believers must possess a faith which is reflected in a total dependence upon the righteousness of Christ and upon His work on the cross for their salvation. On this matter, Whitefield stated:

"Believe in the Lord Jesus Christ, and you shall be saved:" therefore none of you need go away despairing. Come to the Lord Jesus by faith, and he shall receive you. You have no righteousness of your own to depend on. If you are saved, it is by the righteousness of Christ, through his atonement, his making a sacrifice for sin: his righteousness must be imputed to you, otherwise you cannot be saved.[356]

Sinners must place their faith in the shed blood of Christ for their sins as their sole hope of salvation. Whitefield emphasized that Christ's blood is capable to wash away any sin, saying, "No, were our sins more in number than the hairs of our head, or of a deeper die than the brightest scarlet; yet the merits of the death of Jesus Christ are infinitely greater, and faith in his blood will make them white as snow."[357] Thus, Whitefield maintained that the saving faith believers exercise at conversion is a total reliance upon Christ and His shed blood for salvation.

Besides not being a dead faith, this faith, he insisted, is also not a faith of inaction. True faith, he believed, shows through the believer's obedience.[358] Because Whitefield maintained that true converts would evidence faith through fruit in their lives, he was hesitant to identify individuals as converts until seeing such evidence. He stated, "I love now to wait a little, and see if people bring forth fruit; for there are so many blossoms which March winds you know blow away, that I cannot believe they are converts till I see fruit brought forth. It will do converts no harm to keep them a little back; it will never do a sincere soul any harm."[359]

Conclusion. George Whitefield believed that conversion involved individuals acting in repentance and faith in Christ. He acknowledged that such repentance and faith are both gifts from the Holy Spirit granted to the individual. At the same time, the evangelist maintained that, through God's grace, sinners respond to the conviction of the Holy Spirit by turning from their sin and turning towards God. They place their faith in Christ's righteousness and in His work on the cross as their only means of salvation. He emphasized that such faith, if genuine, evidences itself in the believer's obedience.

Justification

The doctrine of justification, a doctrine closely related to the doctrine of conversion, was another part of George Whitefield's theology of evangelism. The itinerant gave the following explanation of justification: "you have your sins forgiven, and are looked upon by God as though you never had offended him at all: for this is the meaning of the word justified, in almost all the passages of holy scripture where this word is mentioned."[360] George Whitefield asserted that the sinner is justified three ways: meritoriously, instrumentally, and declaratively.[361]

Sinners' need for justification. Before entering into a discussion regarding these three aspects of justification, it is imperative that we examine the sinner's need for justification. Whitefield contended that, because of our sinful natures, we are incapable of the holiness required by God to place us in right standing with Him. He held that we have no righteousness of our own. The itinerant asserted:

> For, though we should give all our goods to feed the poor, and our bodies to be burned, yet, if we in the least depend on that, and do not wholly rely on the perfect all-sufficient righteousness of Jesus Christ, it will profit us nothing....We must count all things but dung and dross, so that we may be found in him, not having our own righteousness, but the righteousness which is of God, through Jesus Christ our Lord.[362]

Whitefield opposed the idea that we work for our righteousness and God compensates for the deficiencies in our natures and in our work. He stated that "we are saved, not by any or all the works of righteousness which we have done, or can do; no; we can neither wholly nor in part justify ourselves in the sight of God."[363] Whitefield held that by nature we are spiritually dead and morally unable to gain fellowship with God. He also contended that our every attempt to gain God's favor through religious or moral activity fails because such actions are tainted by our sin and are performed from the wrong motivations.[364] Whitefield gave the following warning to all who attempt to obtain such righteousness through their own works: "Since you will rely on your works, by your works you shall be judged.

They shall be weighed in the balance of the sanctuary; and they will be found wanting. By your works, therefore, shall you be condemned! and you, being out of Christ, shall find God to your poor wretched souls, a consuming fire."[365] Because of our inability to obtain righteousness through our own efforts, the evangelist contended that we must depend upon Christ to grant us righteousness through justification by faith.

Justified meritoriously. Whitefield asserted that sinners are justified meritoriously by grace through the worth of Jesus Christ alone. He emphasized both the full humanity and the full divinity of Christ, stating, "For Christ was not only God, but he was God and man in one person....it is evident, that we do not think rightly of the person of Jesus Christ, unless we believe him to be perfect God and perfect man, or a reasonable soul and human flesh subsisting."[366]

Whitefield held that, as a man, Christ was our representative in obeying the law fully–active obedience–and in bearing our curse of sin upon Himself in death–passive obedience.[367] Whitefield explained his understanding of these two types of obedience and their relationship to righteousness, stating:

> It implies the active as well as passive obedience of the Lord Jesus Christ. We generally, when talking of the merits of Christ, only mention the latter, his death; whereas the former, his life and active obedience, is equally necessary. Christ is not such a Saviour as becomes us, unless we join both together. Christ not only died, but lived; not only suffered, but obeyed for, or instead of poor sinners. And both these jointly make up that complete Righteousness which is to be imputed to us, as the disobedience of our first parents was made ours by imputation.[368]

Only Christ could live a perfect life in the believer's stead, satisfying God's requirement of perfect holiness. Only Christ could satisfy God's justice in the believer's stead, by bearing the wrath upon the cross that the sinner justly deserved. Only Christ could atone for the believer's sin through the shedding of His blood in the atonement.[369] Rather than being based upon human merit, Whitefield maintained that justification is based upon the grace of God in providing His Son as a righteous substitute for the elect.

Justified instrumentally. George Whitefield further preached that man is justified instrumentally by faith. Justifying faith is not a work the believer produces within himself, but is a gift of God given by the Holy Spirit for the believer to exercise in conversion. Thus, he stated, "Not that you must think God will save you because, or on account of, your faith; for faith is a work, and then you would be justified by your works: but when I tell you, we are to be justified by faith, I mean that faith is the instrument whereby the sinner applies or brings home the redemption of Jesus Christ to his heart."[370] In essence, Whitefield believed that faith is the instrument for receiving justification and not the mode of meriting it.

The itinerant contended that believers are justified the moment they exercise faith in Christ.[371] He maintained that the righteousness of Christ, his active and passive obedience, is imputed to the sinner the moment he exercises faith granted in Christ. Otherwise, the sinner would perish without the righteousness of Christ being imputed to him. He stated, "You have no righteousness of your own to depend on. If you are saved, it is by the righteousness of Christ, through his atonement, his making a sacrifice for sin: his righteousness must be imputed to you, otherwise you cannot be saved."[372] When Christ's righteousness is imputed to believers, however, God the Father sees them as righteous because of Christ's righteousness in them.[373] Their faith in the righteousness of Christ is the instrument by which such righteousness is imputed them, by which they are justified, and by which they possess peace with God.[374]

Justified declaratively. Finally, the evangelist also contended that believers are justified declaratively by their works. He clarified that works are not a cause or a condition of justification, "but it requires good works as proof of our having this righteousness imputed to us, and as a declarative evidence of our justification in the sight of men."[375] In other words, he taught, these works naturally follow genuine faith in Christ. He presented Zaccheus as an example of an individual who possessed such works-producing faith.[376]

While he firmly maintained that true faith produces good works that evidence one's justification, Whitefield warned his hearers not to believe that works apart from faith or justification may grant them righteousness. He stated that justification "lays a solid foundation, whereon to build the superstructure of good works,"[377] but the itinerant stressed that justifying faith depends on the righteousness of Christ, not our own righteousness, for salvation. Such justifying faith will produce fruit in the life of the believer that then serves as evidence of its authenticity.

Conclusion. George Whitefield believed that Christians are meritoriously, instrumentally, and declaratively justified by faith. Believers have no merits upon which to base justification other than the active and passive obedience of Christ–His righteousness. When they exercise faith at conversion, this righteousness of Christ is imputed to them and they are justified. Believers then prove the authenticity of such justifying faith through their obedience and good works after conversion.

Sanctification

While Whitefield taught that genuine faith and justification produce good works, he was careful to distinguish between justification and sanctification. He explained that justification is the cause of sanctification and not vice versa. The itinerant viewed the Holy Spirit's work in sanctifying the individual as both a one-time event and a progressive process. He spoke of sanctification as "a total renovation of the whole man: by the righteousness of Christ, believers come legally, by sanctification they are made spiritually, alive; by the one they are entitled to, by the other they are made meet for, glory. They are sanctified, therefore, throughout, in spirit, soul, and body."[378] This aspect of sanctification involves the Holy Spirit setting believers apart as holy based upon the righteousness of Christ imputed to them in justification.

Although holiness is imparted to the human heart through the sanctifying work of the Holy Spirit based upon the imputed righteousness of Christ, Whitefield contended that sanctification is also a "progressive work" in the life of the believer.[379] He held that, through progressive sanctification, the Spirit of God is daily conforming the believer into the image of Christ. The evangelist asserted that, during this process, sin is "gradually more and more weakened as the believer grows in grace, and the Spirit gains a greater and greater ascendancy in the heart."[380] Thus, that progressive sanctification is synergistic. God works within the heart of the believer, motivating and empowering him to perform acts of obedience that are conducive to his growth. Whitefield's understanding of the synergistic nature of this process is evident in a prayer he wrote for new believers. He had the new believer pray that God would "grant I may from henceforward work out my salvation with fear and trembling, since thou hast so graciously wrought in me to will and to do, after thy good pleasure."[381]

While Whitefield believed that believers could grow in holiness through this work of progressive sanctification, he did not agree with John Wesley's contention that one can reach a point of sinless perfection on this side of eternity. In his written response to Wesley's sermon "Free Grace," Whitefield asserted:

> And since the Scriptures declare, 'That there is not a just man upon earth," no, not among those of the

highest attainments of grace, "that doeth good and sinneth not;" we are sure that this will be the case of all the children of God. The universal experience and acknowledgment of this among the godly in every age, is abundantly sufficient to confute the error of those who hold in an absolute sense, *that after a man is born again he cannot commit sin*; especially, since the Holy Ghost condemns the persons who say they have no sin, as deceiving themselves, as being destitute of the truth, and making God a liar, I John I. 8, 10.[382]

In Whitefield's view, believers are never rid of indwelling sin. He stated that the tendency to sin which dwells in us "will never be totally removed until we bow down our heads, and give up the ghost."[383] Whitefield held that, rather than leading them to sinless perfection, the Holy Spirit's work of progressive sanctification leads believers to a more profound and painful knowledge of their indwelling sin. This increased awareness of sin within us, causes believers to rely more upon the righteousness of Christ as their hope and strength in life.[384] The Holy Spirit's work in convicting believers of their sin and in leading them to the righteousness of Christ continues as He works the process of progressive sanctification in their lives, until they are glorified and see Christ face to face.

George Whitefield maintained that sanctification follows the believer's justification, being both a one-time event where God deems the believer holy, and a lifetime process of being conformed more into the image of Christ. He also opposed any idea that one could reach a state of sinless perfection because he believed that the believer struggles with indwelling sin until death.

The Great Commission and Universal Invitations

Although, to my knowledge, George Whitefield never preached or published an exposition focused on the

Great Commission, we may deduce his understanding of the Commission from comments he made in his preaching. In his sermons, Whitefield mentioned to his hearers that he was offering the gospel to them because God had commanded him "to preach the gospel to every creature."[385] He understood that the Commission called for him to proclaim the gospel to as many hearers as he possibly could. Further, Whitefield understood that the Great Commission also called him to persuade and invite his hearers to accept the gospel and come to Christ. He stated that the charge from Christ calls ministers "even to compel poor sinners by the cords of love to come in."[386] Whitefield understood the Great Commission as a command to proclaim the gospel and to persuade his audiences to accept Christ's invitation to salvation. To that end, he maintained that believers may use various means to communicate the gospel in fulfilling the Great Commission.[387]

Universal invitation. In Whitefield's view, the Great Commission called for ministers to present universal invitations to the gospel. He disagreed with Hyper-Calvinists like John Hussey who argued against general offers of grace and contended that persons who believe in particular redemption "cannot preach consistent with general offers of grace."[388] Instead, Whitefield contended that ministers should "offer salvation freely to all by the blood of Jesus."[389]

He further held that, because Christ invites all men to accept His gift of salvation, preachers of the gospel must invite every hearer to accept Christ. Charging a group of women to espouse their hearts to Christ, Whitefield preached:

> We ministers have a commission from the Lord Jesus Christ to invite you, in his name, unto this very thing, and Christ's invitations are real, general, frequent, earnest, free.... Christ's invitations to you, my dear sisters, are general. All of you are invited, none of you are excluded; all sorts of sinners

are invited; the most vile and abominable sinners, the most notorious transgressors, are invited to be Christ's spouse, and shall be as welcome as any unto the embraces of his love.[390]

The English evangelist believed he possessed a mandate to offer salvation to and to invite all to come to Christ.

Whitefield also opposed the idea, proposed by John Gill, that "it is not consistent with our ideas of God, that he should send ministers to offer salvation to men, to whom he himself never intended to give it, which ministers have not power to bestow, nor the men to receive:..."[391] On the contrary, regarding the message, the Great Commission obligates ministers to preach to "every creature." Whitefield stated, "The grand topics Christ's ministers are to preach, are, 'repentance towards God, and faith in our Lord Jesus Christ.'"[392] He maintained that all men, elect or not, have the responsibility to repent and believe in Christ.[393]

Interestingly, Whitefield's position, not Gill's, is consistent with the Calvinist tradition. While Gill accused anyone who would grant general offers of grace as being inconsistent with "our ideas of God," it is actually he who held a position inconsistent with Calvinism. The Synod of Dort supported universal calls to the gospel. This body, which is popularly known for presenting the "five points of Calvinism," asserted:

As many as are called by the gospel are unfeignedly called; for God hath most earnestly and truly declared in his Word what will be acceptable to him, namely, that all who are called should comply with the invitation. He, moreover, seriously promises eternal life and rest to as many as shall come to him, and believe on him.

It is not the fault of the gospel, nor of Christ offered therein, nor of God, who calls men by the gospel, and confers upon them various gifts, that those who are called by the ministry of the Word refuse to come and be converted. The fault lies in themselves...[394]

Clearly, Whitefield was consistent with the Calvinist tradition in offering universal invitations to the gospel. His position in this matter is also consistent with Andrew Fuller's contention that, because all men are responsible to believe in Christ, it is obligatory for Christian clergymen to present universal invitations or offers of salvation.

Universal invitations and election. George Whitefield did not believe he was inconsistent in preaching a universal invitation to the gospel while, at the same time, maintaining a belief in unconditional election. He believed that God intended the preaching of the gospel to all men and the offering of such invitations as a means of drawing the elect to Him through the work of the effectual call of the Holy Spirit. In response to Wesley's contention that unconditional election negates the necessity of gospel preaching, Whitefield wrote:

> Hath not God, who hath appointed salvation for a certain number, appointed also the preaching of the word, as a means to bring them to it? . . . And if so, how is preaching needless to them that are elected; when the gospel is designed by God himself, to be the power of God unto their eternal salvation? And since we know not who are elect, and who reprobate, we are to preach promiscuously to all.[395]

Thus, the itinerant saw universal invitations and gospel preaching in no way inconsistent with the doctrine of unconditional election.

The English evangelist maintained that preachers must share the gospel with all men because they do not know who among their listeners is elect and who is reprobate. Whitefield did not attempt to identify who was elect and who was reprobate among his hearers; rather, he prayed that God would make the preaching of the gospel effectual in drawing the elect to Himself. Touching the issue of ministers offering a general invitation to their hearers without knowing to whom Christ would grant life, Whitefield stated, "We call you to come, being commanded to preach the gospel to every creature, hoping, and praying that Christ's power may accompany the word, and make it effectual to the quickening and raising of your dead souls."[396] Unlike the Hyper-Calvinists who sought to relegate the gospel only to elect hearers, Whitefield chose to be obedient to the Great Commission and invite all of his hearers to come to Christ, leaving secret decrees of God, such as election, to the secret counsel of His perfect will.

Conclusion. Within his theology of evangelism, George Whitefield understood the Great Commission as a mandate to proclaim the gospel to every creature and to persuade his audiences to accept Christ's invitation to salvation. He opposed Hussey's and Gill's contentions that ministers should not offer universal invitations to the gospel. In granting universal invitations, Whitefield was consistent with the Calvinist tradition. The English evangelist viewed preaching as a means by which God draws the elect to Himself. He believed that he was consistent in preaching universal invitations to the gospel while, at the same time, maintaining a belief in unconditional election. It was his responsibility to preach repentance and faith to all and to pray that God would effectually call them.

Conclusion

George Whitefield held a theology of evangelism that referred, in order of emphasis, to the Scriptures and the Thirty-Nine Articles as its two primary sources of authority. While he unapologetically identified himself as a Calvinist, he was more committed to Christ and to the Scriptures than to any theological system. The doctrines of grace formed both the foundation of his theology of evangelism and the content of his preaching. The English itinerant believed that the Great Commission charged him to preach these doctrines of grace to all and to invite all to come to repentance and belief in Jesus Christ.

It is fitting that this chapter close with Whitefield's own words regarding his theology of evangelism and his adherence to the doctrines of grace that formed its foundation. In the words of his will, Whitefield wrote:

> I am more and more convinced of the undoubted reality and infinite importance of the grand gospel truths, which I have, from time to time, delivered; and am so far from repenting my delivering them in an itinerant way, that, had I strength equal to my inclination, I would preach them from pole to pole, not only because I have found them to be the power of God to the salvation of my own soul, but because I am as much assured that the Great Head of the Church hath called me by His Word, Providence, and Spirit, to act in this way, as that the sun shines at noonday.[397]

CHAPTER THREE

George Whitefield's Methodology of Evangelism

George Whitefield was a prolific evangelist, preaching at least eighteen thousand times before his death on September 30, 1770.[398] Approximately 80 percent of the colonists in America heard him preach.[399] Samuel Drew described Whitefield's evangelistic activity after his visit to Philadelphia (1740), noting, "During the journeyings, in seventy-five days, he preached one hundred and seventy-five times in public, besides giving private exhortations; travelled upwards of eight hundred miles; and in goods, provisions, and money collected for his orphan establishment, upwards of seven hundred pounds sterling."[400] While these facts are impressive testimony regarding the scope of Whitefield's involvement in itinerant evangelism, they do not fully depict his methodology of evangelism.

To obtain an understanding of Whitefield's evangelistic methodology, we must begin by asking a number of questions: Since Whitefield claimed to be a Calvinist, did he include Calvinistic doctrines in his evangelistic preaching? How did he present invitations to the gospel? What instructions did he present his hearers regarding receiving Christ? How did he present the cross and Christ's atonement in his preaching? Did he claim to believe particular redemption, yet preach that Christ died for everyone? How did Whitefield counsel with inquirers to the gospel? In addition to his itinerant preaching, was he involved at all in personal evangelism, if so, how? How did he engage societal issues with the gospel? How did he work with other denominations? Finally, did he follow up his preaching with discipleship opportunities for new converts, and if so, how?

The scope of this book does not allow an exhaustive treatment of every aspect of Whitefield's evangelistic methodology, however, I will present in this section the key methodological elements of the English itinerant's evangelistic ministry, including some comparisons between his theology and methodology of evangelism.

George Whitefield's Evangelistic Preaching Ministry

Itinerant preaching was George Whitefield's primary evangelistic methodology. He spent much of his time and effort either preaching or traveling to preaching engagements. Whitefield preached the gospel in numerous towns throughout England, Scotland, Wales, and the American colonies. He preached whenever and wherever he had the opportunity. His methodology of open air traveling evangelism is well documented in his *Journals* and in the numerous biographies written about him. Concerning the amount of territory the English evangelist covered and the large numbers of people who heard him preach, Albert D. Belden reflected, "No man secured such a hearing for the gospel amongst the common people in all the history of Protestant Christianity."[401]

Criticism of Whitefield's Itinerant Preaching Ministry

Eighteenth-century critics did not share Belden's approbation of Whitefield's ministry style. These opponents contended that he had no reasonable or biblical foundation upon which to base his ministry. Charles Chauncy confessed that he could not determine "upon what warrant, either from Scripture or reason, he went about preaching from one province and parish to another, where the gospel was already preach'd, and by parsons well qualified for the work, as he can pretend to be."[402] He questioned Whitefield's motives, inquiring whether the itinerant preached for popularity and the applause of men.[403] This New England minister also questioned Whitefield's method of publicizing his preaching engagements, stating, "And why so ostentatious and assuming as to alarm so many towns, by proclaiming his intentions, in the publick prints, to preach such a day in such a parish, the next day in such a one, and so on, without knowledge, either of pastors or people in most places?"[404] Chauncy vehemently opposed Whitefield's practice of itinerant preaching.

Likewise, President Edward Wigglesworth and some of his fellow scholars at Harvard also criticized Whitefield's ministry. They contended that there were no examples of itinerant evangelists within Scripture; therefore, Whitefield occupied an unbiblical office.[405] While the president and faculty acknowledged that George Whitefield did not preach in a town unless some minister there invited him, these scholars considered such a justification for his itinerating "trifling" because such ministers would not oppose the populace's desire to hear him.[406] Thus, they contended that he had no legitimate basis upon which to found his itinerant preaching ministry.

In response to these criticisms, Whitefield argued that his ministry methodology was founded upon both biblical and reasonable supports. He contended:

> For does not that general commission given by our Lord to his Apostles, "Go ye into all the world, and preach the gospel to every creature," authorize the ministers of Christ, "even to the end of the world," to preach the gospel in every town and country, though not of their own head, yet wherever Providence should open a door, even though it should be a place "where officers are already settled, and the gospel is fully and faithfully preached."[407]

Whitefield viewed the Great Commission not only as a defense for his itinerant preaching ministry, but also as one of his primary motivations. He believed that the Commission calls ministers to preach the gospel to every person.

Whitefield also responded to Chauncy's criticism of his use of publications to advertise his preaching schedule. Regarding this issue, he stated:

> That I give notice in the publick prints of my preaching in different places at different times, is true—but that this proceeded from ostentation, is what the great searcher of hearts can alone determine. As I was a stranger, passing thro' the country, and so many either out of curiosity or some other principle, were desirous to hear me, it was judged expedient by my friends, to give people previous and publick notice of my intention to preach among them, and to the best of my knowledge every advertisement of this kind was pen'd by the direction of some one or more of my brethren and fathers, and as far as I know to the contrary, upon application being made to me or them by either the minister or people, or both belonging to every place where I preached.[408]

Whitefield also maintained that it was fitting that he practice itinerant evangelism because Christ and the disciples were itinerants.[409] He denied that such publications were intended for self-promotion stating, "had I accepted all invitations that were given me by ministers and people, I might have continued in New-England many months longer than I did."[410] Note, however, that he did not discourage the use of this means to advertise his gospel preaching. Some contemporary Christian scholars also raise similar concerns regarding aspects of Whitefield's evangelistic preaching ministry. In his books *"Pedlar in Divinity"* and *Inventing the "Great Awakening,"* Frank Lambert contends that the Great Awakening was partially the result of George Whitefield's strategy "to orchestrate large-scale revivals" in England and the American colonies.[411]

According to Lambert, Whitefield used the press as a means of self-promotion as well as a means of promoting his "Whitefieldian revival."[412] And further, he asserts that, through the press, "Whitefield had carefully crafted his public persona as a special instrument selected by God to proclaim anew the necessity of the new birth. Writing in promotional language as well as in theological discourse, Whitefield presented himself as a well-publicized success."[413] Rather than being sovereign movements of God, Lambert describes the revivals associated with the Great Awakening and Whitefield's itinerant preaching as "a religious invention....alternating between that word's two eighteenth-century meanings: fabrication and invention."[414]

Although Frank Lambert's work displays in-depth primary source research, his conclusions regarding the Great Awakening and the revivals associated with Whitefield's itinerant preaching ministry omit the possibilities that the Great Awakening was, in fact, a spontaneous movement of God and that George Whitefield's use of the press was intended to promote the gospel and not his own "persona." Hidden within Lambert's biography on Whitefield is a statement which might delineate more accurately the itinerant's motivation for publicizing his preaching engagements. "Central to Whitefield's appropriation of print," he wrote, "was his conviction that persons everywhere should hear the gospel."[415] This statement touching Whitefield's intentions for using the press to publicize his preaching also coincides with the itinerant's own testimony regarding his understanding of the Great Commission.[416] Lambert's observation also is more consistent with Whitefield's stated desire that he promote Christ and not himself. In a letter written to a fellow minister, he stated, "Let my name be forgotten, let me be trodden under the feet of all men, if Jesus may thereby be glorified."[417]

Notwithstanding such self-deprecating statements from Whitefield, another modern biographer presents a picture of him that is similar to Lambert's portrayal. Harry Stout maintains that Whitefield's itinerant preaching was a means of self-promotion rather than an effort to preach the gospel to as many persons as possible. He writes:

> Few people achieve fame without aspiring to it, and Whitefield was no exception. But the fame he sought was not that of the metaphysical theologian or the denomination-builder. Rather he strove to achieve the actor's command performance on center stage. From his youth, Whitefield wanted to be a star, and the particular egotistical self-promotion he displayed in his career was very much in the manner of the great actor.[418]

Rather than a concern for his lost hearers, according to Stout, Whitefield's primary concern was to deliver great dramatic performances from the pulpit to augment both his popularity and the revivals he created through this itinerant stage preaching. He claims:

> Whitefield responded to new audiences and gave the performances of his life. What seemed to him in retrospect intuition or providence was, in fact, also a response to acclaim he had already rehearsed endlessly in his imagination. No stage could provide the sense of power and legitimacy he derived from the pulpit.[419]

Stout contends that the English evangelist not only utilized drama to sell himself, but also acted to sell the content of his preaching, stating, "Whitefield was not content simply to talk about the New Birth; he had to sell it with all the dramatic artifice of a huckster."[420]

Stout's contentions and conclusions regarding George Whitefield's aspirations to gain fame as an itinerant stage preacher differ from Whitefield's own testimony and from the observations of his contemporaries. Rather than pursuing popularity, Whitefield referred to aspirations to fame as a danger against which he sought to defend himself. As to his crowds of hearers and their admiration for him, he wrote:

> They grew quite extravagant in their applauses; and, had it not been for my compassionate High Priest, popularity would have destroyed me. I used to plead with Him, to take me by the hand and lead me unhurt through this fiery furnace. He heard my request, and gave me to see the vanity of all commendations but His own.[421]

Whitefield admitted he struggled with his success and the temptation to take pride in it, acknowledging in one letter:

> Success I fear elated my mind. I did not behave towards you, and other ministers of Christ, with that humility which became me. I freely confess my fault; I own myself to be but a novice. Your charity, dear Sir, will excite you to pray that I may not through pride fall into the condemnation of the devil.[422]

While Whitefield struggled with pride and popularity, he wrote of it as something to be avoided and not pursued. It is hard to reconcile this picture of Whitefield with the egotistical dramatist portrayed by Stout in his biography. The witness of Whitefield's contemporaries regarding his itinerant preaching also conflicts with Stout's conclusions. Describing an occasion when he preached in Northampton, Sarah Edwards stated, "A prejudiced person, I know, might say that this is all theatrical artifice and display; but not so will any one think who has seen him and known him. He is a very devout and godly man; and his only aim seems to be to reach and influence men the best way."[423] Joseph Smith, a minister of the era, wrote of Whitefield's character, "Here I may take courage, and challenge his worst enemies to lay any thing to the charge of his morals, or to arraign his sincerity, so visible in his whole deportment."[424] Benjamin Franklin also spoke to Whitefield's integrity and honesty in conduct.[425] Had Whitefield's itinerant preaching ministry merely been an attempt at self-promotion by an egotistical dramatist, one would think that one of these contemporaries, especially Sarah Edwards or Benjamin Franklin, would have mentioned such issues pointedly.

Whitefield's itinerant preaching ministry has been criticized both by some of his contemporaries and by some modern scholars. Critics like Chauncy and Wigglesworth questioned whether he had any biblical foundation for his itineracy. Both eighteenth-century and contemporary critics accused Whitefield of using his itineracy as a means of self-promotion; however, in the midst of such criticisms of his motivations, several contemporaries of the evangelist testified to his godly motives, morals, honesty, and integrity. While he admitted to a spiritual struggle against the pride resulting from his popularity, Whitefield pointed to the Great Commission's mandate to preach the gospel to all people as the driving motivation behind his itinerant preaching ministry.

But what might we further learn from the actual content of his sermons related to the "five points" of Calvinism and his methodology in extending invitations to receive the gospel?

Whitefield's Preaching and the "Five Points" of Calvinism

Undeniably, George Whitefield identified himself as a Calvinist; however, his self-identification of this particular theological persuasion does not necessarily indicate that he incorporated or communicated Calvinist doctrine in his evangelistic preaching. Did he actually include Calvinist doctrines in his sermon content? And if so, how did the inclusion of such doctrines relate to his methodology of evangelism?[426]

Total depravity. The previous chapter on Whitefield's theology of evangelism presents quotes and references from numerous sermons by the itinerant showing his inclusion of the doctrine of total depravity in his preaching.

These citations valuably evidence the incorporation of this Calvinistic doctrine in Whitefield's evangelistic preaching. But just how did he incorporate the doctrine of total depravity in his presentation of the gospel? What did he say regarding total depravity and the state of his hearers? How did he relate the doctrine of total depravity to their need for salvation?

George Whitefield asserted that gospel ministers must inform their hearers of their depravity before presenting the message of the cross. He maintained that people will not desire salvation from Christ until they are aware of their need for such deliverance, exhorting, "We must take care of healing before we see sinners wounded, lest we should say, Peace, peace, where there is no peace... we must first shew people they are condemned, and then shew them how they must be saved."[427] He informed hearers that they must know they are lost or else they will remain condemned by their sins.[428] In other words, Whitefield preached about depravity in order to awaken his hearers to their need for Christ.

He informed his hearers that they stood guilty before a holy God because, according to the doctrine of original sin, Adam's sin was imputed to all human beings. He preached that they were enemies of God and objects of his wrath due to their depravity. Speaking of the effects of original sin and their relationship with Adam's sin, Whitefield declared:

> Now, we are all by nature naked and void of God, as he was at the time, and consequently until we are changed, renewed, and clothed with a divine nature again, we must fly from God also...we are all equally included under the guilt and consequences of our first parent's sin, even as others; and, to use the language of our own church article, "bring into the world with us, a corruption, which renders us liable to God's wrath and eternal damnation."[429]

It was imperative, he insisted, that his hearers understand that they are fallen and separated from God because of their inherent sin.

Then further, Whitefield also revealed to them that they were unable to find acceptance with or gain favor from God by depending upon their own "free will," exercises of reason, moral activity, or upon their religious activity. He stated that, when his hearers became aware of their sinful condition, "you would no more flatter yourselves with your abilities and good wishes: no, you would see how unable you were, how incapable to save yourselves; that there is no fitness, no free-will in you: no fitness but for eternal damnation, no free-will, but that of doing evil; and that when you would do good, evil is present with you, and the thing that ye would not, that do ye."[430] Whitefield told his audiences that they could not depend upon their own understandings to find God, because they suffered from fallen minds.[431] Without the intervention of the Holy Spirit's regenerating work, they would continue to sin and rebel against God.[432]

Whitefield warned his audiences that death is also a result of the Fall and an aspect of their depravity. He stated that, left in their depravity and sin, they would justly be condemned for eternity to hell, declaring, "Are there enemies of God here? . . . For you without repentance is reserved the blackness of darkness for ever."[433] For those persons who refused to repent of their sin and their sinfulness, the itinerant said that they could see "hell gaping ready to receive you."[434] He depicted their plight as hopeless without Christ.

Plainly, George Whitefield included the doctrine of total depravity in his gospel preaching. He believed sinners must know their sinful condition before they will desire salvation. He included the doctrines of original sin, moral inability, and reprobation in his preaching. The following quote is a fitting conclusion to this section regarding man's condition apart from the grace of God:

If I were to paint man in his proper colours, I must go to the kingdom of hell for a copy: for man is by nature full of pride, subtlety, malice, envy, revenge, and all uncharitableness; and what are these, but the tempers of the beast. Thus, my brethren, man is half a beast, and half a devil, a motley mixture of beast and devil.[435]

Unconditional election. George Whitefield debated, through written correspondence, with his good friend John Wesley over the doctrine of election. In a letter written on June 25, 1740, Whitefield admonished Wesley, "For God's sake, if possible, dear Sir, never speak against election in your sermons: no one can say that I ever mentioned it in public discourses, whatever my private sentiments may be. For Christ's sake, let us not be divided amongst ourselves: nothing will so much prevent our division as your being silent on this head."[436] After Wesley preached and published his sermon "Free Grace," Whitefield asked his friend, "Why did you throw out a bone of contention? Why did you print your sermon against predestination? . . . But I must preach the gospel of Christ, and that I cannot now do, without speaking of election."[437]

Whitefield's claim that he never mentioned the doctrine of election in public discourses prior to writing his letter in June of 1740 is inaccurate based upon his own activity and testimony. He mentioned election as early as July 31, 1739 in his sermon "The Seed of the Woman, the Seed of the Serpent."[438] In this message, Whitefield spoke about the elect and about the covenant of grace by which the elect were granted redemption.[439] He also published a sermon in 1739 in which he mentioned that Zaccheus was one of the individuals that God the Father gave Christ the Son "from all eternity."[440] The itinerant explained further that Zaccheus' salvation was related to God's work in predestination. In addition to these two sermons, Whitefield wrote a letter claiming that he preached on the doctrine of election prior to his departure for America in 1739.[441]

While it is not clear what the itinerant meant when he claimed he never mentioned election in public discourse prior to June 25, 1740, it is apparent, based upon Whitefield's own activity and testimony, that his statement to Wesley was inaccurate.[442]

George Whitefield preached on the doctrine of election from as early as 1739, to the end of his evangelistic ministry. He repeatedly reminded his hearers that they could not be saved by their own free will or action. They are only saved by God's having chosen them in election and not by their own initiative. Speaking to believing hearers, the itinerant preached, "Think often how highly you are favoured; and remember, you have not chosen Christ, but Christ has chosen you. Put on (as the elect of God) humbleness of mind, and glory, but let it only be in the Lord; for you have nothing but what you have received of God. By nature ye were as foolish, as legal, as unholy, and in as damnable condition, as others."[443] He instructed his hearers that God is the "first cause" of salvation.[444] God chooses them based upon His sovereign will and not upon any merit within them or upon any activity they perform. He exhorted his listeners, "To check therefore all suggestion to spiritual pride, let us consider that we did not apprehend Christ, but were apprehended of him: that we have nothing but what we have received: that the free grace of God has alone made the difference between us and others; and was God to leave us to the deceitfulness of our own hearts but one moment, we should become weak and wicked, like other men."[445] Salvation is totally dependent upon God's free grace in election.

Whitefield preached that to deny unconditional election is essentially to glory in oneself; however, the affirmation of unconditional election brings humility, leading one to look towards God for succor.[446] He contended that, when one comes to realize the truth of unconditional election intellectually and experientially through salvation, one possesses a "sure bottom, the believer may build upon" in the midst of persecution and life's storms.[447] Their hope and joy is found in the Father's decision to elect them and to fulfill the covenant of grace He made with Christ the Son to redeem them.

Although Whitefield preached the above aspects of unconditional election, he warned his unregenerate hearers not to become preoccupied with questions regarding election; rather, they must focus upon whether or not they have experienced salvation through repentance and faith in Jesus Christ. He stated, "Do not go and quarrel with God's decrees, and say, If I am reprobate, I shall be damned; if I am elected, I shall be saved; and therefore I will do nothing. What have you to do with God's decrees? Secret things belong to him; it is your business to 'give all diligence to make your calling and election sure.'"[448] Rather than speculate about election, he encouraged his hearers to pursue salvation in Christ.

The English evangelist believed that it was more important that his audiences hear that they must repent and believe in Christ for their salvation than it was necessary that they be instructed regarding the doctrine of unconditional election. He communicated this priority on preaching the gospel over the doctrine of unconditional election in his journal. Whitefield wrote, "But I would be tender on this point, to leave persons to be taught it of God. I am of the martyr Bradford's mind. Let a man go to the grammar school of faith and repentance, before he goes to the university of election and predestination."[449]

In summary, George Whitefield included the doctrine of unconditional election in his preaching. While he spoke of unconditional election being a firm foundation upon which believers' salvation is based, he discouraged his hearers from speculating about election, asking whether they were elect or reprobate; rather, the itinerant emphasized their need to pursue Christ and the salvation He offers to all men who will repent and believe.

Particular redemption. In an article in the *Journal of the American Society for Church Growth*, Seth Polk asserts that "Whitefield did not preach or write in terms of a limited or particular atonement."[450] While focus on Whitefield's theology and methods is commendable, Polk's conclusions on this matter are inaccurate. George Whitefield included the doctrine of particular redemption in his evangelistic preaching.

He spoke of Christ dying for the elect or for believers. In his sermon "The Righteousness of Christ, an Everlasting Righteousness," Whitefield stated that Christ suffered and died "for an elect world–for all that will believe in him."[451] He asserted that Christ offered Himself up as "an offering for the sins of the elect world."[452] Christ's death was intended for believers. Referring to the connection between election and redemption, Whitefield preached, "Now this word chosen, refers us to God's eternal election; it comprehends, and is the source of all that God has done for believers, for every individual believer in particular, when Jesus bowed his head and gave up the ghost."[453] In an even more direct reference to the particular nature of the atonement, Whitefield said of Christ, "On him God the Father has laid the iniquities of all that shall believe on him; and in his own body he bare them on the tree."[454]

Although Whitefield clearly included the doctrine of particular redemption in his preaching, a cursory reading of his sermons reveals several instances where he made statements regarding the extent of the atonement which seemingly contradict his belief in particular redemption. In the few sermons in which he stated, "Christ died for you," the English itinerant referred such claims to the "brethren."[455] While a discussion of his use of the term "brethren" may appear to be an exercise in semantics, this term is significant, because it relates to the issue of the itinerant's consistency in preaching particular redemption.

It is possible that Whitefield used the term "brethren" in a sociological context, referring to the brotherhood of humanity. Preaching to "guilty brethren," the evangelist implored them to "turn unto the Lord of love, the Jesus who died for you, that in the day when he shall come to take his people to the mansions of everlasting rest, you may hear his voice."[456] In this example of Whitefield's use of the term "brethren," his intended audience is not quite clear. Although by referring to "guilty brethren" he likely used the phrase in a sociological context, he could also be exhorting wayward believers to "turn unto the Lord." Whitefield's intended audience in this first example is not clear. In his sermon "Christ the Support of the Tempted," Whitefield admonished, "O consider, my brethren, the love of the Lord Jesus Christ in dying for you; and are you resolved to slight his dying love? Your sins brought Christ from heaven, and I humbly pray to the Lord, that they may not be a means of sending you to hell."[457] It does not appear, in praying that the sins of the "brethren" will not send them to hell, that the English itinerant referred to "brethren" in a theological sense. Using the term theologically would contradict Whitefield's strong-held and well-documented belief in the perseverance of the saints by implying that they might go to hell. While it is possible that he spoke of the "brethren" in a sociological context in the first example, it is very likely that he intended such a meaning in referring to the group of hearers he prayed would not perish in hell.

Additionally, Whitefield might have intended a theological meaning for the term. Speaking against the false doctrine of Socinianism, Whitefield admonished, "O my brethren, do not think so dishonourably of the Lord who bought you; of the Jesus who died for you: he must be all in all unto your souls, if ever you be saved by him: Christ must be your active, as well as passive obedience; his righteousness must be imputed to you."[458] In this admonition, he might refer to believers he sought to protect from false doctrine. He also may have intended his words for Socinian hearers or audience members tempted to follow the doctrine. Whitefield discussed the theological use of the terms "brother" or "brethren" in his sermon "Saul's Conversion," stating, "It is remarkable that the primitive Christians much used the word brother and brethren; I know this is a term now much in reproach; but those who despise it, I believe, would be glad to be of our brotherhood, when they see us sitting at the right hand of the Majesty on high."[459] Clearly, Whitefield sometimes viewed the term brethren as a means of identifying believers.

There are also occasions in which George Whitefield utilized the term "brethren" to address both believers and nonbelievers. In one sermon, he stated:

> O my brethren, consider what Christ hath done, and you will be astonished that he has done so much for such wicked wretches as you and I are. If you are easy under the storm and tempest of sin, and do not cry to Christ for salvation, thou art in a dangerous condition: and it is a wonder to consider, how a man that is not sure of having made his peace with God, can eat, or drink, or live in peace; that thou art not afraid when thou liest down, that thou shouldest awake in hell: but if Christ speak peace unto thy soul, who can then speak trouble?[460]

Here, the preacher may be calling both believers and nonbelievers to "consider what Christ hath done" and to ask themselves questions regarding whether Christ is their source of security for salvation. He exhorted another audience:

> Examine yourselves therefore, my brethren, whether you are in the faith; prove yourselves, and think it not sufficient to say in your creed, I believe in Jesus Christ; many say so, who do not believe, who are reprobates, and yet in a state of death.
> You take God's name in vain when you call him Father, and your prayers are turned into sin, unless you believe in Christ, so as to have your life hid with

him in God, and to receive life and nourishment from him, as branches do from the vine.[461]
Whitefield's reference to "brethren" in this passage might also refer to both believers and nonbelievers. He asked his hearers to examine themselves to see if they have been hid with Christ in God. Both believers and nonbelievers might benefit from such an examination. Although these two examples do not explicitly mention Christ's atonement, they do give insight into the itinerant's use of the term "brethren" as it relates to his preaching on particular redemption.

With the exception of the instances in which Whitefield told the "brethren" that he prayed their sins would not send them to hell and where he mentions the "brethren" being bought by Christ, Whitefield was somewhat ambiguous in his use of the term "brethren" in treating the subject of Christ's redemption.[462] At times, he apparently used the term in a sociological context. In other cases, it is possible the evangelist intended a theological meaning for "brethren." In some sermons, Whitefield's use of the term "brethren" appears in statements that seem to be directed to both believers and nonbelievers. Taken together, his use of the term "brethren" in relation to particular redemption is rather equivocal.

Otherwise, though, Whitefield clearly preached the doctrine of particular redemption. He stated often and in no uncertain terms that Christ died for "the elect" and for those who "shall believe on him." Inexactness aside, the English itinerant clearly held to and held out the doctrine of particular redemption in the majority of his comments touching Christ's atoning work.

Effectual calling. A casual reading of Whitefield's sermons also reveals that the he included the doctrine of effectual calling in his preaching. He preached that the Holy Spirit must grant sinners life and faith before they can come to Christ. Whitefield also preached that the Holy Spirit changes their wills, granting them a willingness to follow Christ rather than death and sin. He repeatedly emphasized the Holy Spirit's effectiveness in these tasks.

Only the Holy Spirit, he insisted, can bring sinners from spiritual death to spiritual life. He expressed that all by nature are dead, like Lazarus, and need the Holy Spirit to make them alive, draw them to Christ, and grant them faith in Jesus. Describing this process of effectual calling, Whitefield stated that God cries "'Lazarus, come forth,' comes by his mighty power, removes the stone of unbelief, speaks life to thy dead soul, looses thee from the fetters of thy sins and corruptions, and, by the influences of his blessed Spirit, enables thee to arise, and to walk in the way of his holy commandments."[463] In addition, he contended, the Holy Spirit draws believers by granting "a particular call that the sheep understand" and placing within these individuals a voluntary desire to follow Christ.[464] He further emphasized the Spirit's role in unveiling the meaning of Scripture to his lost hearers and giving them spiritual understanding regarding the gospel.[465]

Thus, Whitefield maintained that the Spirit is effectual in granting life, in drawing lost sinners to Christ, and in giving them spiritual understanding regarding the gospel and the meaning of Scripture. He asserted that God prevents sinners from continuing in their sin and "calls them effectually by his grace."[466] The Holy Spirit not only unveils the eyes, resulting in spiritual understanding, but He irresistibly draws the person to follow Christ.[467] Whitefield contended that the Holy Spirit makes sinners willing to come to Christ as they are "made willing to accept salvation upon our Lord's own terms, and receive him as their all in all: thus Christ is made to them wisdom."[468] The call of the Holy Spirit is effectual upon their lives.

Perseverance of the Saints. George Whitefield also included the doctrine of the perseverance of the saints in his preaching. He believed that true believers cannot lose their salvation. To believers, he stated, "God, if he has freely justified you by faith in his Son, and given you his Spirit, has sealed you to be his; and has secured you, as surely as he secured Noah, when he locked him in the ark."[469]

His audiences also heard that Christ is the Good Shepherd who will not allow anyone to snatch His sheep from His hand. Believers are secure because they are among the sheep for whom Jesus died. Regarding John's depiction of Christ as the Good Shepherd (John 10), Whitefield preached:

> O my brethren, if it were not for keeping you too long, and too much exhausting my own spirits, I could call upon you to leap for joy; there is not a more blessed text to support the final perseverance of the saints; and I am astonished any poor soul, and good people I hope too, can fight against the doctrine of the perseverance of the saints: . . . upon this text I can leave my cares, all my friends, and all Christ's sheep, to the protection of Christ Jesus' never-failing love.[470]

He stressed that the imputed righteousness of Christ holds believers secure because His righteousness cannot fail to accomplish their salvation; therefore, nothing can separate them from Him.[471]

Moreover, Whitefield contended that God protects believers against Satan, sin, and persecution. To a group of women, the evangelist declared:

> It is your safety to be espoused unto the Lord Jesus Christ; he will protect and defend you, even from sin and Satan, and eternal ruin; and therefore thus far you are safe: he hath a regard for you in times of danger from men, and these times of danger seem to be hastening; it is now arising as a black cloud no bigger than a man's hand, and by and by it will overspread the heavens, and when it is full it will burst; but if you are espoused to Christ, you are safe.[472]

This divine protection against attacks from men and devils should grant believers boldness in at serving Christ. He also reminded Christians that their guarantee of a heavenly destination should grant them encouragement and fearlessness in the face of such persecution. Whitefield fortified them, saying, "You must expect to go through evil report, and good report; fear not the violence of unreasonable men; let them hate you, and cast you out for the Lord's sake, behold he shall appear to your joy, and they shall be ashamed: therefore hold on, and hold out to the end. Be steadfast and patient, and bear the troubles of the world; if you be people of God, there is a rest provided for you, which you shall certainly obtain."[473]

George Whitefield considered the doctrine of the perseverance of the saints a great help and hope to believers. He included the doctrine in his preaching, maintaining that God through Christ holds true believers fast to the day of their glorification, even in the midst of persecution from Satan, sin, and evil men.

Conclusion. George Whitefield not only identified himself a Calvinist, but included Calvinist doctrines in his sermons. He often mentioned the doctrine of total depravity in his preaching, emphasizing the doctrines of original sin, moral inability, and reprobation. Whitefield included the doctrine of unconditional election in his preaching; however, he encouraged his hearers to focus on the need to pursue Christ and salvation rather than speculating whether or not they are among the elect. Whitefield clearly preached the doctrine of particular redemption, stating that Christ died for "the elect" or for those "who shall believe on him;" some ambiguous references to "brethren" aside. He also included the doctrine of effectual calling in his preaching, proclaiming that the Holy Spirit is effectual in drawing the elect to Christ. Finally, Whitefield preached that true saints persevere to the day of their glorification and cannot lose their salvation.

Whitefield and Invitations

George Whitefield did not invite his hearers to come forward and walk an aisle in response to his gospel preaching; however, he did invite people to repent and believe in Christ. So, what part did invitations play as a component of his evangelistic methodology, and what were the various methods he utilized in inviting his hearers to come to Christ?

Universal invitations. George Whitefield invited all his hearers to come to Christ. It did not matter how many or what type of sins his listeners committed, they could receive forgiveness through the shed blood of Christ. He mentioned various categories of sins in his invitations in order to reveal Jesus' willingness to forgive anyone who will come to Him. In his sermon "Christ the Only Preservative Against a Reprobate Spirit," Whitefield entreated:

> Come then unto Christ every one that hears me this night; I offer Jesus Christ, pardon, and salvation, to all you who will accept thereof. Come, O ye drunkards, lay aside your cups, drink no more to excess; come and drink of the water which Christ will give you, and then you will thirst no more: come, O ye thieves; let him that has stolen, steal no more, but fly unto Christ and he will receive you. Come unto him, O ye harlots; lay aside your lusts, and turn unto the Lord, and he will have mercy upon you, he will cleanse you of all your sins, and wash you in his blood. Come, all ye liars; come all ye Pharisees; come, all ye fornicators, adulterers, swearers, and blasphemers, come to Christ, and he will take away all your filth, he will cleanse you from your pollution, and your sins shall be done away.[474]

The English itinerant also called people from all socioeconomic backgrounds to come to Christ. He preached, "Therefore, let me, by way of application, exhort all of you, high and low, rich and poor, one with another, to come unto the Lord Jesus Christ, that he may give you strength to undergo whatsoever he in his wisdom calls you to."[475] He also invited African and Caribbean slaves included among his hearers to come to Christ.[476] Whitefield excluded no one from his invitations to the gospel, they were universal calls for his hearers to come to Christ. He exhorted all of his hearers to come to Jesus.

Invitations to groups. In his invitations to the gospel, Whitefield also often addressed specific groups within his audiences. He focused his comments towards his listeners' various spiritual conditions. In his sermon "The Eternity of Hell Torments," he admonished each of the following groups: sinners, lukewarm professors, and true believers. To each group, Whitefield presented a different invitation or admonition. To sinners, he told them to imagine suffering under eternal torments. He warned the lukewarm professors, "O think, think within yourselves, how deplorable it will be to lose the enjoyment of heaven, and run into endless torments, merely because you will be content to be almost, and will not strive to be altogether Christians." To the believers, however, the evangelist encouraged them not to be terrified of such torments because, "Christ never said that the righteous, the believing, the upright, the sincere, but the wicked, merciless, negatively good professors before described, shall go into everlasting punishment."[477]

In his sermon, "The Care of the Soul Urged as the One Thing Needful," Whitefield addressed persons wrestling with various levels of concern regarding the condition of their souls. To persons totally unconcerned about their eternal destiny, he queried whether it is being rational for a man "to go on with your eyes open towards a pit of eternal ruin, because there are a few gay flowers on the way? or what if you shut your eyes, will that prevent your fall?" He also exhorted persons who believe they can defer accepting Christ to another time. "Talk not of a more convenient season; none can be more convenient; and that to which you would probably refer it, is least of all so, a dying time. You would not choose then to have any important business in hand; and will you of choice refer the greatest business of all, to that languishing, hurrying, amazing hour?"[478]

George Whitefield also spoke directly to any who rely on outward religious activity for their spiritual security. He warned this group that such efforts are not sufficient to grant anyone salvation. In his sermon "Spiritual Baptism," the evangelistic preacher entreated, "Sinners in Zion, baptized heathens, professors but not possessors, formalists, believing unbelievers, talking of Christ, talking of grace, orthodox in your creeds, but heterodox in your lives, turn ye, turn ye, Lord help you to turn to him, turn ye to Jesus Christ, and may God turn you inside out to-night; may the power of the highest overshadow you, and may that glorious Father that raised Christ from the dead, raise your dead souls!"[479] Whitefield emphasized that these religious individuals must rely upon the new birth and the righteousness of Christ for their salvation. He invited such sinners to come to Christ and depend upon Him alone, and not upon their religious activity, to save them.

Whitefield also directed invitations to individuals belonging to different age groups. His sermon "The Lord Our Righteousness" presents numerous examples of the itinerant's invitations to various age groups. To children, the evangelist admonished:

> Come then, ye little children, come to Christ; the Lord Christ shall be your righteousness. Do not think that you are too young to be converted. Perhaps many of you may be nine or ten years old, and yet cannot say, the Lord is our righteousness; which many have said, though younger than you. . .. Do not stay for other people. If your fathers and mothers will not come to Christ, do you come without them. Let children lead them, and shew them how the Lord may be their righteousness.[480]

The English itinerant also directed his invitations towards youth. He warned adolescents not to take for granted that they will live long enough to accept Christ in their own time. Whitefield admonished his young hearers:

> But say you, all in good time, I do not choose to be converted yet; why, what age are you now? I will come down to a pretty moderate age; suppose your are fourteen: and do not you think it time to be converted? . . . There was a young man buried last night at Tottenhamcourt but seventeen, an early monument of free grace!
>
> . . . If it is time for them, it is time for you, for you may be dead before them.[481]

He asserted that the happiness they believe their sinful activities bring them actually leads to their eternal condemnation.[482] Rather than playing the prodigal, they should leave their life of sin and answer the Father's call to repentance and faith.[483] Only Christ could grant them eternal life and joy.

Whitefield also called middle-aged hearers to respond to the gospel. He emphasized that their pursuit of wealth and a comfortable life would not help them when they face the Lord after their deaths. To these hearers, he declared:

> Alas! what profit will there be of all your labour under the sun, if you do not secure this pearl of invaluable price? this one thing so absolutely needful, that it only can stand you in stead, when all other things shall be taken from you. Labour therefore, no longer, so anxiously for the meat which perisheth, but henceforward seek for the Lord to be your righteousness, a righteousness that will entitle you to life everlasting.[484]

Older persons also received specific invitations from Whitefield to receive Christ. He reminded these hearers that they were not far from their deaths. They also could not find security in being long-time members of the church. To one elderly group of hearers, the English evangelist stated:

> O grey-headed sinners, I could weep over you! Your grey hairs, which ought to be your crown, and in which perhaps you glory, are now your shame. You know not that the Lord is your righteousness: O haste then, haste ye, aged sinners, and seek an interest in redeeming love! Alas, you have one foot already in the grave, your glass is just run out, your sun is just going down, and it will set and leave you in an eternal darkness, unless the Lord be your righteousness! Flee then, O flee for you lives! Be not afraid.... If you come, though it be at the eleventh hour, Christ Jesus will no wise cast you out.[485]

George Whitefield's method of offering invitations to specific groups of hearers within his audiences allowed these listeners to personalize the gospel call to their own lives. His listeners knew that his call to receive Christ applied to each one of them. They also heard that their response to such invitations would have an eternal impact upon their lives. His intentionality in appealing to various groups of hearers also reflects Whitefield's belief in granting universal invitations to the gospel. He wanted young and old, rich and poor, religious and profligate to know that Christ calls them to repentance and faith in Him.

Invitations and questions. George Whitefield also presented inquiries to his hearers as a means of exciting their minds and affections to respond affirmatively to his gospel invitations. His questions dealt with numerous aspects of salvation. Though not an exhaustive treatment of the matter, we should consider several categories of questions included in Whitefield's invitations.

The evangelist often asked his hearers whether they had experienced conviction over their own sins and sinfulness. In his sermon "Self-Inquiry Concerning the Work of God," Whitefield asked listeners to take stock of the Holy

Spirit's convicting work upon their lives. He inquired of them:

> Now, has God wrought in you? Has he given this conviction to you; not a little flight now and then, or a qualm of thy conscience; the devil and natural conscience may do this; but when it is wrought in thy heart by the Spirit of God, it goes to the bottom, the arrow sticks fast, and a poor soul sometimes endeavours to pray, endeavours to pull it out, but in vain. Hath God wrought this in thy soul? . . . It is God wounds the soul, and it is he that heals it; has he wrought in thee not only a deep and humbling sense of the outward acts of sin, but a humbling sense of the inward corruptions of thy heart?[486]

In another sermon on the story of the Pharisee and the publican, he asked his hearers if they had experienced conviction like the publican. He encouraged them to place themselves in the position of the publican and to ask themselves if he would have been angry if a minister told him he was damned or that he was "half a devil and half a beast."[487] Such questions regarding the individual experiencing conviction of sin reflects Whitefield's belief that sinners must be convicted of their sinful condition before they will desire salvation.

Whitefield also questioned audience members about their total dependence upon Christ's righteousness for their salvation. He asked whether listeners had been convicted of relying upon their own righteousness, rather than the righteousness of Christ, to save them.

> Were you ever made to abhor yourselves for your actual and original sins, and to loathe your own righteousness; for, as the prophet beautifully expresses it, "your righteousness is as filthy rags?" Were you ever made to see and admire the all- sufficiency of Christ's righteousness, and excited by the Spirit of God to hunger and thirst after it? Could you ever

say, My soul is athirst for Christ, yea, even for the righteousness of Christ?[488]

He emphasized that his hearers could not depend upon their own righteousness to justify them before God, but must rely upon the righteousness of Christ for their justification. He asked one assemblage whether they understood that the law requires their perfect obedience and that the curse of sin upon their lives prevents them from fulfilling the law.[489] Whitefield questioned whether, faced with such teaching regarding the doctrine of justification, his hearers would rely upon their own efforts even if they knew that their very lives might be asked of them that evening.[490] All of these questions concerning the righteousness of Christ led hearers to determine whether they relied on such righteousness and experienced the resulting justification.

Questions about the new birth comprised another category George Whitefield included in his invitations. He encouraged his audiences to examine whether they ever experienced a change of their natures wrought by the Holy Spirit. He asked his hearers, "Has God by his blessed Spirit wrought such a change in your hearts? I do not ask you whether God has made you angels, that I know will never be; I only ask you whether you have any well-grounded hope to think that God has made you new creatures in Jesus Christ?"[491] He encouraged his hearers to determine whether they had experienced the renewing power of the Holy Spirit. Their pursuit to be like Christ would serve as evidence that such a transformation had occurred. Whitefield also asked whether their hearts had been changed to the point that their affections were set upon Jesus.[492] Because of his belief in the ability of believers to feel the inner workings of the Holy Spirit, the English evangelist asked such questions with the confidence that those in whom the Spirit was working would be able to determine whether such a change had occurred in their natures.

George Whitefield also asked listeners why they would not come to Christ. He reasoned with them to examine their hearts and determine what would prevent them from accepting the salvation Jesus offers. He inquired, "And why will not all that hitherto are strangers to this blessed restoration of their fallen natures, (for my heart is too full to abstain any longer from an application,) why will you any longer dispute or stand against it? Why will you not rather bring your clay to this heavenly potter, and say from your inmost souls, 'Turn us, O good Lord, and so shall we be turned.'"[493] Whitefield asked what else his hearers would expect from Christ in order to warrant them giving their lives to Him.[494] Why would they not come to Christ when they hear that He alone can save them from death and hell?[495] The evangelist questioned why they would risk dying in their condemnation when Christ can take them out of the captivity of their sin.[496] He pressed these questions to cause hearers to compare their excuses for not receiving the gospel with the great hope and salvation offered in the gospel. His questions revealed the folly of rejecting an invitation to accept Christ and also displayed his belief that sinners are responsible for responding in repentance and faith to the gospel. Whitefield longed for the questions to lead his hearers to that end.

Further still, he asked questions related to the condemnation sinners will experience apart from a relationship with Jesus Christ. He powerfully delineated the plight of all without Christ, stating:

> How miserable will your life be when all your joys are over, when your pleasures are all past, and no more mirth or pastime! Do you think that there is one merry heart in hell? one pleasing countenance? or jesting, scoffing, swearing tongue? A sermon now is irksome: the offer of salvation by the blood of Jesus Christ, is now termed enthusiasm; but then you would give thousands of worlds, if in your power,

for one tender mercy, for one offer of grace, which now you so much despise.[497]

As to the unsaved sinner's relation to the devil, Whitefield asked, "And how can you bear to be ruled by one, who is such a professed, open enemy, to the most high and holy God? which will make a drudge of you whilst you live, and be your companion in endless and extreme torment, after you are dead."[498] He called his hearers to count the cost of their sins to determine whether the short pleasures they gain from them are worth an eternity of suffering in hell. He warned that the failure or refusal to entertain such questions regarding hell and suffering would not excuse them when their lives are demanded of them.[499] Whitefield presented them with questions regarding hell and eternal suffering because of the deadly seriousness of the gospel. He wanted listeners to ponder such crucial questions.

Invitational questioning was an integral part of George Whitefield's methodology of evangelism. He wanted his hearers to deal seriously with issues such as conviction over sin, the occurrence of the new birth in their lives, dependence upon Christ's righteousness alone for their justification, issues hindering them from accepting Christ, and the possibility of their eternal damnation. The English itinerant intended such questions to stir those who had not yet received the gospel to turn to Jesus Christ for their salvation.

Instructions and invitations. And yet there is more! George Whitefield also provided his hearers with instructions regarding what they must do to receive Christ. How did he do this? What directions did he give to listeners to lead them to Christ?

For one thing, Whitefield included directions regarding repentance in his invitations to the gospel. He encouraged listeners that, if they confessed their sins and repented of them, God would have mercy on them, wash their sins, make them clean, and grant them the Holy Spirit. He implored, "And O if you repent and come to Jesus, I would rejoice on your accounts too; and we should rejoice together to all eternity, when once passed on the other side of the grave....The arms of Jesus Christ will embrace you; he will wash away all your sins in his blood, and will love you freely."[500] He often directed audience members to leave their sins and come to Christ for their salvation.[501] While, as noted, Whitefield believed that God grants believers the gift of repentance, he held that the process of conversion involved believers taking action by turning from their sin and placing faith in Christ; therefore, he instructed his hearers to repent and believe the gospel.[502]

This call to repentance and belief led, necessarily, to another instruction. Should the sinner ask, "What must I do to be saved?" the directions are both simple and biblical. For example, in his sermon "The Folly and Danger of Not Being Righteous Enough," he spoke to sinners "who ask what you must do to be saved? how uncomfortable would it be to tell you, by good works, when perhaps you have never done one good work in your life: this would be driving you to despair, indeed: no; 'Believe in the Lord Jesus Christ, and you shall be saved:' therefore none of you need to go away despairing. Come to the Lord Jesus by faith, and he shall save you."[503] With such instructions, Whitefield called listeners to exercise the second of the two aspects of conversion mentioned earlier—belief in Jesus Christ. Such directions for hearers to repent and believe reflect a convergence of the itinerant's theology of conversion and his methodology of evangelism.[504]

George Whitefield also called his listeners to forsake any dependence upon their own ability, righteousness, or works to save them. He entreated one audience to:

> come in full dependence upon the Lord Jesus Christ, looking on him as the Lord who died to save sinners: Go to him, tell him you are lost, undone, miserable sinners, and that you deserve nothing but hell; and when you thus go to the Lord Jesus Christ, you will find him an able and a willing Sav-

iour: he is pleased to see sinners coming to him in a sense of their own unworthiness; and when their case seems to be most dangerous, most distressed, then the Lord in his mercy steps in and gives you his grace; he puts his Spirit within you, takes away your heart of stone, and gives you a heart of flesh. Stand not out then against the Lord, but go unto him, not on your own strength, but in the strength of Jesus Christ.[505]

They should come as sinners who have no hope and are helpless to obtain for themselves their own salvation. Their only hope must be in the righteousness of Christ to save them. Such instructions regarding a full dependence on Christ are consistent with Whitefield's theological understanding of humanity's inability and with the doctrine of justification.[506]

In light of the sinner's total dependence upon God for their salvation, Whitefield also instructed his hearers to plead with and pray to God that He might deliver them from their sin. He instructed one group of hearers to "beg of God to make you willing to be saved in this day of his power; for it is not flesh and blood, but the Spirit of Jesus Christ that can alone reveal these things unto you."[507] They should plead with God to grant them salvation and not rest until they feel they have obtained it. Whitefield also encouraged his hearers to pray for their own salvation upon returning home from hearing him preach.[508] To persons under the conviction of the Holy Spirit, he admonished, "Stifle not, but rather encourage these convictions; and who knows, but that Lord, who is rich in mercy to all that call upon him faithfully, may so work upon you, even by this foolishness of preaching, as to make you wise virgins before you return home."[509] In such admonitions, Whitefield proclaimed God's sovereignty over salvation and the fact that His invitations do not cease at the conclusion of the sermon. His hearers should continue to plead with God after the sermon to grant them the salvation they so desperately needed.

Notice that, in all of the above instructions, Whitefield expected his hearers to respond to such directions. He did not call listeners to be immobile and wait for God to save them. These instructions reflect his theology of conversion. The itinerant believed that conversion involves action on the part of his hearers. They should turn from their sinful lives and place faith in Christ for their salvation. They should renounce their own righteousness and trust fully in the righteousness of Christ to save them. Their total dependence should be on Christ and not on themselves. He also did not want listeners to cease from striving for their salvation until they knew it had been granted by God to them. Within all of these factors, Whitefield believed that God is the One who sovereignly grants salvation; therefore, he admonished hearers to pray that He would bestow upon them that precious gift.

Whitefield's treatment of the cross. Closely related to instructing his hearers, Whitefield called his audiences to come to the cross. His treatment of the cross in his invitations was bound to the doctrine of particular redemption in his theology and methodology of evangelism. Whitefield occasionally made the statement "Christ died for you" in references to the "brethren." More often, when he spoke of the cross in his invitations, he stated that Christ died for "sinners," "rebels," or the "lost." He asked one group of hearers, "Can you bear to think of a bleeding, panting, dying Jesus, offering himself up for sinners, and you will not accept of him?"[510] Whitefield marveled that the Savior would "die for such rebels as you and I are."[511] He also preached that Christ came to save "that which is lost."[512] Such statements are consistent with Whitefield's belief in particular redemption; yet, they also communicate the truth that Christ did die for sinners.

Christ's willingness to accept all persons who would place faith in his atoning blood for their forgiveness and righteousness was another element that George Whitefield emphasized in his treatment of the cross. He contended that only a lack of faith in Christ's shed blood would serve as his hearers' condemnation. The evangelist encouraged them to "look by an eye of faith, to the God-man whom ye have pierced. Behold him bleeding, panting, dying upon the cross, with arms stretched out ready to embrace you all."[513] Whitefield preached that Christ's blood possesses infinite value "to atone for the sins of millions of worlds."[514] He asserted that, if his hearers would only place their faith in Christ's shed blood for their forgiveness, He would cleanse them whiter than snow.[515] Whitefield wanted his listeners to know that Christ's atonement on the cross was their only hope for forgiveness of sins and a relationship with God. He called them to come to the cross for their salvation.

The other side of the gospel. At the same time he offered his hearers the hope of the cross, Whitefield also included strong admonitions about hell in his invitations. He warned audience members that they must repent now because they are not guaranteed the time to do so later. He told one audience that "the time is hastening when you will have neither time nor call to repent."[516] Whitefield admonished young and old alike that they should heed his invitation to the gospel "lest God should cut you off before you have another invitation to hear him."[517] The English evangelist wanted hearers to realize the somber truth that there would be no second chances after death for them to respond in repentance and faith to the gospel.

Some of Whitefield's admonitions regarding his hearers' potential refusal of the gospel message were not pleasant. To one assemblage, the itinerant preached:

> If you refuse to humble yourselves, after hearing this parable, I call heaven and earth to witness against you this day, that God shall visit you with all his storms, and pour all the vials of his wrath upon your rebellious heads: you exalted yourselves here,

and God shall abase you hereafter; you are as proud as the devil, and with devils shall you dwell to all eternity. "Be not deceived, God is not mocked;" he sees your hearts, he knows all things. And, notwithstanding you may come up to the temple to pray, your prayers are turned into sin, and you go down to your houses unjustified, if you are self-judiciaries; and do you know what it is to be unjustified? Why, if you are unjustified, the wrath of God abideth upon you; you are in your blood; . . . everything you do, say, or think, from morning to night, is only one continued series of sin.[518]

Although Whitefield did not use such strong language often in his invitations, it is important to note these examples, because they reveal the deadly seriousness with which he viewed rejection of the gospel and make plain how he communicated this somber reality to his listeners.

He proclaimed that, ultimately, God would be glorified whether or not individuals accepted the good news of the gospel. The Lord would either gain glory through their salvation or in their just condemnation.[519] Whitefield stated that the love of God would remain, whether or not his hearers accepted it. If they would not accept such condescending love, they would see His justice.[520] Regardless, God would receive all the glory.

Whitefield's dependence upon God. While George Whitefield incorporated such methods in inviting his hearers to come to Christ, he realized that only God could grant them saving repentance and faith. The itinerant knew that his persuasive words alone would not suffice to convert them, only the Holy Spirit could accomplish such a task. With this knowledge in mind, he included within his invitations prayers that God would grant his listeners conversion. In one sermon, Whitefield prayed, "God convince you; God convert you: God help those that never believed, to believe."[521] He entreated the Holy Spirit to excite his hearers to choose God.[522] The English evangelist also prayed that God would draw his listeners and allow them to hear the voice of the Good Shepherd.[523] Such supplications clearly reveal Whitefield's dependence upon the Lord to draw souls to Himself through the itinerant's invitations to the gospel.

Conclusion. Invitations to the gospel comprised a vital part of George Whitefield's methodology of evangelism. The English itinerant presented universal invitations, calling all of his hearers to come to Christ. He admonished separate groups in his audiences, personalizing his invitations to their relative contexts. Whitefield also asked questions of his hearers to cause them to think about various matters related to their salvation. He instructed them to repent of their sins and place their faith in Christ. The evangelist also invited sinners to come to the cross where Christ is willing to accept all who place faith in Him. Although he spoke mainly of the glorious aspects of salvation, Whitefield also exhorted listeners regarding hell and the eternal condemnation they would experience apart from Christ. But in all of these invitational methods, George Whitefield acknowledged that God alone is the one who can grant salvation; therefore, the itinerant did not rely on his own persuasive words to save his hearers, but prayed that the Holy Spirit would draw them.

Whitefield and Personal Evangelism

Personal evangelism constituted another element of George Whitefield's evangelistic methodology. In his sermon "Jacob's Ladder," the English itinerant stated, "God forbid I should travel with any body a quarter of an hour without speaking Christ to them."[524] He shared the gospel verbally through personal interactions with people he encountered during his travels and through letters that he sent to unconverted persons. His efforts towards personal evangelism were many and varied, but reviewing several of them will be instructive and helpful.

Personal Interaction

George Whitefield made an intentional effort to share the gospel verbally with people he encountered during his travels and daily activities. This habit of personal evangelism began shortly after the itinerant's conversion. Whitefield shared his new-found faith with a woman and several young people who, as a result, experienced conversion.[525] He shared the gospel with the poor people of Oxford, leading a number of them to Christ. The English evangelist also brought the gospel to inmates imprisoned in the Gloucester jail.[526]

Whitefield shared the gospel with fellow travelers who sailed with him on his numerous journeys across the Atlantic Ocean. He witnessed to sick family members, leading one fever-stricken boy to Christ.[527] He shared the gospel with the captain and sailors of the ship as well as with the British Army troops on board, walking the decks late at night to gain a hearing from the sailors.[528] He sometimes witnessed to individuals for hours at a time, answering any of their questions regarding the gospel. The itinerant sought to speak to each person on the ship regarding his or her spiritual condition.[529]

Numerous inquirers to the gospel approached the evangelist with questions regarding salvation, as we shall see. Each of these encounters granted him an opportunity to share the gospel with these individuals. So precious were these that Whitefield made himself available for extended periods of time to accommodate such visits and the personal evangelism efforts for which they called.

George Whitefield witnessed one-on-one as an evangelistic method. He spoke to the poor and to persons in local prisons and jails, and shared Christ with his traveling companions at sea. The numerous inquirers who visited Whitefield with questions regarding the gospel also afforded him opportunities to communicate the gospel privately with them.

Written Correspondence and
Personal Evangelism

George Whitefield also wrote letters to declare the good news of salvation to unconverted people. Some of these lost individuals were members of the itinerant's immediate family. Whitefield wrote a letter to his mother entreating:

> O my honoured mother, my soul is in distress for you: Flee, flee I beseech you to Jesus Christ by faith. Lay hold on Him, and do not let Him go. God hath given you convictions. Arise, arise, and never rest till they end in a sound conversion. Dare to deny yourself. My honoured mother, I beseech you by the mercies of God in Christ Jesus, dare to take up your cross and follow Christ.[530]

In another letter to his brother James, the itinerant admonished his sibling not to mistakenly call himself a Christian. He asked James, "But does not my dear brother find, that he yet lacks something? Have not his tempers and corruptions; nay, hath not sin itself dominion over him? Are his affections weaned from the world? Does he feel himself a poor lost sinner? Is he willing the Lord Jesus should be his whole righteousness? Is he convinced of the freeness, as well as of the riches of his grace?"[531] These citations indicate how Whitefield served as an evangelist to his family members as well as to the masses of people to whom he preached.

Whitefield further made known the gospel through letters written to unconverted individuals he met or heard about as he traveled. The following examples represent the content within such letters of personal evangelism. In a thank you letter written to a woman who allowed him the use of her coach, Whitefield wrote:

> But what is of greater concern, I think it my duty to write to you about a more important affair; I mean the salvation of your precious and immortal soul.

God was pleased to incline your heart, Madam, to hear and receive the word with joy. . .

Pure and undefiled religion consists in a lively faith in Jesus Christ, as the only mediator between God and man. A faith that changes and renews the whole soul, takes it entirely off the world and fixes it wholly upon God. This, Madam, is the faith that you so often heard me preach, and of which I pray God you may be a partaker. Though you have it not yet, you need not despair; God will give it to all who sincerely ask of him.[532]

To a man who spoke with Whitefield regarding the state of his own soul, he wrote, "What therefore you have to do, dear Sir, but to throw yourself as a poor sinner at the feet of the holy Jesus? You need not doubt his holding out the golden sceptre to you. Whoever cometh to him by faith, he will in no-wise cast out."[533]

The itinerant also addressed those who relied upon their outward religious performances or moral activity to save them. Responding to the request to write a hearer's father, Whitefield wrote:

Assure yourself that Christianity is something more than a name and bare outward profession. Morality itself, dear Sir, will never carry us to heaven; no, Jesus Christ is the way, the truth, and the life. There is no being happy without a lively faith in him, wrought in the heart by the blessed Spirit of God. This faith transforms the whole man, delivers him from the tyranny of his passions, and makes him entirely a new creature.[534]

He warned a woman who had extended kindness to him during one of his visits that "what the world calls an innocent, harmless, decent, sober life, will not be sufficient to carry us to heaven. Such a life I suppose you have led, and assure yourself, you will find it an hard work to give up such a life in point of dependence, and to come as a poor, ill and hell deserving wretch, to be washed in the blood and clothed with the righteousness of Jesus Christ."[535] In this written correspondence, Whitefield emphasized that baptism, church membership, moral acts, or religious activity cannot grant one right standing with God. Only repentance and faith in the righteousness of Christ, imputed to the heart of the individual, can bring salvation.

Besides writing to people from common backgrounds, George Whitefield also wrote letters explaining the gospel to those of nobility and fame. To his friend Benjamin Franklin, the English evangelist wrote:

> As you have made a pretty considerable progress in the mysteries of electricity, I would now humbly recommend to your diligent unprejudiced pursuit and study the mystery of the new-birth. It is a most important, interesting study, and when mastered, will richly answer and repay you for all your pains. One at whose bar we are shortly to appear, hath solemnly declared, that without it, "we cannot enter the kingdom of heaven." You will excuse this freedom. I must have *aliquid Christi* in all my letters.[536]

Whitefield also witnessed through written correspondence with the Earl of Leven and Melville. He wrote:

> Here is the fountain to which you and I must apply, to wash away all our sins. And is it yet open for all poor sinners? Come then, my Lord, and lay yourself at the feet of the blessed Jesus. He can, he will, if you believe on him, abundantly pardon you. But faith is the gift of God. I pray God to give you no rest, 'till you have received the full assurance of faith. . .. Your Lordship need not remind me to pray for you. Your eternal welfare is much upon my heart. My Lord, now is the accepted time, now is the day of salvation.[537]

Plainly, the English evangelist acknowledged the need for the noble and famous to come to Christ, and he was not timid in communicating the gospel to them.

These few examples make the point.[538] In letter after letter, the itinerant emphasized the individual's need to forsake sin and place his or her faith in Christ alone for salvation, whether to members of his family, strangers, hearers of his sermons, or men of fame and nobility. Written correspondence comprised a significant element of his evangelistic methodology.

Conclusion

Personal evangelism played a notable part in George Whitefield's methodology of evangelism. He witnessed through his personal interaction with the poor, prison inmates, town inhabitants, inquirers, and fellow travelers. He also wrote evangelistic letters through which he proclaimed and applied the gospel. All were further means by which the itinerant sought to fulfill the Great Commission by sharing the gospel with as many people as possible.

Whitefield and Follow Up[539]

But the Great Commission is more than just evangelism. What were George Whitefield's methods for discipling new believers and providing further information to inquirers? What were his methods for counseling inquirers following his sermons, and how did he track conversions resulting from his preaching? What part did societies and local ministers play as a means of discipleship and follow up, and how did Whitefield use written correspondence to investigate and facilitate his evangelistic efforts?

Counseling Inquirers

Answering inquirers was a key element of George Whitefield's efforts at follow up. Numerous hearers approached the English itinerant with questions about the gospel and salvation. He mentioned in his letters and journals that they sometimes passed notes to him while he preached or sent them to him after the sermon's conclusion.[540] One such note he received while eating dinner–after preaching a sermon–in which the writer entreated him to "help in the way of salvation."[541] Again, in one of his letters, Whitefield wrote of having his "pockets full of notes from persons brought under concern."[542] Often, those who sent these notes to him signed their names to them so that he could find them and meet with them after the conclusion of the sermon.

More often, inquirers met with Whitefield in the homes in which he stayed as a guest. They often followed him home after he concluded his sermon or visited him there the following day. The evangelist described large numbers of people coming to these residences, often throughout the day, to ask him questions about the gospel and the welfare of their souls. He often spent from early in the morning to late in the evening talking with inquirers,[543] even, at times, sacrificing eating or writing correspondence in order to talk with the considerable number of people calling on him.

A few specific examples may prove helpful in understanding this aspect of the evangelist's methodology of evangelism. Describing one encounter with two inquirers who had fallen under conviction, Whitefield recounted, "Afterwards, one or two more came under similar circumstances, crying out, in the bitterness of their souls, after the Lord Jesus. I prayed with each of them, and exhorted them not to rest till they found rest in Jesus Christ."[544] He mentioned another meeting with inquirers, stating, "Was employed for two hours this morning in giving answers to several who came to me under strong convictions; amongst whom was a negro or two, and a young girl of about fourteen years of age, who was turned out of the house where she boarded, because she would hear me, and would not learn to dance."[545] Describing meetings with inquirers in London, Whitefield stated, "From seven in the morning till three in the afternoon, people came, some telling me what God had done for their souls, and others crying out, 'What shall we do to be saved?'...God enabled me to give them answers of peace."[546]

Beyond meeting with individual inquirers, the English evangelist also addressed groups of persons wanting to hear more about the gospel. Frequently, Whitefield would finish preaching and, upon returning to his lodgings, encounter large groups of inquirers and believers alike awaiting further exhortation from him. These crowds, at times, followed him to his guest house. Of one of these encounters in Boston, the itinerant wrote, "After the sermon, the Governor went with me to my lodgings. I stood in the passage, and spoke to a great company, both within and without doors; but they were so deeply affected, and cried so loud, that I was obliged to leave off praying."[547] In another case, Whitefield visited a girl who had fallen under deep conviction by the Holy Spirit. While in her room, he gave a strong exhortation to twenty people which resulted in much weeping and earnest prayer to God.[548] While the crowds involved in such encounters likely included a number of believers, the habit of inquirers to come to Whitefield's lodging to speak with him following a sermon suggests that many of them had questions regarding salvation.

George Whitefield made himself available to a great many inquirers who visited him at the homes in which he stayed as he traveled throughout England and the American colonies. He devoted large segments of his time to answering their questions and exhorting them in the gospel. He met with both individuals and groups to provide follow up to his preaching. And he did this, methodically, as a crucial aspect of faithfully fulfilling the Great Commission.

Tracking Conversions

It is helpful to focus on how Whitefield tracked conversions resulting from the Holy Spirit's work. A number

of questions are pertinent: Did Whitefield present defini-
tive numbers of claimed conversions or was there a sense
of caution in his presentation of conversion figures? How
did he obtain information regarding conversions?

George Whitefield claimed that he exercised caution in labeling individuals as believers or converts until
he saw evidence supporting such a conclusion.[549] And the
language the itinerant used in reporting converts bears
this out. Regarding one group who followed him to hear
him preach, Whitefield stated that "near fifty or sixty more
joined us, most of whom I hope, had been effectually called
by the grace of God."[550] Writing of a fellow traveler on one
of his overseas passages, he stated that the man was "one
I hope effectually converted."[551] Describing the results of
his preaching in Bristol, Whitefield wrote, "Many sinners,
I believe, have been effectually converted; numbers have
come to me under convictions; and all the children of God
have been exceedingly comforted."[552]
Note in each of these examples, the phrases "I hope" or
"I believe" in referring to conversion numbers. Such language demonstrates Whitefield's caution against identifying people as converts prematurely. While the itinerant
did mention estimates of people on whom God was working, such figures were not exact and were presented with
cautious enthusiasm.[553]

Whitefield obtained information about conversion
numbers from a number of sources. The inquirers who
regularly came to his lodgings for counseling on salvation gave him some idea of how many persons in a given
town had been saved. Describing the results of preaching
in Charleston, South Carolina, Whitefield surmised that "a
good work is begun in many. Generally, every day several came to me, telling me how God had been pleased to
convince them by the Word preached, and how desirous
they were of laying hold on and having an interest in the
complete and everlasting righteousness of the Lord Jesus
Christ. Numbers desired privately to converse with me."[554]

After preaching a morning sermon in Hertford, England, the itinerant wrote, "Many came to me under strong convictions of their fallen estate, and their want of a God-man to be their Mediator."[555] Thus, through such conversations with others, he received an idea of how many conversions occurred in any particular town.

Closely related to the issue of inquirers, Whitefield also gained insight on conversions in any particular town from notes he received during and after preaching his sermons. He told one congregation, "I have reason to believe, from the notes put up at both ends of the town, that there are many of you that have arrows of conviction stuck fast in your souls; I have taken in near two hundred at the other end of town, within a fortnight; if this be the case, that God is thus at work, let the devil roar, and we will go on in the name of the Lord."[556] Notes to him, then, also helped fill in the picture of conversion work occurring from his preaching.

Sometimes, Whitefield could fairly assess the work in a particular place only after he had left the area or upon returning years later. Ministers and others wrote to him of God's convicting work among the townspeople. One minister wrote stating that Whitefield "had left the town under a deep and universal concern. Many were greatly affected, and I hope abiding impressions are left upon some. Some who were before very loose and profligate, now look back with shame upon their past lives and conversations, and seem resolved upon a thorough reformation."[557] New converts also wrote Whitefield after he had gone to preach in another town.[558] Upon returning to towns in which he had preached years before, he was approached by individuals told him stories of conversions resulting from the earlier visit.[559] All of these sources of information enabled the itinerant preacher to gain an good idea of the number of conversions in these locations.

Remembering, though, George Whitefield exhibited caution in communicating conversion figures. When he mentioned such figures, he stated that he "hoped" or "believed" the particular number of individuals were converts. He gathered his information on these matters from counseling inquirers, getting notes, receiving letters, and from conversations with townspeople. Sometimes he found additional data on results only upon returning to a town in which he had preached previously.

Religious Societies

In his historical work *Religion in England 1688-1791*, Gordon Rupp writes, "Religious Societies were the soil in which the Evangelical Revival was rooted."[560] These religious societies comprised an essential element of George Whitefield's methodology for follow up. Their significance is evidenced by the fact that the first sermon the young evangelist preached bore the title "The Necessity and Benefits of Religious Society."[561] Whitefield made establishing such societies a priority in his evangelistic ministry. He emphasized that the purpose of these groups was not to compete with public worship in area churches; rather, they served as an "imitation of the primitive Christians, who continued daily with one accord in the Temple, and yet in fellowship building up one another, and exhorting one another from house to house."[562] The members of societies studied Scripture together, prayed together, and sang praises to the Lord together. Various local ministers, like Gilbert Tennent, even led some of these societies. Overall, these groups of believers provided an excellent environment in which new converts from Whitefield's evangelistic ministry could be discipled.

Whitefield's *Journals* bear record of his activity in establishing such groups for discipleship and exhortation. As early as March 7, 1739, he met with another evangelist, Howell Harris, to coordinate the formation and follow up of several societies.[563] He set up societies for both men and women in the American colonies and the British

Isles, and intended to form a society for slaves in Philadelphia.[564] Whitefield formed these societies in the towns through which he traveled and considered it incumbent upon believers to create and participate in such societies. Whitefield stated:

> And first, if 'two are better than one,' and the advantages of religious society are so many and so great; then it is the duty of every true Christian to set on foot, establish, and promote as much as in him lies, societies of this nature. And I believe we may venture to affirm, that if ever a spirit of true Christianity be revived in the world, it must be brought about by some such means as this.[565]

He also encouraged new converts to join such societies for their spiritual growth.

However, and rightly, Whitefield declined to attempt to manage each one of them. He knew that involving himself in overseeing the daily activities of the societies would hinder his itinerant preaching ministry. He wrote, "I believe my particular province is to go about and preach the gospel to all. My being obliged to keep up a large correspondence in America, and the necessity I am under of going thither myself entirely prevents my taking care of any societies."[566] But his refusal to care for societies he established should lead no one to think Whitefield did not provide for their care through other means. He passed on the welfare of his societies to other ministers within each area. For example, prior to his departure on his second journey to the American colonies, Whitefield left the numerous societies he had established in the areas of Bristol and Kingswood in the hands of John Wesley to provide follow up to the new converts there.[567] He also mentioned commending societies in Wales to the care of Howell Harris.[568] Not bearing the responsibility for the daily care of the societies enabled Whitefield to focus on his ministry of itinerant evangelism.

It would be a mistake, however, to conclude that he failed to provide follow up to these groups he established. He frequently preached at the societies, both those he founded and others, whenever he was in their respective areas. He sometimes preached to two or three of these societies after having just preached, on the same day, in a meeting house or in the open air.[569] Having left a town and its societies, Whitefield would often return months later and follow up with these groups. For example, from December of 1738 to January of 1739, he exhorted the members of the Fetter Lane Society in London on several occasions, then returned in May of 1739 to follow up with and preach to them again.[570] Such return visits allowed Whitefield to exhort new converts that might have joined the society after he left and to encourage the more mature believers within the group. In one of his letters, Whitefield said of such exhortations, "I exhorted them to stedfastness and patience under the cross. They seemed much strengthened and ready for suffering; for God was with us."[571]

Plainly, George Whitefield utilized religious societies as an important element of his methodology of evangelism. Through these societies new converts received follow up and discipleship from other believers. So useful were they, Whitefield himself established numerous societies throughout his itinerant ministry. Although he did not personally oversee the daily activities of these groups of believers, he coordinated with other ministers in whose care he left the societies. He often returned to these societies to follow up with and encourage their members and to new converts who came to Christ as a result of his preaching.

Written Correspondence and Follow Up

Further still, George Whitefield used written correspondence as another means of follow up within his methodology of evangelism. He wrote numerous letters to both individuals and groups to assist them in their spiritual growth. He wrote letters of encouragement and exhortation to the many societies where he had preached. In one of these letters, the itinerant admonished the members of a society not to stake their salvation upon their involvement in that religious body.[572] In a letter to the religious societies in England and Scotland, Whitefield encouraged the members to pray for and encourage each other. He also exhorted:

> How to improve your meetings, so as best to promote God's glory, and the good of your own souls, ought to be your constant and chief concern: for as christians in general, so members of religious societies in particular, are as cities built upon a hill; and therefore it more highly concerns them to let their light shine before men, that they seeing their good works, may glorify our Father who is in heaven.[573]

Whitefield also wrote letters of encouragement to society leaders. In one, he encouraged a leader to remind his society's members of the importance of "being wounded deeply, before they can be capable of healing by Jesus Christ."[574] He encouraged another leader of a newly-formed society not to be discouraged by small beginnings.[575] In one more letter, Whitefield directed the leader of a society to continue the habit of reading Scripture to the society.[576] His comments in such letters are further evidence of his efforts at following up his ministry to the societies and their leaders.

George Whitefield also addressed follow up correspondence to ministers from towns in which he preached. He charged one pastor to continue to preach the gospel and not retreat from it.[577] To a pastor who faced opposition, Whitefield stated, "However, let us behave with meekness, my dear brother, and we shall soon find that every plant that our heavenly father hath not planted, shall be plucked up. 'He that believeth doth not make haste.' Jesus reigneth; let our eyes wait on Him. All things shall work and even now are working, together for good to all that love him."[578] He also frequently told these ministers that he prayed for God's direction and protection over their lives. He intended the follow up letters he sent to ministers to encourage them to continue the work of spreading the gospel and discipling believers.

Whitefield again wrote to believers to exhort them in the faith, encouraging one man converted under his preaching to "let a sense of God's distinguishing love to you above others, excite you to distinguish yourself by your obedience; still remembering that the Lord Jesus is our whole and everlasting righteousness."[579] He charged another new convert, "Strive as much as in you lies, by your life and conversation, to win others to the blessed God. The eyes of men and angels will now be upon you. May the Lord enable you to walk circumspectly to those that are without."[580] Whitefield also encouraged mature believers to persevere in the midst of hardships and trials. He pointed the recipients to Christ for their strength. These letters to believers encouraged both new and older believers to grow in the faith.

Whitefield, then, put all these forms of correspondence to good follow up use. He encouraged society members and leaders he met during his visits to various towns across England, Wales, Scotland, and the American colonies. He wrote letters of encouragement to ministers from these areas. He corresponded with new believers who were converted under his ministry and exhorted mature believers to be a witness and to endure hardships and trials. Such correspondence enabled Whitefield to continue his ministry to these individuals even though he was separated from them geographically.

Conclusion

Follow up was a critical aspect of Whitefield's ministry, and he used a variety of means to undertake this work faithfully. He counseled with numerous inquirers who approached him with questions about the gospel and salvation. He tracked estimates of conversion figures through counseling sessions, getting notes, receiving letters, and talking with townspeople. Whitefield established societies in which new converts could be effectively disciple by ministers and mature believers, while leaving the care of such societies in the hands of local ministers. Then over and above all this, he used written correspondence for exhorting society members, ministers, and new believers.

Gospel Action and the Orphan House

Gospel action refers to ministering to physical, emotional, spiritual, societal, and cultural needs by living out the gospel. Such "care for the city," so to speak, opens the door to share the gospel hope as well. As noted, Whitefield visited people in prison and ministered to the poor with a view to sharing the life-changing gospel with them. Perhaps his most significant effort at gospel action was the founding of an orphan house in Bethesda, Georgia.

Early on in his ministry to the colonists in Georgia, Whitefield developed the desire to found an orphan house to minister to the physical needs of orphans, to educate them to become self-sustaining citizens contributing positively to the colony. During his first visit to Georgia, Whitefield wrote:

> I also enquired into the state of their children, and found there were many who might prove useful members of the Colony, if there was a proper place provided for their maintenance and education. Nothing can effect this but an Orphan House, which might easily be erected in Savannah, would some of those who are rich in the world's good contribute towards it.[581]

Whitefield also wanted the orphanage to be a place where the orphans could hear the gospel, come to faith in Christ, and perhaps follow the call to vocational ministry. He wrote of such intentions for the orphan house, stating:

> I have digged low, and intend to build it high, because I have a great God to pay the charges. I have about thirty-six children which I maintain and clothe, and have upwards of forty persons more who are employed in the work. The plantation is in great forwardness—Many families are kept here by my employing them, and I hope to see many a youth bred up for God; for I design to breed up for the ministry, all that at any time shall perceive to be renewed by the Holy Ghost, and endued with suitable natural abilities. The work, I am persuaded, is of God, and I know he will raise up instruments to support it.[582]

He utilized his preaching opportunities to raise support for the orphan house, preaching throughout the colonies, England, and Scotland and receiving offerings to support the effort.

While we should commend Whitefield for his ministry through the orphan house, his mention of the plantation in the above excerpt points to a significant problem in the evangelist's efforts at gospel action. While opposing the slave trade, Whitefield bought slaves to work as servants in the orphan house and in the fields of its plantation. The following excerpt taken from one of Whitefield's letters helps clarify the English evangelist's stance on slavery:

> As for the lawfulness of keeping slaves, I have no doubt, since I hear of some that were bought with Abraham's money, and some that were born in his house. —And I cannot help thinking, that some of those servants mentioned by the Apostles in their epistles, were or had been slaves. It is plain, that the Gibeonites were doomed to perpetual slavery, and though liberty is a sweet thing to such as are born

free, yet to those who never knew the sweets of it, slavery perhaps may not be so irksome.

However this be, it is plain to a demonstration, that hot countries cannot be cultivated without negroes. What a flourishing country might Georgia have been, had the use of them been permitted years ago? How many white people have been destroyed for want of them, and how many thousands of pounds spent to no purpose at all? Had Mr Henry been in America, I believe he would have seen the lawfulness and necessity of having negroes there. And though it is true, that they are brought in a wrong way from their own country, and it is a trade not to be approved of, yet as it will be carried on whether we will or not; I should think myself highly favoured if I could purchase a good number of them, in order to make their lives comfortable, and lay a foundation for breeding up their posterity in the nurture and admonition of the LORD. You know, dear Sir, that I had no hand in bringing them into Georgia; though my judgement was for it, and so much money was yearly spent to no purpose, and I was strongly importuned thereto, yet I would not have a negro upon my plantation, till the use of them was publicly allowed in the colony. Now this is done, dear Sir, let us reason no more about it, but diligently improve the present opportunity for their instruction. The trustees favour it, and we may never have a like prospect. It rejoiced my soul, to hear that one of my poor negroes in Carolina was made a brother in CHRIST. How know we but we may have many such instances in Georgia ere it be long?[583]

As already discussed here and as evidenced in the above quote, Whitefield desired the salvation of African slaves and preached to them on occasion. He also wrote against slaveholders who abused their slaves, stating in a work entitled "A Letter to the Inhabitants of Maryland, Virginia, and North and South Carolina":

> I must inform you, in the meekness and gentleness of CHRIST, that I think GOD has a quarrel with you, for your abuse of and cruelty to the poor negroes. Whether it be lawful for Christians to buy slaves, and thereby encourage the nations from whence they are brought to be at perpetual war with each other, I shall not take upon me to determine; but sure I am it is sinful, when bought, to use them as bad as, nay worse than brutes: and whatever particular exceptions there may be, (as I would charitably hope there are some) I fear the generality of you that own negroes, are liable to such a charge; for your slaves, I believe, work as hard, if not harder, than the horses whereon you ride.[584]

He reminded slaveholders of their accountability before God regarding their treatment of their slaves and of the need for them to seek the salvation of their slaves.

While Whitefield's concern for the compassionate treatment of slaves and his desire that they would hear and receive the gospel is commendable, his support of slavery, ownership of slaves, and failure to utilize his popularity and preaching platform to speak against slavery are all tragic weaknesses in his theology and methodology of evangelism. While he sought the care of prisoners, the poor, and orphans, Whitefield also should have extended his efforts at gospel action to speaking and working against the evil institution of slavery.[585]

Chapter Summary

Numerous components comprised George Whitefield's methodology of evangelism. Whitefield preached evangelistic messages containing the Calvinist doctrines of total depravity, unconditional election, particular redemption, effectual calling, and perseverance of the saints.

Whitefield offered universal invitations to the gospel, appealing to all of his hearers to repent and trust Jesus Christ for their salvation. He personalized these entreaties by addressing particular groups within his audiences. The itinerant also offered thought-provoking questions in his invitations to encourage his hearers to think about the state of their souls and their need for Christ. Within these invitations, he offered instructions regarding how his listeners may be saved. He emphasized Christ's willingness to accept all persons who place faith in His atoning blood for their forgiveness and salvation. Whitefield also did not neglect to inform hearers about the eternal torments of hell that awaited them if they rejected Christ. Within all of these aspects of his evangelistic preaching, the itinerant acknowledged that God alone could grant his hearers repentant hearts and saving faith.

In addition to his preaching efforts, George Whitefield also incorporated personal evangelism into his evangelistic methodology. He shared the gospel through personal encounters with individuals and witnessing to the poor, imprisoned, fellow travelers, and inquirers to the gospel. The itinerant also witnessed to family members, strangers, hearers of his sermons, and men of fame and nobility through evangelistic letters.

Follow up was another vital aspect of Whitefield's methodology of evangelism. He counseled with numerous inquirers to the gospel, answering their questions regarding the gospel and salvation. He also established various societies that encouraged spiritual growth in both new converts and mature believers. Whitefield wrote letters to society members, ministers, new converts, and mature believers to follow up on his evangelistic efforts and to encourage them in ministry.

He sought to live out the gospel through gospel action, ministering to the needs of others, opening an effective door for a verbal witness of the gospel. Whitefield founded an orphan house for the care of orphans, with the intent that they would accept Christ and, perhaps, pursue calls to vocational ministry. While such gospel action is commendable, Whitefield's stance in support of slave ownership is indefensible. He missed an opportunity to serve as a pivotal voice against such an evil institution.

Overall, these methods reflect George Whitefield's concern for reaching unconverted people with the gospel of Jesus Christ. Clearly, the English itinerant took seriously the Great Commission to preach the gospel to every creature. Although this brief review does not exhaust every means Whitefield utilized to fulfill that Commission, it does highlight the key methods involved in his effort.

CONCLUSION

In the introduction of this book I mentioned that, up to this point, no Christian scholar has examined thoroughly George Whitefield's theology and methodology of evangelism. I also presented the research question that forms the basis for this work: What was the relationship between George Whitefield's theology and methodology of evangelism? The goal, then, has been to analyze and describe Whitefield's theology and methodology of evangelism and provide conclusions about the relationship between these two aspects of his ministry.

In chapter one we put in place the larger historical and theological context surrounding Whitefield's ministry. Elements included the decline of the Church of England in the eighteenth century, the intermingling of politics within the clergy, and the problem of unconverted ministers within the Church of England and American churches. Also bearing on the whole were the negative impacts of rationalism, Deism, and Latitudinarianism upon eighteenth-century churches. Further complications included the problem of unregenerate church membership within churches in the American colonies and the British Isles, as well as debates between Calvinists and Hyper-Calvinists over offering universal invitations and over whether non-elect hearers are responsible to respond affirmatively to the gospel.

In chapter two we began discussing and analyzing the English itinerant's theology of evangelism. The two primary sources of authority to which Whitefield referred in the formation of his theology were, in order of emphasis, the Scriptures and the Thirty-Nine Articles. Whitefield, remember, identified himself as a Calvinist; however, he was more committed to the Scriptures than to any theological system and was more concerned that people hear the cross preached than he was interested in promoting Calvinism. However, the great doctrines of grace formed the foundation of Whitefield's theology of evangelism and the primary content of his evangelistic preaching, including total depravity, unconditional election, particular redemption, effectual calling, perseverance of the saints, new birth, conversion, justification, and sanctification. With this sturdy theological undergirding, Whitefield went into the world, believing that the Great Commission calls ministers to preach the gospel to every creature and to offer universal invitations to the gospel.

In the third chapter, we examined Whitefield's methodology of evangelism. He clearly included all of the "five points" of Calvinism in his evangelistic preaching. But an intriguing aspect of his evangelistic method was his use of invitations. He also engaged in personal evangelism to communicate the gospel through direct interaction and through a variety of evangelistic letters. I mentioned Whitefield's efforts at follow up through counseling inquirers, tracking conversions, establishing religious societies, and writing letters to society members, ministers, and new believers. A final crucial piece of Whitefield's ministry method were his efforts at gospel action through the orphan house and a discussion of his support of slavery and failure to oppose that evil institution.

With that historical and analytical review established, we are now in a place to draw conclusions about the relationship between George Whitefield's theology and his methodology of evangelism. Then we can discuss how Whitefield's theology and methodology of evangelism apply to contemporary evangelism.

The Relationship Between George Whitefield's Theology and Methodology of Evangelism

What might we confidently say about the relationship between George Whitefield's theology and methodology of evangelism?[586] Given the various methodologies explored, what framework do we have to guide our discussion, and how do the conclusions illustrate the effect Whitefield's theology of evangelism had on his methodology?

Evangelistic Preaching

We can learn quite a bit about the relationship between Whitefield's theology and methodology of evangelism from his evangelistic preaching, especially as it pertains to his belief in and treatment of the "five points" of Calvinism and his invitations to the gospel.

The "five points" of Calvinism. George Whitefield not only identified himself as a Calvinist, but he regularly unpacked the "five points" of Calvinism in his evangelistic preaching. Whitefield believed that all are totally depraved and that this depravity corrupts every aspect of their persons including their minds, wills, emotions, abilities, affections, and souls. He held that, because of their depravity, sinners are spiritually dead and at enmity with God. He believed that Adam's sin is imputed to the entire human race and that, because of their sin, original and actual, all deserve eternal condemnation in hell. In Whitefield's view, the only will sinners possess in this depraved state is the will to sin. By nature, all possess a moral inability to find or pursue God.

This belief in total depravity and his concern for his hearers motivated the English itinerant to declare plainly these truths to his audiences. He believed that his hearers needed to become aware of their terrible plight before they would desire salvation from such a sinful condition.

Whitefield preached that ministers "must first shew people they are condemned, and then shew them how they must be saved."[587] He preached on total depravity to inform his hearers about their desperately lost state.

Whitefield emphasized the doctrine of original sin in his theology and in his evangelistic preaching, because he wanted to counter the false belief that anyone is born naturally good. In his sermon "Of Justification by Christ," he called this doctrine "the foundation of Christian religion" and asserted that "it is nothing but a want of being well grounded in the doctrine of original sin . . . that makes so many infidels oppose" the gospel.[588] Because of his belief in original sin, Whitefield preached that all by nature are fallen and at enmity with God due to their inherent sin. The itinerant also believed and preached that sinners cannot come to God on their own power because of their moral inability. Because he held the doctrine of moral inability, Whitefield told his hearers that, although they may attempt to gain favor by participating in morally good acts, their sin corrupts every one of these efforts at self-righteous behavior to gain God's favor. His theological adherence to this truth also led him to declare that all by nature are unable to find God through the mere exercise of reason because their minds are fallen and infected with sin. Whitefield also preached against the concept that humans are able to exercise free will to choose God on their own volition. He repeatedly emphasized that sinners' only will is to sin and not to worship God with their hearts. Thus, he plainly told his hearers that "thou art as unable to raise thyself out of this loathsome, dead state, to a life of righteousness and true holiness, as ever Lazarus was to raise himself from the cave in which he lay so long."[589]

Whitefield also preached on the doctrine of unconditional election. He believed that God does not base his choice in election upon any foreseen merit or choice on the part of the human being. He held that God chose the elect before the foundation of the earth and entered into a covenant of grace with Christ to redeem them. The itinerant maintained that election is based upon God's sovereign choice and not upon man's free will. God must initiate salvation, no one by nature will choose Him. Whitefield also held that God's choice to elect was one of his secret decrees that is beyond our knowledge or comprehension.

All of these views regarding unconditional election Whitefield included in his evangelistic preaching. He preached that sinners are like clay in the hands of God, who can make them vessels of grace or vessels of destruction as He wills.[590]   Regarding who initiates salvation, the itinerant evangelist pointed out to a group of women believers that "you did not, you would not, have chosen him; but when once, my dear sisters, he hath chosen you, then, and not till then, you make a choice of him for your Lord and Husband."[591] He preached that God, from all eternity, initiated the salvation of the elect by choosing them and entering into a covenant of grace with Christ for their redemption. Whitefield also declared that this choice is based solely upon God's sovereign will and not upon man's free will.[592] However, he discouraged his hearers from speculating whether or not they were among the elect. On this, Whitefield preached that his hearers should seek their own salvation and leave God's secret decrees to Him.[593] His sermons clearly indicate that what he believed regarding election, he included in his evangelistic preaching.

Whitefield's theology of evangelism also included the doctrine of particular redemption. He maintained that, in the covenant of grace, God the Father presented Christ the Son with the elect for their redemption. Thus, it would be a travesty upon the blood of Christ to assert that Christ died for non-elect or reprobate individuals who did not fall within this covenant.[594] While Whitefield believed that Christ "is the Saviour of all men, that is, of all sorts of men," he did not agree with the doctrine of universal redemption.[595] The English itinerant maintained that such a doctrine logically leads to universalism.

Whitefield incorporated the doctrine of particular redemption in his evangelistic preaching. He preached that Christ died and offered Himself as an atonement for the sins of "an elect world,"[596] and that God laid the "iniquities of all that shall believe on him" upon Christ.[597] The influence of Whitefield's belief in particular redemption is also evident in his extending invitations to the gospel. Although the itinerant made statements such as "Christ died for you" in a number of somewhat ambiguous references to the "brethren," more often, he stated that Christ died for "sinners," "rebels," or the "lost."[598]

While Whitefield communicated the particular nature of the atonement in his preaching, he also emphasized Christ's willingness to embrace all who would believe in Him. The itinerant also preached that Christ's blood consists of infinite worth "to atone for the sins of millions of worlds."[599] Thus, while preaching the doctrine of particular redemption, Whitefield also held open wide the invitation for all sorts of people to come to Christ.

The English itinerant also believed in the doctrine of effectual calling. He believed that the Holy Spirit fulfills His role in the covenant of grace by drawing and sanctifying the elect. As with the doctrine of election, the evangelist held that God must take the initiative in drawing sinners to Christ because of their moral inability. He maintained that the Holy Spirit makes them willing to come to Christ in repentance and faith. The Spirit takes away a sinner's heart of stone and grants him a heart of flesh that is convicted over sin and willing to pursue Christ. The itinerant believed that, without such intervention by the Holy Spirit, sinners would continue in darkness and sin, ignorant of their terrible plight. But, he maintained, the Spirit cannot fail in this endeavor of drawing and sanctifying the elect.

Of course, Whitefield included the doctrine in his sermons. He preached that, through the work of the Holy

Spirit, sinners are "made willing to accept salvation" and come to Christ through repentance and faith.[600] He emphasized the ability of the Holy Spirit to irresistibly draw individuals to follow Christ.[601] Regarding the elect, Whitefield preached that the Holy Spirit "calls them effectually by his grace."[602] It is evident from these examples that Whitefield preached what he believed regarding effectual calling.

Perseverance of the saints was another doctrine that George Whitefield espoused in his theology of evangelism. He maintained that God is the sovereign keeper of the believer's salvation, and so true believers cannot lose their salvation. The righteousness of Christ imputed to the believer cannot fail to save him and keep him secure. God also protects His children from sin, Satan, and persecution. He will uphold them in each of these trials.

The English itinerant encouraged his hearers by preaching this doctrine of perseverance of the saints. He reminded them that Scripture teaches that Christ is the Good Shepherd, and no one can snatch His sheep from His hand.[603] He preached that Christ's righteousness cannot fail to secure their eternal salvation. Through redemption, Christ secures them from the eternal effects of sin. Whitefield also told believers that God would secure them from "sin and Satan, and eternal ruin."[604] His strong belief in perseverance of the saints was clearly evident in his evangelistic preaching,[605] and offered it as a great encouragement to all persons who come to Christ through repentance and faith.

It is evident that George Whitefield's incorporated his Calvinistic theology into his evangelistic preaching. The Reformed doctrines he maintained stood in close relationship to the doctrinal content of his gospel sermons. Throughout his ministry, the English itinerant not only identified himself as a Calvinist, but also exemplified its theology in his preaching.

Whitefield's invitations. But what are we to make of his invitations to the gospel? Whitefield believed that the Great Commission called him to preach the gospel to every creature.[606] Unlike Hyper-Calvinists such as John Hussey and John Gill, George Whitefield extended universal invitations to the gospel. He maintained that ministers should "offer salvation freely to all by the blood of Jesus."[607] Whitefield's theological beliefs regarding preaching the gospel to every creature and extending offers of salvation to all are reflected in his evangelistic methodology.

The English itinerant offered invitations to salvation through Christ to all of his hearers. He preached that it did not matter what sins his listeners committed in the past or whether they were rich or poor, black or white.[608] He declared, "Come then unto Christ every one that hears me this night; I offer Christ, pardon, and salvation, to all you who will accept thereof."[609] Because he believed that Christ died for "all sorts of men," he offered Christ to a wide variety of groups. His conviction regarding the Great Commission's command to preach the gospel to every creature also motivated him to travel and preach the gospel extensively. His theology of the Great Commission and of universal invitations to the gospel motivated him to invite as many people as possible to come to Christ.

Whitefield's theology of conversion also affected his invitations to the gospel. He maintained that, while salvation is entirely a gift of God, coming to Christ involves sinners acting in repentance and faith. Individuals respond to the convicting work of the Holy Spirit and repent of their sin. They forsake their own righteousness and place their trust in the righteousness of Christ for their salvation. The itinerant believed that repentance and faith are both gifts from God, as well as actions that humans perform and involve the exercise of humans' faculties: their minds, wills, and affections.

The English itinerant's invitations reflect his understanding of conversion. Because he understood conversion to involve individuals acting in repentance and faith, Whitefield felt it incumbent upon himself to persuade them to such actions in his invitations. He preached that Christ calls ministers "even to compel poor sinners by the cords of love to come in."[610] His efforts to persuade them through questions reflect this understanding of conversion. They were not to sit on their hands and wait for God to save them. He wanted them to ask if they had ever experienced conviction, placed their faith in the righteousness of Christ, or experienced the new birth; or if they would deny Christ's call for their salvation.[611] Thus, he passionately called hearers to think about and act upon the answers to such questions.

Whitefield's instructions to his hearers also reflect his theology of conversion. Because Whitefield believed the two aspects of conversion to be repentance and faith, he called his hearers to repent of their sins.[612] Responding to the question, "What must I do to be saved?" Whitefield instructed, "'Believe in the Lord Jesus Christ, and you shall be saved.'"[613] Such directions to hearers to repent and believe are consistent with his theological understanding of the doctrine of conversion.

Also evident in his instructions to hearers is his theological understanding of justification. Whitefield believed that sinners are justified by the righteousness of Christ and not by any righteousness of their own. By nature, all attempts at righteousness fail because they are corrupted by depravity and sin.[614] This perspective on justification influenced the questions and instructions the evangelistic preacher posed in his invitations. He questioned his hearers whether they ever abhorred their own "righteousness" and totally trusted the righteousness of Christ for their salvation.[615] He instructed them to forsake their own attempts at righteousness and to rely solely upon Christ's righteousness for their salvation. His direction to every listener was to "come in full dependence upon the Lord Jesus Christ, looking on him as the Lord who died to save sinners."[616] All such questions and instructions for sinners to trust in the righteousness of Christ to save them are consistent with Whitefield's understanding of the doctrines of justification and conversion.

The doctrine of regeneration also shaped Whitefield's evangelistic invitations. He believed firmly in the necessity of the new birth. He held that church membership, religious involvement, and moral activity are not sufficient for one's salvation. The sinner must experience the inner workings of the Holy Spirit in changing his or her nature and heart, resulting in new birth or regeneration. He further held that individuals can feel this inward change when the Holy Spirit grants them new birth. They will sense a change in their lives as they forsake their sinful nature and pursue Christ. And that such a transformation, he held, is necessary for one to experience salvation.

Thus, Whitefield's evangelistic preaching, including his invitations to the gospel, reflected this theological emphasis on and understanding of the new birth. In addressing various groups of people, Whitefield warned them of the danger of relying on their own religious activity for their salvation. He preached that baptism, church membership, and moral acts were not sufficient for anyone's salvation. He confronted them with their need for God to raise them from spiritual death and grant them new birth.[617] So, he encouraged his hearers to ask themselves whether they had ever experienced the Holy Spirit's work in the new birth. He asked them questions such as, "Has God by his blessed Spirit wrought such a change in your hearts?"[618] And such questions reflected his belief in inner feelings of the change. These queries regarding the new birth reveal the close relationship between his belief in that truth and his method in evangelism.[619]

The doctrine of hell is another teaching that helped form and inform Whitefield's theology and methodology of evangelism. He believed that all those who do not accept Christ while they are alive will experience torment in hell for eternity after their death.[620] He did not believe anyone has another chance to accept Christ after dying. Whitefield, then, incorporated his belief in hell into his evangelistic invitations. He asked his hearers if their short-lived happiness gained from sinning on earth was worth an eternity of suffering in hell.[621] His preaching expressed the urgency of the gospel and the fact that some of his hearers might not live long enough for another chance to accept Christ.[622] He stated that, in either case, God would gain glory in their salvation or in their condemnation. Such evangelistic preaching about the reality and terrors of hell is a direct reflection of Whitefield's convictions about this truth.

Another of Whitefield's theological tenets relating to his invitations to the gospel is his belief in the sovereignty of God over conversion and effectual calling. The English itinerant believed that repentance and faith are both gifts given by God and maintained that God sovereignly calls whom he wills through the process of effectual calling. Because of this theological stance, Whitefield prayed that God would open his hearers' ears and hearts to the gospel.[623] He also instructed his hearers to pray that God would save them.[624] Such prayers and encouragements to pray clearly reflect the incorporation of his understanding of the sovereignty of God in effectual calling and conversion into his evangelistic preaching.

It is quite evident then, given these examples, that Whitefield's invitations to respond to the gospel arose directly and were shaped by his theology of evangelism. His theological views regarding the Great Commission, universal invitations, conversion, justification through Christ's righteousness, the new birth, hell, and God's sovereignty in effectual calling and conversion are all directly reflected in his invitations to the gospel, further indicated the close relationship between his theology and methodology.

Personal Evangelism

The close relationship between George Whitefield's theological convictions and methodological practices is also evident in his efforts at personal evangelism. Though he may never have expressly related his understanding of the Great Commission to his witnessing efforts, such a connection is not presumptuous. Whitefield clearly understood Christ's command as a mandate to share the gospel with all people. His clear conviction regarding the Great Commission is apparent in his statement that he would not travel with an individual for fifteen minutes without sharing Christ with him.[625]

So, his passion for the Great Commission and his belief in universal invitations are evidenced in his efforts to share Christ through personal interactions. Although Whitefield did not record any accounts of the exact words he shared during these personal interactions, he does mention that he led individuals to Christ during such encounters.[626] He shared with prisoners and poor persons. He spoke about matters of salvation with the travelers and sailors he accompanied on his overseas voyages, leading at least one young boy to Christ on one journey.[627] He shared the gospel with the numerous inquirers who visited him with questions about salvation. Clearly, a close relationship stood between Whitefield's theological understanding of the Great Commission and universal invitations, on one hand, and his actions in witnessing through personal encounters, on the other.

Letters as a means of personal evangelism also help reveal the close relationship between Whitefield's theology of evangelism and his personal practice of evangelism. His belief that conversion involves placing one's faith in Christ for salvation is evident in the content of letters he wrote to his mother and to a woman who allowed him to use her coach during one of his journeys.[628] His views on justification based on the righteousness of Christ alone are evident in his explanation, sent to his brother and to a woman who showed him kindness during one of his journeys, that outward acts of religious expression or moral actions are not sufficient to merit salvation. He urged them both to depend upon the righteousness of Christ to save them.[629] Whitefield also communicated his belief in and the sinner's need for the new birth. For example, in a letter to Benjamin Franklin, he urged the American colonist to pursue and "study the mystery of the new- birth."[630] Such samples from only a few of his many evangelistic letters reveal the close relationship between Whitefield's theology of evangelism and the content of his evangelistic correspondence.

Undeniably, Whitefield's theology of evangelism was reflected in his methodology of personal evangelism. Because of his belief in the Great Commission and universal invitations, he regularly sought to share the gospel through his personal interactions and the evangelistic letters he wrote to lost individuals. Whitefield's efforts at individual gospel engagement are yet another example of the close relationship between his theology and methodology of evangelism.

Follow Up

Is there anything we might learn from his methods of follow up? Remember, one way that Whitefield demonstrated his concern for the Great Commission was by making himself available for extended periods of time to the numerous inquirers who came to him with questions regarding salvation.[631] His theology of conversion is reflected in the fact that he did not tell such inquirers to just sit and wait for God to save them, but encouraged them to "find no rest until they found rest in Jesus Christ."[632]

Something of Whitefield's theology of evangelism is also displayed in his method of tracking conversions. As noted, Whitefield exhibited caution in not identifying individuals as converts until they displayed fruit in their lives that was indicative of true faith.[633] This caution relates to his belief in declarative justification, the idea that one who is truly justified will show he possesses justifying faith through his good works.[634] When referring to conversion numbers, Whitefield generally used the phrases "I hope" or "I believe."[635] His caution in identifying converts and his use of such tentative phrases in reference to conversion estimates clearly reflect his theological understanding of declarative justification.

As a further means of follow up, the English evangelist established religious societies. Whitefield believed in the doctrine of progressive sanctification. He maintained that, through this synergistic process, the Holy Spirit daily conforms the believer into the image of Christ.[636] He intended for the religious societies to promote such spiritual growth in new converts and in mature believers.[637] However, beacuse he believed the Great Commission called him to share the gospel with as many people as possible, the itinerant refused to manage these societies. He felt that the responsibility of managing societies would detract from his efforts to obey the Great Commission through itinerant preaching.[638] While his belief in the necessity of spiritual growth led him to establish such societies, his understanding of the Great Commission motivated him to leave their management in the hands of other ministers.[639] These methodological decisions touching the establishment and management of the religious societies clearly reflect Whitefield's theological views on both progressive sanctification and the Great Commission.

Whitefield also wrote letters to society members, new converts, and ministers to follow up his evangelistic efforts and to promote their spiritual growth. He often exhorted society members to "promote God's glory, and the good of your own souls."[640] He reminded and encouraged one society on the importance of "being wounded deeply" over one's own sin.[641] Such counsel reflects the itinerant's belief that as believers grow spiritually, through the work of the Holy Spirit in progressive sanctification, they become more mindful and grieved over sin in their lives.[642] His concern for spiritual growth and progressive sanctification is also evident in his words to new converts. Whitefield wrote letters exhorting new believers to show their love for Christ by their obedience and to walk circumspectly in Christ.[643] He also encouraged the spiritual growth of ministers. Through written correspondence, he emboldened and energized pastors to preach without apology and to show meekness and love to others.[644] These examples reveal Whitefield's theological concern for the spiritual growth and progressive sanctification of believers and reflect his theology of evangelism in practice.

Gospel Action and the Orphan House

Whitefield's involvement in ministering to the imprisoned, poor, and orphaned in society coincides with his theological conviction that everyone should hear the gospel and receive and invitation to repent and believe in Jesus Christ. His orphan house is an example of how his biblical compassion for the lost, in this case lost children, motivated him to gospel action to found an orphanage for their care and spiritual instruction. He is not consistent, however, in his theology and methodology of evangelism as they relate to the issue of slavery. Whitefield's support of slavery and his failure to oppose the institution in his preaching reveal a significant inconsistency in his theology and methodology of evangelism. While he did mention the need for slaves to hear the gospel and for slave owners to treat their slaves well, his support of the institution and failure to speak against it is indefensible.

Conclusion

With the exception of Whitefield's treatment of slaves and slavery, there is a close relationship between

George Whitefield's theology and methodology of evangelism. Though hardly exhaustive, this suggestive review of the methods he used in his itinerant ministry does clearly reflect Whitefield's theology of evangelism. He not only identified himself as a Calvinist, but also included the "five points" of Calvinism in his evangelistic preaching. His theological views on the Great Commission, universal invitations, conversion, justification, regeneration, hell, and God's sovereignty over new life and effectual calling are clearly reflected in the itinerant's invitations and instructions to his hearers. Whitefield's witnessing efforts through personal interactions display his beliefs about the Great Commission and the universal offer of the gospel. The content of his evangelistic letters arises from his theological understanding of conversion, justification, and new birth. Whitefield's follow up methods also reveal the bond between his theology and the means of evangelism. Whitefield's treatment of inquirers reflects his beliefs about conversion and the Great Commission. His treatment of conversion estimates reveals his theological understanding of declarative justification and effectual calling. Whitefield's practice of establishing and managing religious societies reflects his belief in and concern for progressive sanctification and the Great Commission. His follow up letters further reveal the itinerant's views on the importance of spiritual growth through progressive sanctification in the life of believers. At every turn, though, George Whitefield's methods of evangelism reveal the closest and most vital relationship with his theology of evangelism.

Applications to the Modern Church

Contemporary Christians and ministers of the gospel can glean numerous lessons from George Whitefield's theology and methodology of evangelism, beginning with Whitefield's emphasis on doctrinal preaching. It would be wise for contemporary preachers to emulate the evangelist's practice of preaching doctrinally. In their book *Vanishing Boundaries*, Dean R. Hoge, Benton Johnson, and Donald A. Luidens cite an absence of biblical and doctrinal teaching as one of the reasons for the decline of mainline denominations.[645] On the other hand, Thom Rainer, in his book *Effective Evangelistic Churches,* contends that churches that experience significant conversion growth have pastors who preach expository and textual messages.[646] Such expository messages communicate biblical doctrines from their text. The statistics in both books verify the need for ministers to incorporate Whitefield's practice of preaching doctrinal messages into their evangelistic strategy. Just as He did for Whitefield, God will empower evangelistic preaching that is biblically sound and doctrinally focused. By preaching such messages, contemporary ministers will offer lost persons the truth of Scripture while, at the same time, teaching doctrine to them and to the believers within the congregation.

Another aspect of Whitefield's theology and methodology of evangelism that contemporary ministers and lay persons should emulate is the itinerant's passion for the Great Commission. Churches would likely experience tremendous revival if members would merely adopt Whitefield's method of not allowing fifteen minutes of time spent with anyone to pass before sharing the gospel with them. We all should learn from Whitefield's willingness to share Christ anywhere, anytime, regardless of the circumstances. In a time when 71% of non-Christian Americans state that no Christian has ever shared with them how to come to Christ and 79% claim that they would listen to their Christian friends share their faith, we are in need of Christians committed like Whitefield to personal evangelism.[647] American Christians are tempted to fall into the surrounding culture's obsession with self-gratification, we must pray for the same determination that Whitefield possessed and displayed in obeying the Great Commission. From the English itinerant's ministry, our churches can learn to be single-minded in the priority they place upon evangelism and in the willingness to do whatever it takes to reach their communities for Christ to the glory of God.

Further, contemporary Christians can also learn from Whitefield's response to the problem of unregenerate church membership within churches in the American colonies and the British Isles. He repeatedly reminded his hearers that mere church attendance or membership is not sufficient for salvation. One must experience new birth through the transforming power of the Holy Spirit. He also believed and preached that true faith in Christ will reveal itself through the believer's obedience to the Lord in doing good works. He was rightly hesitant to identify anyone as converts until he or she demonstrated their faith through obedience. Contemporary churches should learn both from Whitefield's practice and from his preaching about the importance of regenerate church membership.

Contemporary Christians-both laypersons and pastors-should also adopt Whitefield's practice of showing meekness and love towards fellow Christians who hold contrary theological views and so work to find commonality with them in the preaching of the cross. Although George Whitefield vehemently disagreed with John Wesley over the issues of unconditional election and particular redemption, he strove to show love towards Wesley and sought to avoid the conflict. Contemporary believers should adopt the spirit in which Whitefield wrote Wesley, stating, "And in one word, how would the cause of our common Master every way suffer by our raging disputes about particular points of doctrines? Honoured Sir, let us offer salvation freely to all by the blood of Jesus, and whatever light God has communicated to us, let us freely communicate to others."[648] The church would be edified and Christ would be glorified if contemporary believers adopt and practice such charity towards one another and, rather than wasting time arguing over particular doctrines, focus upon obeying the Great Commission's mandate to make disciples of all peoples.

Finally, we must learn from Whitefield's focus on gospel action as a means to gain a hearing to the gospel with the lost people we encounter. We must live out the gospel in our culture and address needs in our communities like Whitefield did in establishing the orphan house. We must also be aware of theological blind spots in our lives as they related to people of other races and ethnicities and not fall into the trap into which Whitefield fell of supporting institutions and movements that detract from the gospel's teaching that people from every tribe, tongue, and nation are equally dear to God and have equal value. We must learn from Whitefield's tragic mistake and uphold the dignity and worth of every human being as we share the gospel in our actions and our words.

The scope of this book does not permit a delineation of every possible application from George Whitefield's ministry to the contemporary church. If believers, ministers, and churches would merely apply the lessons mentioned above, they would bring God great glory and likely see fruit from their evangelistic efforts.

Conclusion

In this book, I have attempted to describe George Whitefield's theology and methodology of evangelism and the relationship between them. Throughout his evangelistic ministry, Whitefield was both a Calvinist and a passionate evangelist. Overall, there was the closest and most vital union between his theology and his practice of evangelism. The English itinerant was compelled by his understanding of the Great Commission to share the gospel with all peoples. In his preaching, he emphasized the sovereignty of God in regeneration and conversion, extended universal invitations to respond to the gospel, and emphasized the responsibility of sinners to repent of their sins and trust in the righteousness of Christ for their salvation. White-field's burden for the Great Commission also led him to share Christ through personal evangelism. He also offered means for follow up because of his concern for the spiritu-al growth of his converts. The contemporary church can benefit greatly by studying his evangelistic ministry and by emulating his passion for sharing the gospel. Know that even as we seek to imitate George Whitefield in his minis-try, he would still guard and guide our efforts at adulation, "No, let the name of Whitefield die, so the cause of Jesus Christ may live."[649]

NOTES

Introduction

1   Thomas S. Kidd, *George Whitefield: America's Spiritual Founding Father* (New Haven & London: Yale University Press, 2014), 1-2.

2   Throughout this book, the term "awakening" means a movement of the Holy Spirit in which spiritually dead individuals are converted from death to life through repentance and faith in Jesus Christ. Such an awakening may occur within the life of a single individual or may involve multitudes of individuals over wide geographic spans. The term "revival" means a movement of the Holy Spirit in which believers are convicted to live lives that reflect greater holiness and commitment to Christ. Revivals also result in believers becoming more involved in evangelism. For a discussion regarding the meaning of the terms "awakening" and "revival" see Errol Hulse, *Give Him No Rest* (Durham, UK: Evangelical Press, 1991), 10-11; and J. Edwin Orr, *The Event of the Century* (Wheaton, IL: International Awakening Press, 1989), xi-xvi.

3   Kevin A. Miller, "Did You Know?" *Christian History* 38, no. 2 (1993): 2.

4   Mark A. Noll, *The Rise of Evangelicalism: The Age of Edwards, Whitefield, and the Wesleys* (Downers Grove, IL: InterVarsity Press, 2003), 13.

5   George Whitefield, *George Whitefield's Journals* (London: The Banner of Truth Trust, 1960), 284.

6   John Gillies, *Memoirs of Rev. George Whitefield* (New Haven: Whitmore & Buckingham and H. Mansfield, 1834), 284.

7   Ibid., 221.

8   Benjamin Franklin, *The Life of Benjamin Franklin* (Auburn and Buffalo, NY: Miller, Orton, & Mulligan, 1854), 118.

9   Luke Tyerman, *The Life of the Reverend George Whitefield* (London: Hodder and Stoughton, 1876-1877; reprint, Azle, TX: Need of the Times Publishers, 1995), 1:94.

10   Gillies, *Memoirs,* 11.

11   The servitors were servants for the students from higher socioeconomic backgrounds. These servants cleaned rooms, polished shoes, ran errands, and washed clothes for their student employers. The servitors were not allowed to initiate conversations with students in higher positions. Special times for the partaking of the Sacrament were arranged so that servitors did not socialize with the rest of the student body. These servants were also required to wear particular clothes that distinguished them from the other students.

12   George Whitefield, *George Whitefield's Letters* (Carlisle, PA: The Banner of Truth Trust, 1976), 19. Because this source is easier for readers to find than *TWRGW*, I will include references from it along with references to letters presented from the first volume of *TWRGW*.

13   Whitefield's self designation was "itinerant preacher." Throughout the dissertation, I will use the terms "evangelist" and "itinerant" interchangeably when referring to Whitefield. Both terms refer to his efforts to share the gospel with as many persons as possible in as many places as possible so they might repent and place their faith in Christ for their salvation.

14   Joseph Belcher, *George Whitefield: A Biography* (New York: American Tract Society, 1857), 468.

15   For Wesley's sermon and Whitefield's response, see John Wesley, "Free Grace," in *The SAGE Digital Library* [CD ROM] (Albany, OR: Ages Software, 1996), 415-28; George Whitefield, "A Letter to the Reverend Mr. John Wesley: in Answer to His Sermon, Entituled *Free-Grace*," in *TWRGW* (London: Printed for Edward and Charles Dilly, in the Poultry; and Messrs. Kincaid and Bell, at Edinburgh, 1771-1772), 4:52-73. A later chapter of this book focusing on Whitefield's theology of evangelism contains a thorough treatment of this interchange between the two evangelists.

16   Arnold Dallimore, *Geroge Whitefield* (Carlisle, PA: The Banner of Truth Trust, 1980), 2:426.

17   George Whitefield, "Letter MCCCCVI," in *TWRGW*, 3:382.

18   For this book, the term "Calvinism" refers to the five points of Calvinism as outlined and explained by the Synod of Dort in 1618. While the five points of Calvinism do not exhaust every aspect involved in the theological system known as Calvinism, they do represent the Calvinist's understanding of soteriology and the gospel.

In his preface to John Owen's work entitled *The Death of Death in the Death of Christ*, J. I. Packer writes of the five points of Calvinism, "They stem from a very different principle-the biblical principle that 'salvation is of the Lord;' and they may be summarized thus: (1.) Fallen man in his natural state lacks all power to believe the gospel, just as he lacks all power to believe the law, despite all external inducements that may be extended to him. (2.) God's election is a free, sovereign, unconditional choice of sinners, as sinners, to be redeemed by Christ, given faith and brought to glory. (3.) The redeeming work of Christ had as its end and goal the salvation of the elect. (4.) The work of the Holy Spirit in bringing men to faith never fails to achieve its object. (5.) Believers are kept in faith and grace by the unconquerable power of God till they come to glory. These five points are conveniently denoted by the mnemonic TULIP: Total depravity, Unconditional election, Limited atonement, Irresistible grace, Preservation of the saints." J. I. Packer, "Introductory Essay," in *The Death of Death in the Death of Christ*, by John Owen (Carlisle, PA: The Banner of Truth Trust, 1995), 4.

19   Harry S. Stout, *The Divine Dramatist: George Whitefield and the Rise of Modern Evangelicalism* (Grand Rapids: Eerdmans, 1991), xxiii.

20   Ibid., 95.

21   Ibid., 192.

22   Frank Lambert, *Pedlar in Divinity: George Whitefield and the Transatlantic Revivals, 1737-1770* (Princeton: Princeton University Press, 1994), 72

23   Ibid., 227.

24   Frank Lambert, *Inventing the "Great Awakening"* (Princeton: Princeton University Press, 1999), 105.

25 Tyerman, *The Life of the Reverend George Whitefield*, 1:407-08.

26 Ibid., 479.

27 Dallimore, *George Whitefield*, 2:87.

28 Ibid., 1:85.

29 Mark Noll, *A History of Christianity in the United States and Canada* (Grand Rapids: William B. Eerdmans Publishing Company, 1992), 91.

30 D. M. Lloyd-Jones, "John Calvin and George Whitefield," in *The Puritans: Their Origins and Successors* (Carlisle, PA: The Banner of Truth Trust, 1996), 103.

31 J. I. Packer, "The Spirit and the Word," in *The Bible, the Reformation, and the Church*, ed. W. P. Stephens (Sheffield, UK: Sheffield Academic Press, 1995), 174.

32 Stuart C. Henry, *George Whitefield: Wayfaring Witness* (Nashville, TN: Abingdon Press, 1957), 100, 103-105, 113.

33 This book will use the term "evangelism" to refer to sharing the gospel, through the power of the Holy Spirit, with the hope that individuals repent of their sins, place their faith in the righteousness of Christ for their salvation, and display evidence of true faith through their obedience to Christ in doing good works.

34 John Wesley, *A Sermon on the Death of the Rev. Mr. George Whitefield. Preached at the Chapel in Tottenham-Court-Road, at the Tabernacle near the Moorfields, on Sunday, November 18, 1770* (London: J. and W. Oliver, 1770; reprint, Atlanta: The Library of Emory University, 1953), 14-15.

35 Tyerman, *The Life of the Reverend George Whitefield,* 1:iii-iv.

36 J. C. Ryle, "George Whitefield and His Ministry," in *Select Sermons of George Whitefield* (Carlisle, PA: The Banner of Truth Trust, 1997), 41.

37 Edwin C. Dargan, *A History of Preaching* (Grand Rapids: Baker Book House, 1954), 2:307.

38 Dallimore, *George Whitefield*, 2:536.

39 Lloyd-Jones, *John Calvin and George Whitefield*, 126.

40 Packer refutes Harry Stout's assertion that Whitefield was a model for revivalists like Charles Finney. He points out that Whitefield did not give an "altar call," but sent people away from his preaching to "pray for a change of heart

through the new birth...." He contends that Whitefield's evangelistic methodology was consistent with the Calvinist theology to which he adhered. Packer, "The Spirit with the Word," 185-89.

41   Packer, "A Calvinist—and an Evangelist!" 205, 209. Although Packer does not present an in-depth examination of Whitefield's theology and methodology of evangelism, he mentions the English itinerant as an example of a Calvinist evangelist's theology and methodology of evangelism.

42   Henry, *George Whitefield*, 122-132.

43   Ibid., 131. In this statement, Henry argues that Whitefield was not consistent in his theology and methodology. He contends that the English itinerant believed in Calvinism, yet preached like an Arminian.

44   Wesley, "Free Grace," 418.

45   George Whitefield, "A Letter to Wesley," in *TWRGW*, 4:59. As stated previously, a more detailed analysis of this interchange between Whitefield and Wesley will appear in the second chapter of this dissertation.

46   For the purpose of this paper, this writer accepts Toon's definition of hyper-Calvinism. He wrote, "It was a system of theology, or a system of the doctrines of God, man, and grace, which was famed to exalt the honour and glory of God and did so at the expense of minimising the moral and spiritual responsibility of sinners to God. It placed excessive emphasis on the immanent acts of God—eternal justification, eternal adoption, and the eternal covenant of grace. In practice, this meant that 'Christ and Him crucified,' the central message of the apostles, was obscured. It also often made no distinction concerning the secret and revealed will of God, and tried to deduce the duty of men from what it taught concerning the secret, eternal decrees of God. Excessive emphasis was also placed on the doctrine of irresistible grace with the tendency to state that an elect man is not only passive in regeneration but also in conversion as well. The absorbing interest in the eternal, immanent acts of God and in irresistible grace led to the notion that grace must only be offered to those for whom it was intended.... So Hyper-Calvinism led its adherents to hold that evangelism was not necessary and to place much emphasis on introspection in order to discover whether or not one as

elect." Peter Toon, *The Emergence of Hyper-Calvinism in English Nonconformity, 1689-1765* (London: The Olive Tree, 1967), 144-145.

47   The eighteenth-century debate between Calvinism and hyper-Calvinism will receive more attention in the first chapter.

48   See Lambert, *Inventing the "Great Awakening"*; Lambert, *Pedlar in Divinity*

49   See Stout, *The Divine Dramatist*

50   Although this writer knows of no such word study of Whitefield's sermons, a word study of the evangelist's letters exists in print. See Michael T. McCarty, "The Internal Congruity of George Whitefield's Letters, 1735-1742: A Word Frequency Analysis" (M.A. thesis, Mississippi State University, 1990).

Chapter 1

51   Alfred Plummer, *The Church of England in the Eighteenth Century* (London: Methuen & Company, 1910), 4.

52   E. J. Poole-Connor, *Evangelicalism in England* (Worthing: Henry E. Walter Ltd., 1966), 139.

53   Charles J. Abbey and John H. Overton, *The English Church in the Eighteenth Century* (London: Longmans, Green, and Co., 1878), 1:238.

54   David Hartley, *Observations on Man, His Frame, His Duty, and His Expectations* (Bath: James Leake and Wm. Frederick, 1749; reprint, Gainesville: Scholar's Facsimiles & Reprints, 1966), 441.

55   Joseph Butler, *The Analogy of Religion to the Constitution and Course of Nature* (Philadelphia: J. B. Lippincott & Co., 1857) 66

56   For an informative, thorough, and well-researched treatment of this relationship, see Norman Sykes, *Church and State in England in the XVIIIth Century* (Hamden, CT: Archon Books, 1962).

57   Plummer, *Church in the Eighteenth Century*, 2.

58   This chapter will discuss further this issue of bishop appointments in its section regarding the state of the clergy in England.

59 Gerald Cragg, *The Church and the Age of Reason, 1648-1789* (London: Penguin Books, 1970), 120.

60 Plummer, *Church in the Eighteenth Century*, 41.

61 E. Gordon Rupp, *Religion in England 1688-1791* (Oxford: Clarendon Press, 1986), 53.

62 Plummer, *Church in the Eighteenth Century*, 41.

63 Dissenters consisted of members of various denominations that refused to conform to the Act of Uniformity. The following section will include a more thorough discussion of this group.

64 Cragg, *The Church and the Age of Reason*, 120.

65 The Latitudinarians will receive attention in a later section of this chapter.

66 Rupp, *Religion in England*, 55.

67 For a detailed discussion of the controversy between High and Low Churchmen, see E. Gordon Rupp, *Religion in England 1688-1791* (Oxford: Clarendon Press, 1986), and Charles J. Abbey and John H. Overton, *The English Church in the Eighteenth Century*, 2 vols. (London: Longmans, Green, and Co., 1878).

68 Not all Nonconformists separated from the Church of England.

69 Cragg, *The Church and the Age of Reason*, 53. See Cragg, *The Church and the Age of Reason, 51-55,* for an excellent overview of the era's issues regarding Dissenters.

70 Roy Porter, *English Society in the Eighteenth Century* (London: Penguin Books, 1990), 179.

71 Rupp, *Religion in England*, 125.

72 A later section of this chapter will include a more thorough discussion regarding the issue of unregenerate church members prior to the First Great Awakening.

73 For examples of some of these confessions of faith, see William Latane Lumpkin, *Baptist Confessions of Faith* (Chicago: Judson Press, 1959).

74 Poole-Connor, *Evangelicalism in England*, 145. Despite all of the differences between the Dissenting denominations and between the Church of England and the Nonconformists, all of these religious bodies agreed in their opposition of the Catholic Church. Concerning this unifying factor, Alfred Plummer wrote, "The intense prejudice against Romanists pervaded all classes,--High Churchmen and Lati-

tudinarians, Dissenters of all kinds, Socinians, Deists, infidels, Whigs, and Tories. Not even among the Nonjurors or other Protestant Jacobites were there any as yet who were disposed to show any inclination towards Rome." Plummer, *Church in the Eighteenth Century*, 34.

75 Noll, *Rise of Evangelicalism*, 39.

76 Plummer, *Church in Eighteenth Century*, 114.

77 Gilbert Burnet, *Discourse of the Pastoral Care* (Lampeter, UK: The Edwin Mellen Press, 1997), 54-55.

78 Ibid., 55.

79 Sykes, *Church and State in England*, 93.

80 Regarding Bishop Hoadly, Cragg noted, "During his six years as Bishop of Bangor he never set foot within his diocese—an even worse record than Laud's at St. David's—but Hoadly was a cripple, who should never have accepted a bishopric; since that presupposes a degree of self-denial that few clerics of the age could not have comprehended, the position should never have been offered to him." Cragg, *The Church and the Age of Reason*, 123.

81 Ibid.; Sykes, *Church and State in England*, 99, 105.

82 Cragg, *The Church in the Age of Reason*, 123; Sykes, *Church and State in England*, 111.

83 Sykes, *Church and State in England*, 110.

84 John Henry Overton, *The Evangelical Revival in the Eighteenth Century* (London: Longmans, Green, and Co., 1907), 7.

85 Cragg, *The Church and the Age of Reason*, 128.

86 John Locke, *An Essay Concerning Human Understanding and a Treatise on the Conduct of Understanding* (Philadelphia: Troutman & Hayes, 1852), 452-53.

87 Ibid., 449.

88 John Locke, *The Reasonableness of Christianity as Delivered in the Scriptures* (Bristol, UK: Thoemmes Press, 1997), 133.

89 A subsequent section will discuss a group of clergymen, known as the Latitudinarians, who were influenced by rationalism and the teachings of John Locke.

90 Abbey and Overton, *The English Church in the Eighteenth Century*, 1:177.

91 Plummer, *Church in the Eighteenth Century*, 89. For more descriptions of Deism, see Abbey and Overton, *The En-*

glish Church in the Eighteenth Century, 1:178; also refer to Cragg, *The Church and the Age of Reason*, 77.

92 Matthew Tindal, *Christianity as Old as the Creation* (London: n.p., 1730), 202.

93 Thomas Woolston, *A Discourse on the Miracles of Our Saviour, in View of the Present Controversy between Infidels and Apostates* (London: n.p., 1728; reprint, London: Garland Publishing, 1979), 4.

94 Thomas Woolston, *A Sixth Discourse on the Miracles of our Saviour, in View of the Present Controversy between Infidels and Apostates* (London: n.p., 1729); reprint, London: Garland Publishing, 1979), 26.

95 Butler, *The Analogy of Religion*, 204.

96 For other eighteenth-century arguments against Deism, see William Law, *The Case of Reason* (London: W. Innys, 1731), and George Berkeley, *Alciphron* (London: Printed for J. Tonson, 1732).

97 Abbey and Overton, *The English Church in the Eighteenth Century*, 1:233.

98 Ibid., 1:266.

99 Plummer, *Church in the Eighteenth Century*, 52.

100 The Arians adopted Arius' proposition that the Father and Son are distinctly different, the Son being subordinate to the Father in every aspect. They asserted that the Father alone is the one supreme God and identified Christ as a created being higher than all other created beings. This viewpoint eventually led to the Unitarian movement in the eighteenth century that taught that Christ was a mere man who should be commended for his morality.

The Socinians believed that Christ possessed a human nature alone and became the Son of God only when God adopted Him after the Resurrection. They advocated that people interpret Scripture through the lens of reason. The individual should eliminate those aspects or parts of Scripture that do not agree with their rational understanding.

The inclusion of members of these two groups into the clergy of the Church of England drew understandable criticism. George Whitefield spoke against their presence among the ministers of the Anglican Church. In his sermon "Christ the Only Preservative against a Reprobate Spirit," Whitefield lamented, "Many of those who call themselves members, yea, teachers of the church of England, have got into this polite scheme. Good God! My very soul shudders at the thoughts of the consequences that will attend such a belief." Whitefield, "Christ the Only Preservative against a Reprobate Spirit," in *TWRGW*, 6:294; idem, "Christ the Only Preservative against a Reprobate Spirit," in *SIS*, 565-66. Throughout this book, when applicable, I will include the same sermon from *SIS* because this source is more accessible.

101 Hartley, *Observations on Man*, 290-91.

102 John Tillotson, "Sermon LVI," in *The Works of the Most Reverend Dr. John Tillotson, Lord Archbishop of Centerbury* (London: T. Birch, 1820), 35.

103 Cragg, *The Church in the Age of Reason*, 70.

104 The Latitudinarians' opposition to Whitefield's preaching regarding the new birth and inner feelings stemmed from their emphasis upon faith being the result of the application of reason. They criticized Whitefield and labeled him an "enthusiast" because of this preaching regarding the Spirit's work in the life of believers. Whitefield's beliefs regarding the Holy Spirit will receive more attention in the next chapter, which addresses his theology of evangelism.

105 *The Thirty-Nine Articles of the Church of England*, in *A History of the Creeds of Christendom*, ed. Phillip Schaff (Grand Rapids: Baker Books, 1998), 3:486-516. The next chapter will reveal more information regarding the Reformed nature of the Thirty-Nine Articles and George Whitefield's attitude towards them. This section focuses on the Articles' teaching on baptism and the way eighteenth-century clergymen in the Church of England interpreted them in relation to church membership.

106 This Article read, "Baptism is not only a sign of profession and mark of difference whereby Christian men are discerned from other that be not christened: but is also a sign of regeneration or new birth, whereby, as by an instrument, they that receive Baptism rightly are grafted into the Church; the promises of the forgiveness of sin, and of our adoption to be the sons of god by the Holy Ghost are visibly signed and sealed: faith is confirmed: and grace increased by virtue of prayer unto God. The Baptism of young children is in any wise to be retained in the Church, as most

agreeable with the institution of Christ." Gilbert Burnet, "Article XXVII," in *An Exposition of the Thirty-Nine Articles of the Church of England* (New York: D. Appleton and Company, 1866), 391.

107 Ibid., 401.

108 Ibid., 397.

109 In the chapter on Whitefield's theology of evangelism, I will present a more thorough discussion on his attention to the relationship between baptism, church membership, and regeneration.

110 George Whitefield, *George Whitefield's Journals* (London: The Banner of Truth Trust, 1960), 252.

111 Ibid., 249.

112 Rupp, *Religion in England*, 290.

113 Ibid., 292.

114 Plummer, *Church in the Eighteenth Century*, 21.

115 Ibid., 301.

116 Derek Jarrett, *England in the Age of Hogarth* (New Haven: Yale University Press, 1992), 151.

117 Ibid., 52.

118 Rupp, *Religion in England*, 304.

119 Jarrett, *England*, 65.

120 I will present more information on Whitefield's use of societies in the chapter on George Whitefield's methodology of evangelism.

121 Rupp, *Religion in England*, 330.

122 Porter, *English Society*, 167.

123 Lawrence Stone, "Literacy and Education in England 1640-1900," *Past and Present* 42 (1969): 85, 110.

124 For the purposes of this book, the term "Arminianism" refers to the theological system based upon the teachings of Jacob Arminius and the Five Articles of the Remonstrance. These five articles propose: (1) That Christ, before the foundation of the world, chose to save those persons who would believe in Him and persevere in their faith in and obedience to Him. (2) That Christ died for all men and for the sins of every man; however, only those persons who believe in Him receive forgiveness of sins. (3) That man does not possess saving grace in himself, but must be born again and renewed by the power of the Holy Spirit. (4) That man is saved and sustained by prevenient, assisting, awakening,

following, and cooperative grace; however, this grace is not irresistible. (5) That believers can persevere over and resist temptation; however, it is also possible that they might turn from grace and actually lose their salvation. For a copy of the Five Articles, see *The Five Arminian Articles*, in *A History of the Creeds of Christendom*, ed. Phillip Schaff (Grand Rapids: Baker Books, 1998), 2:545-49.

125 Because most American readers are more familiar with American history than they are with English history, this book grants more attention to historical and theological factors in eighteenth- century England. For more information regarding the historical and theological context of eighteenth- century America, refer to Richard Bushman, *The Great Awakening: Documents on the Revival of Religion*, 1740-1745 (Chapel Hill: The University of North Carolina Press, 1969); John Gillies, *Historical Collections Relating to Remarkable Periods of Success of the Gospel Compiled by the Rev. John Gillies* (Kelso, UK: John Rutherford, Market Place, 1845; reprinted as *Historical Collections and Accounts of Revival*, Fairfield, PA: The Banner of Truth Trust, 1981); Alan Heimert and Perry Miller, eds., *The Great Awakening: Documents Illustrating the Crisis and Its Consequences* (Indianapolis: The Bobbs-Merrill Company, Inc., 1967); Michael Crawford, *Seasons of Grace: Colonial New England's Revival Tradition in Its British Context* (Oxford: Oxford University Press, 1991); Robert L. Ferm, ed., *Issues in American Protestantism* (Gloucester, UK: Peter Smith, 1976); Edwin Scott Gaustad, *A Documentary History of Religion in America: To the Civil War*, 2nd ed. (Grand Rapids: Eerdmans Publishing Company, 1993); idem, *The Great Awakening in New England* (New York: Harper & Brothers, 1957); Keith Hardman, *Seasons of Refreshing: Evangelism and Revivals in America* (Grand Rapids: Baker Books, 1994); Franklin Talley Lambert, *Inventing the "Great Awakening"* (Princeton: Princeton University Press, 1999); William G. McLoughlin, *Revivals, Awakenings, and Reform: An Essay on Religion and Social Change in America, 1607-1977* (Chicago: The University of Chicago Press, 1978); Iain H. Murray, *Revival and Revivalism* (Edinburgh: The Banner of Truth Trust, 1996); Mark A. Noll, *A History of Christianity in the Unit-*

ed States and Canada (Grand Rapids: Eerdmans Publishing Company, 1992); Joseph Tracy, *The Great Awakening* (Boston: Tappan and Dennet, 1842; reprint, Edinburgh: The Banner of Truth Trust, 1997); and Jon Butler, *Becoming America: The Revolution before* 1776 (Cambridge, MA: Harvard University Press, 2000).

126 Ferm, *Issues in American Protestantism*, 40.

127 Gaustad, *The Great Awakening*,11.

128 Solomon Stoddard, "The Inexcusableness of Neglecting the Worship of God," in *Issues in American Protestantism*, ed Robert L. Ferm (Gloucester, UK: Peter Smith, 1976), 41-42.

129 Tracy, *The Great Awakening*, 8.

130 Jonathan Edwards, "A Faithful Narrative of the Surprising Work of God, in the Conversion of Many Hundred Souls, in Northampton, and the Neighbouring Towns and Villages of New Hampshire, in New England," in *The Works of Jonathan Edwards* (Carlisle, PA: The Banner of Truth Trust, 1995), 1:347.

131 Tracy, *The Great Awakening*, 7.

132 Stoddard, "The Inexcusableness of Neglecting the Worship of God," 43.

133 Whitefield, *Journals*, 482. Whitefield's opponents criticized the itinerant for publishing such statements regarding unconverted ministers in New England. Charles Chauncy argued that the itinerant was a new comer to New England and did not possess sufficient knowledge of the ministers there to know whether or not they were unregenerate. Although he did not believe Whitefield wrote these critical comments with the intent to damage New England churches, Chauncy asserted that "what he delivered; especially, at some certain time, had an evident tendency to fill the minds of the people with evil surmisings against the ministers, as tho' they were, for the most part, carnal, unregenerate wretches." Charles Chauncy, *Seasonable Thoughts on the State of Religion in New England* (Hicksville, NY: The Regina Press, 1975), 141.

President Edward Wigglesworth and the scholars at Harvard agreed with Chauncy's criticisms of Whitefield's censoriousness against unconverted ministers. Concerning Whitefield's comments regarding the spiritual condition of New England ministers, the administrators and faculty of Harvard asked if "it is not one of the most uncharitable things he cou'd have done, to manifest these fears to all the world, without ground?" *The Testimony of the President, Professors, Tutors, and Hebrew Instructor of Harvard College, against George Whitefield*, in *The Great Awakening*, ed. Alan Heimert and Perry Miller (Boston, n.p., 1744; reprint, Indianapolis: Bobbs-Merrill Educational Publishing, 1967), 348 (page citations are to the reprint edition).

In response to these critics, George Whitefield acknowledged fault concerning the rashness and public nature of his comments against New England ministers. In response to Chauncy's rebuke on the matter, Whitefield admitted, "I confess this was too unguarded–For whether in fact it was or is true or not, the most that preach in *New England* did not experimentally know Christ, yet I ought to have taken more time before I deliver'd my judgment.–I thank you, Reverend Sir, for pointing out this fault unto me." George Whitefield, *A Letter to the Reverend Dr. Chuancy, on Account of Some Passages Relating to the Rev. Mr. Whitefield, in His Book Intitled Seasonable Thoughts on the State of Religion in New-England* (Boston: S. Kneeland and T. Green, 1745), 9. In the 1756 revision of his *Journals*, Whitefield apologized for his statements regarding these unconverted ministers. He wrote, "In my former Journal, taking things by hearsay too much, I spoke and wrote too rashly of the colleges and ministers of New England, for which, as I have already done it when at Boston last from the pulpit, I take this opportunity of asking public pardon from the press. It was rash and uncharitable and though well-meant, I fear, did hurt." Whitefield, *Journals*, 462. While the itinerant did not retract his claim that there were unconverted ministers in New England, he did apologize for the rashness of publishing such a statement in his *Journals*.

134 Whitefield, *Journals*, 478.

135 Heimert and Miller, *The Great Awakening*, xxi.

136 Edwards, "A Faithful Narrative," 347.

137 Gaustad, *Great Awakening*, 22.

138 Dallimore, *Whitefield*, 1:414-15.

139 For more information regarding the use of the press to promote Whitefield's preaching, see Lambert, *Inventing the "Great Awakening"*; and idem, *"Pedlar in Divin-*

ity": George Whitefield and the Transatlantic Revivals 1737-1770 (Princeton: Princeton University Press, 1994). Although this writer does not agree with all of Lambert's conclusions regarding Whitefield and the First Great Awakening, both works are well researched treatments of the subject.

140 Luke Tyerman, *The Life of the Reverend George Whitefield* (London: Hodder and Stoughton, 1876-1877; reprint, Azle, TX: Need of the Times Publishers, 1995), 1:128.

141 For a thorough treatment of this subject, see Peter Toon, *The Emergence of Hyper-Calvinism in English Noncon-formity 1689-1765* (London: The Olive Tree, 1967). This source was an invaluable reference to this writer in developing an understanding of this eighteenth-century debate.

142 Ibid., 147.

143 The lapsarian arguments focus on the order of God's secret decrees to allow the Fall, create human beings, adopt and save the elect, and to redeem through the death of Christ. In his description of the supralapsarian position, Lorraine Boettner wrote, "According to the supralapsarian view the order of events was: (1) to elect some createable men (that is, men who were to be created) to life and to condemn others to destruction; (2) to create; (3) to permit the fall; (4) to send Christ to redeem the elect; and (5) to send the Holy Spirit to apply this redemption to the elect." Lorraine Boettner, *The Reformed Doctrine of Predestination* (Philadelphia: The Presbyterian and Reformed Publishing Company, 1965), 127.

144 John Hussey, *God's Operations of Grace but No Offers of Grace* (Elon, NC: Primitive Publications, 1973), 72.

145 Ibid., 17. Interestingly, John Wesley presented a similar argument against Calvinism in his sermon "Free Grace." He contended that Calvinists cannot present a universal invitation to the gospel with logical consistency if they believe in particular redemption.

146 John Brine, *The Certain Efficacy of the Death of Christ* (London: Aaron Ward, 1743), 75.

147 John Gill, "Answer to the Birmingham Dialogue-Writer, Part II," in *A Collection of Sermons and Tracts: In Two Volumes* (London: George Keith, 1773), 2:146. Concerning Gill's view that unconverted men are excused from respond-

ing positively to the gospel, Tom Nettles writes, "Although I think the judgment should still be surrounded with cautions and caveats, there may be compelling evidence that Gill held to the distinctive Hyper-Calvinist tenet." Tom Nettles, "John Gill and the Evangelical Awakening," in *The Life and Thought of John Gill (1697-1771)*, ed. Michael A.G. Haykin (New York: Brill, 1997), 153.

148 Peter J. Morden, *Offering Christ to the World: Andrew Fuller (1754-1815) and the Revival of Eighteenth Century Particular Baptist Life* (Bletchley, UK: Paternoster, 2003), 20.

149 Regarding the relationship between the activities of Brine, Gill, and Whitefield, Peter Toon noted, "Also, as W. T. Whitley has pointed out, in the very years when Gill shut himself in his study to expound the New Testament, George Whitefield was preaching several times daily to thousands of people on Newington Common, Blackheath, and Kennington Common; and in the same year that Brine published a refutation of the tract, *The Modern Question*, Newton of Olney went to Moorfields and by the light of lanterns saw Whitefield preaching to thousands, leading to repentance on one occasion more than eleven times as many sinners as there were saints listening to Brine a quarter of a mile away." Toon, *Hyper- Calvinism*, 150.

150 Richard Lovett, *The History of the London Missionary Society 1795-1895* (London: Oxford University Press, 1899), 1:3.

In addition to Lovett, Bernard Manning commented, "The confluence of Calvinism and the Evangelical revival produced at the end of the century the modern missionary enthusiasm of our Churches. The foundation of the London Missionary Society in 1795 may stand as a reminder of what was accomplished when, as Watts had prayed, the heavenly wind came and, blowing over the garden of the churches, made their best spices flow abroad." Bernard Manning, quoted in N. Carr Sargant, "Calvinists, Arminians, and Missions," *London Quarterly and Holborn Review* 177 (January 1952): 45.

151 These hyper-Calvinist sentiments were made famous by John Collett Ryland, Sr.'s rebuke of William Carey: "Young man, sit down. When God pleases to convert the heathen,

He will do it without your aid or mine!" Ryland, quoted in Timothy George, *Faithful Witness: The Life and Mission of William Carey* (Birmingham, AL: New Hope, 1991), 53.

152 Andrew Fuller, "The Gospel Worthy of All Acceptation, or the Duty of Sinners to Believe in Jesus Christ, With Corrections and Additions; to Which is Added an Appendix, On the Necessity of a Holy Disposition in Order to Believing in Christ," in *The Complete Works of the Rev. Andrew Fuller: With a Memoir of His Life, By Andrew Gunton Fuller*, vol. 2, ed. Joseph Belcher (Harrisonburg, VA: Sprinkle Publications, 1988), 343-66.

153 Andrew Fuller, *The Work of Faith, the Labour of Love, and the Patience of Hope, Illustrated; in the Life and Death of the Rev. Andrew Fuller, Late Pastor of the Baptist Church of Kettering, and Secretary to the Baptist Missionary Society, From Its Commencement, In 1792*, ed. John Ryland (Charlestown, UK: Samuel Etheridge, 1818), 346.

154 Andrew Fuller, *The Last Remains of the Rev. Andrew Fuller: Sermons, Essays, Letters, and Other Miscellaneous Papers, Not Included in His Published Works* (Philadelphia: American Baptist Publication Society, 1856), 218.

155 Fuller, *Works*, 712. In a letter to John Ryland, Jr., written in the same year as his response to the hyper-Calvinist mentioned above, Fuller asserted that "Christ did not lay down his life but by covenant—as the elect were given to him, to be as the *trevail of his soul, the purchase of his blood*—he had respect in all that he did and suffered to this recompense of reward. It was for the covering of *their* transgressions that he became obedient unto death. To them his substitution was the same, *in effect*, as if their sins had by number been literally transferred to him." Ibid., 708.

Chapter 2

156 Stuart C. Henry, *George Whitefield, Wayfaring Witness* (Nashville: Abingdon Press, 1957), 96.

157 Harry S. Stout, *The Divine Dramatist: George Whitefield and the Rise of Modern* Evangelicalism (Grand Rapids: Eerdmans, 1991), 39.

158 Regarding Stout's comment, Tom Nettles writes, "Concerning Whitefield's sermon on 2 Corinthians 5:17, *The Nature*

and Necessity of Our Regeneration or the New Birth, Harry S. Stout observes that 'throughout, he showed no interest in theology. Instead of doctrine, he explored the feelings of the New Birth' and invited his hearers to imagine what a new state of being might be and to experience it for themselves. While it is true that Whitefield always urged the necessity of the new birth and described how one might palpably sense its presence in one's life, he did not avoid doctrinal expositions of it in his sermons." Tom Nettles, "John Gill and the Evangelical Awakening," in *The Life and Thought of John Gill (1697-1771)*, ed. Michael A.G. Haykin (New York: Brill, 1997), 165-66.

159 Stout, *The Divine Dramatist*, 94.

160 Kidd, *George Whitefield*, 261.

161 As I mentioned in the introduction, this book does not attempt to present an exhaustive treatment of George Whitefield's theology. Because Whitefield concentrated most of his thought, preaching, and writing upon the doctrines of grace and the doctrine of the new birth, this chapter will discuss the evidence of these doctrines in his life and preaching

162 Whitefield refers to the infallibility of Scripture in his sermon entitled "The Potter and the Clay." George Whitefield, "The Potter and the Clay," in *TWRGW* (London: Printed for Edward and Charles Dilly, in the Poultry; and Messrs. Kincaid and Bell, at Edinburgh, 1771-1772), 5:216; idem, "The Potter and the Clay," in *SIS* (London: Henry Fisher, Son, & P. Jackson, 1828), 174.

163 Whitefield, "Walking with God," in *TWRGW*, 5:36; Whitefield, "Walking with God," in *SIS*, 50.

164 George Whitefield, "Letter III," in *TWRGW*, 1:12-13; idem, *George Whitefield's Letters* (Carlisle, PA: The Banner of Truth Trust, 1976), 12-13.

165 Speaking of Scripture, Whitefield stated, "This is my rock, this is my foundation, it is now about thirty-five years since I have begun to read the Bible upon my pillow. I love to read this book.. . ." Whitefield, "God a Believer's Glory," in *SIS*, 764.

166 George Whitefield, *George Whitefield's Journals* (London: The Banner of Truth Trust, 1960), 256.

167 I will present a more thorough discussion of critics' concerns regarding inner feelings and experience in a later section.

168 Whitefield, "Walking with God," in *TWRGW*, 5:39; Whitefield, "Walking with God," in *SIS*, 52-53.

169 Whitefield, "The Potter and the Clay," in *TWRGW*, 5:227; Whitefield, "The Potter and the Clay," in *SIS*, 182.

170 In his sermon entitled "The Extent and Reasonableness of Self-Denial," Whitefield stated, "We must, with all humility and reverence, embrace the truths revealed to us in the holy scriptures; for thus only can we become truly wise, even 'wise unto salvation.'" George Whitefield, "The Extent and Reasonableness of Self-Denial," in *TWRGW*, 5:448; George Whitefield, "The Extent and Reasonableness of Self-Denial," in *SIS*, 334.

171 The English itinerant stated, "What do you think of Jesus Christ and his Apostles? Were they not field-preachers? Was not the best sermon that was ever delivered, delivered from a mount? Was not another very excellent one preached some a place called Mars-Hill? And did not Peter and John preach above seventeen hundred years ago in Solomon's Porch, and elsewhere, though the clergy of that generation commanded them to speak no more in the name of Jesus? These were the persons that I had in view, when I begun my adventures of field-preaching." Whitefield, "Remarks on a Pamphlet, Entitled, the Enthusiasm of Methodists and Papists Compared; Wherein Several Mistakes in Some Parts of My Past Writings and Conduct Are Acknowledged, and My Present Sentiments Concerning the Methodists is Explained," in *TWRGW*, 4:250.

172 Whitefield, "The Eternity of Hell Torments," in *TWRGW*, 5:412-13; Whitefield, "The Eternity of Hell Torments," in *SIS*, 310-11.

173 Whitefield, "The Indwelling of the Spirit, the Common Privilege of All Believers," in *TWRGW*, 6:102; Whitefield, "The Indwelling of the Holy Spirit, the Common Privilege of All Believers," in *SIS*, 432.

174 Arnold A. Dallimore, *George Whitefield* (Carlisle, PA: The Banner of Truth Trust, 1980), 2:24.

175 Ibid., 1:383.

176 D. M. Lloyd-Jones, "John Calvin and George Whitefield," in *The Puritans: Their Origins and Successors* (Carlisle, PA: The Banner of Truth Trust, 1996), 103. A later section of this chapter will address the theological division between Whitefield and Wesley.

177 The candidate's support of the Articles was a condition of ordination in the Church of England.

178 Whitefield, *Journals*, 68.

179 Whitefield, "Answer to the Bishop of London's Last Pastoral Letter," in *TWRGW*, 4:18.

180 The English itinerant reminded the recipients of this message that "all that are to be ordained to the office of a deacon, are, in the sight of GOD, and in the presence of the congregation, to declare, that "they trust they are inwardly moved by the Holy Ghost, to take upon them that administration;" and to those, who are to be ordained priests, the bishop is to repeat these solemn words, "Receive thou the Holy Ghost, now committed unto thee, by the imposition of our hands." Whitefield, "The Indwelling of the Spirit," in *TWRGW*, 6:106; idem, "The Indwelling of the Spirit," in *SIS*, 434.

181 Whitefield, "The Indwelling of the Spirit," in *TWRGW*, 6:106; idem, "The Indwelling of the Spirit," in *SIS*, 435. Throughout his ministry, Whitefield grieved over such unfaithful ministers within the Church of England. Regarding his fidelity to the Church of England and her Articles, the itinerant asserted, "I keep close to her Articles and Homilies, which, if my opposers did, we should not have so many dissenters." Idem, *Journals*, 250.

182 Whitefield, "The Potter and the Clay," in *TWRGW*, 5:226; idem, "The Potter and the Clay," in *SIS*, 181.

183 Whitefield, "Of Justification by Christ," in *TWRGW*, 6:227-28; idem, "The Potter and the Clay," in *SIS*, 520. Article IX of the Thirty-Nine Articles states, "Original sin standeth not in the following of Adam, but it is the fault or corruption of the nature of every man, that naturally is engendered of the offspring of Adam, whereby man is very far gone from original righteousness, and is of his own nature inclined to evil, so that the flesh lusteth always contrary to the Spirit, and therefore in every person born into the world it deserveth God's wrath and damnation." Gilbert Burnet, *An Exposi-*

tion of the Thirty-Nine Articles of the Church of England (New York: D. Appleton and Company, 1866), 139.

184 Whitefield, "The Indwelling of the Spirit," in *TWRGW*, 6:109; idem, "The Indwelling of the Spirit," in *SIS*, 437.

185 Whitefield, "Answer to the Bishop of London's Last Pastoral Letter," in *TWRGW*, 4:24.

186 In his sermon entitled "The Lord Our Righteousness," Whitefield quoted Article XII in response to an objection that Matthew 25 teaches justification by works. The evangelist contended, "This, I confess, is the most plausible objection that is brought against the doctrine insisted on from the text; and that we may answer it in as clear and brief a manner as may be, we confess with the article of the Church of England, 'That albeit good works do not justify us, yet they will follow after justification, as fruits of it; and though they can claim no reward in themselves, yet forasmuch as they spring from faith in Christ, and a renewed soul, they shall receive a reward of grace, though not of debt; and consequently, the more we abound in such good works, the greater will be our reward when Jesus Christ shall come to judgement.'" Whitefield, "The Lord Our Righteousness," in *TWRGW*, 5:239; idem, "The Lord Our Righteousness," in *SIS*, 190.

Whitefield made reference to this sermon and the above citation of Article XII in one of his journals. He wrote, "I produced the Articles of our Church to illustrate it, and concluded with an exhortation to all to lay aside reasoning infidelity, and to submit to Jesus Christ, Who is the end of the law for righteousness, to every one that believeth." Whitefield, *Journals*, 356.

187 I will present a more thorough treatment of the theological dispute between Whitefield and Wesley in a later section.

188 Whitefield admonished Wesley, "In the mean while, I cannot but blame you for censuring the clergy of our church for not keeping to their articles, when you yourself by your principles, positively deny the 9th, 10th, and 17th. Dear Sir, these things ought not so to be. God knows my heart, as I told you before, so I declare again, nothing but a single regard to the honour of Christ has forced this letter from me. I love and honour you for his sake; and when I come to judgement, will thank you before men and angels, for what

you have, under GOD, done for my soul." Whitefield, "A Letter to the Reverend Mr. John Wesley in Answer to His Sermon Entitled, *Free-Grace*," in *TWRGW*, 4:83; idem, *Journals*, 588.

189 The English itinerant maintained, "I believe they who have experienced it, will agree with our 17th article, 'That the godly consideration of predestination, and election in Christ, is full of sweet, pleasant, unspeakable comfort to godly persons, and such as feel in themselves the working of the Spirit of Christ, mortifying the works of the flesh, and their earthly members, and drawing their minds to high and heavenly things, as well because it does greatly establish and confirm their faith of eternal salvation, to be enjoyed through Christ, as because it doth fervently kindle their love towards GOD, &c.' This plainly shows, that our godly reformers did not think election destroyed holiness, or the comforts of religion." Whitefield, "A Letter to the Reverend Mr. John Wesley in Answer to His Sermon Entitled, *Free-Grace*," in *TWRGW*, 4:72; idem, *Journals*, 578.

190 Whitefield, "Letter CCXXI," in *TWRGW*, 1:211; idem, *Letters*, 211. The Article to which Whitefield referred was Article IX.

191 In his famous description of the Church of England in the eighteenth century, Lord Chatham stated, "We have a Calvinistic creed, a Popish liturgy, and an Arminian clergy. J. Wesley Bready, *England: Before and After Wesley* (London: Harper and Brothers Publishers, 1938), 53; Lloyd-Jones, *The Puritans*, 193.

192 Whitefield, "A Letter to the Rev. Thomas Church, M. A. Vicar of Battersea, and Prebendary of St. Paul's; in Answer to His Serious and Expostulary Letter to the Rev. George Whitefield, On Occasion of His Late Letter to the Bishop of London, and Other Bishops," in *TWRGW*, 4:127.

193 George Whitefield, *Additional Letters*, in *The Works of George Whitefield* [CD-ROM] (Shropshire, UK: Quinta Press, 2000), 39.

194 Whitefield, "A Letter to the Reverend and the President, and Professors, Tutors, and Hebrew Instructor, of Harvard-College in Cambridge; in Answer to A Testimony Published by Them Against the Reverend Mr. George Whitefield, and His Conduct," in *TWRGW*, 4:225.

195 Whitefield, "Letter CCCCLVII," *TWRGW*, 1:442; idem, *Letters*, 442.
196 Whitefield, "Letter CCXIV," in *TWRGW*, 1:205; idem, *Letters*, 205.
197 Whitefield, "The Beloved of God," *SIS*, 680.
198 Whitefield, "Letter DCCCCXII," in *TWRGW*, 2:428-29.
199 Whitefield, "Self-Inquiry Concerning the Work of God," in *SIS*, 711.
200 Whitefield, "Letter CCCCLVI," in *TWRGW*, 1:439; idem, *Letters*, 439.
201 Whitefield, "Letter CCCCXXIX," in *TWRGW*, 1:406; idem, *Letters*, 406.
202 Whitefield, "Letter CLXIX," in *TWRGW*, 1:156; idem, *Letters*, 156.
203 It would be a mistake, however, to conclude, from the above comments regarding Whitefield's emphasis upon love and unity, that the English itinerant avoided preaching against or opposing the Arminian theology that was prevalent among ministers within the Church of England during the eighteenth century. He particularly viewed Arminianism as an affront to the righteousness of Christ because of the theological system's emphasis upon individuals' ability to come to Christ based upon their own effort, power, or activity.

In a sermon entitled "The Lord Our Righteousness," Whitefield lamented opposition from Arminians against that idea that Christ's righteousness must be imputed to individuals to receive salvation. He asserted that "being once born under a covenant of works, it is natural for us all to have recourse to a covenant of works for our everlasting salvation. And we have contracted such a devilish pride by our fall from God, that we would, if not wholly, yet in part at least, glory in being the cause of our own salvation. We cry out against popery, and that very justly; but we are all Papists; at least, I am sure, we are all Arminians by nature; and, therefore, no wonder so many natural men embrace that scheme. It is true, we disclaim the doctrine of merit, are ashamed directly to say we deserve any good at the hands of God; therefore, as the apostle excellently well observes, 'we go about,' we fetch a circuit, 'to establish a righteousness of our own, and,' like the Pharisees of old, 'will not wholly submit to that righteousness which is of God through Jesus Christ our Lord.'" Whitefield, "The Lord Our Righteousness," in *TWRGW*, 5:216; idem, "The Lord Our Righteousness," *SIS*, 184.

Whitefield also opposed Arminians' rejection of the doctrines of total depravity and original sin. He preached, "Though the doctrine of original sin is a doctrine written in such legible characters in the word of God, that he who runs may read it; and though, I think, every thing without us, and every thing within us, plainly proclaims that we are fallen creatures; though the very heathen, who had no other light but the dim light of unassisted reason, complained of this, for they felt the wound, and discovered the disease, but were ignorant of the cause of it; yet there are too many persons, of those who have been baptised in the name of Christ, that dare to speak against the doctrine of original sin, and are angry with those ill-natured ministers, who paint man in such black colours. Say they, 'It cannot be that children come into the world with the guilt of Adam's sin lying upon them.'" Whitefield, "Marks of a True Conversion," in *TWRGW*, 5:339-40; idem, "Marks of a True Conversion," in *SIS*, 270-71.

204 The doctrines of grace include, but are not limited to, the "five points" of Calvinism. The format and organization of these doctrines that composed Whitefield's theology of evangelism is the creation of this writer. Although he preached all of the doctrines mentioned in this section, the English evangelist may not have adopted the same order and outline structure of the doctrines. The fact that George Whitefield never systematized his theology of evangelism makes it incumbent upon this writer to create his own outline.

205 Whitefield, *Letters*, 515. The last words of this quote indicate Whitefield's teaching that one can adhere to the doctrines of grace mentally, while not experiencing them through conversion spiritually.

206 Whitefield, "Marks of a True Conversion," in *TWRGW*, 5:348; idem, "Marks of a True Conversion," 277.

207 Whitefield, "The Conversion of Zaccheus," in *TWRGW*, 6:58; idem, "The Conversion of Zaccheus," 408.

208 Whitefield referred to this doctrine as "universal depravi-ty." I utilize the term "total depravity" because it is more familiar to the modern reader. For the English itinerant's use of "universal depravity," see Whitefield, "Observations on Some Fatal Mistakes, in a Book Lately Published, and Entitled, 'The Doctrine of Grace; or, the Office and Oper-ations of the Holy Spirit Vindicated From the Insults of Infidelity, and the Abuses of Fanaticism. By William Lord Bishop of Gloucester,'" in *TWRGW*, 4:285; idem, "Spiritual Baptism," in *SIS*, 730.

209 Whitefield, "The Potter and the Clay," in *TWRGW*, 5:208; idem, "The Potter and the Clay," in *SIS*, 179. In a descrip-tion of man's rejection of the gospel, Whitefield asserted, "For unless a man was very much disordered indeed, as to his understanding, will, affections, natural conscience, and his power of reasoning, he could never possibly deny such a revelation, which is founded on a multiplicity of infalli-ble external evidences, hath so many internal evidences of divine stamp in every page, is so suited to the common ex-igencies of all mankind, so agreeable to the experience of all men, and which hath been so wonderfully handed and preserved to us, hath been so instrumental in convicting, converting, and comforting so many millions of souls, and hath stood the test of the most severe scrutinies, and exact criticisms, of the most subtle and refined, as well as of the most malicious and persecuting enemies, that ever lived, even from the beginning of time to this very day." Idem, "The Potter and the Clay," in *TWRGW*, 207; idem, "The Potter and the Clay," in *SIS*, 178.

210 Whitefield, "The Wise and Foolish Virgins," in *TWRGW*, 5:387; idem, "The Wise and Foolish Virgins," in *SIS*, 305.

211 Whitefield, "The Potter and the Clay," in *TWRGW*, 5:205; idem, "The Potter and the Clay," in *SIS*, 176.

212 Whitefield, "The Potter and the Clay," in *TWRGW*, 5:203; idem, "The Potter and the Clay," in *SIS*, 175.

213 In his sermon entitled "The Care of the Soul Urged as the One Thing Needful," Whitefield contended that fallen men view God as "the one thing needless: the vainest dream, and the idlest amusement, of the mind." Whitefield, "The Care of the Soul Urged as the One Thing Needful," in *TWRGW*,

5:470; idem, "The Care of the Soul Urged as the One Thing Needful," in *SIS*, 364.

214 Whitefield, "The Potter and the Clay," in *TWRGW*, 5:202; Idem, "The Potter and the Clay," in *SIS*, 174.

215 Whitefield, "A Penitent Heart, the Best New Year's Gift," in *TWRGW*, 6:4; Idem, "A Penitent Heart, the Best New Year's Gift," in *SIS*, 369.

216 Whitefield, "Walking with God," in *TWRGW*, 5:23; Idem, "Walking with God," in *SIS*, 47.

217 Whitefield, "Walking with God," in *TWRGW*, 5:24; idem, "Walking with God," *SIS*, 48.

218 Whitefield, "The Indwelling of the Spirit," in *TWRGW*, 6:96; idem, "The Indwelling of the Spirit," in *SIS*, 435-36.

219 Whitefield, "The Seed of the Woman and the Seed of the Serpent," in *TWRGW*, 5:5; idem, "The Seed of the Woman and the Seed of the Serpent," in *SIS*, 34. In his sermon "The Righteousness of Christ, an Everlasting Righteousness," Whitefield stated, "God left Adam to his own free will; he was pleased to enter into a covenant with him, which indeed is an amazing instance of God's condescension." Whitefield, "The Righteousness of Christ, an Everlasting Righteousness," in *TWRGW*, 5:241; idem, "The Righteousness of Christ, an Everlasting Righteousness," in *SIS*, 201.

220 Regarding Adam and Eve, Whitefield preached, "But what an alteration is here! Instead of rejoicing at the voice of their beloved, instead of meeting him with open arms and enlarged hearts, as before, they now hide themselves in the trees of the garden....Whither could they flee from his presence? But, by their fall, they had contracted an enmity against GOD: they now hated, and were afraid to converse with God their Maker." Whitefield, "The Seed of the Woman," in *TWRGW*, 5:10; idem, "The Seed of the Woman," in *SIS*, 38.

221 Whitefield, "The Seed of the Woman," in *TWRGW*, 5:14; idem, "The Seed of the Woman," in *SIS*, 40.

222 Whitefield, "Christ the Only Preservative Against a Reprobate Spirit," in *TWRGW*, 6:289; idem, "Christ the Only Preservative Against a Reprobate Spirit," in *SIS*, 563. In his sermon "Of Justification By Christ," Whitefield asserted "that in the first covenant God made with man, Adam acted as a public person, as the proper representative of all man-

kind, and consequently we must stand or fall with him."
Idem, "Of Justification By Christ," in *TWRGW*, 6:219;
idem, "Of Justification By Christ," in *SIS*, 521.

223 Whitefield, "The Righteousness of Christ," in *TWRGW*,
5:242; idem, "The Righteousness of Christ," in *SIS*, 202.

224 To impute means "to think of as belonging to someone,
and therefore to cause it to belong to that person." Wayne
Grudem, *Systematic Theology* (Grand Rapids: Zondervan
Publishing House, 1994), 495.

Regarding the relationship between original sin and
imputation, Joseph Smith stated, "By original sin, I mean
nothing less than the imputation of Adam's first sin to all
his posterity, by ordinary generation; which imputation is
the resultance of his being constituted to act for them in
the extensive capacity of a legal representative; the con-
sequence of which is, that inherent corruption of nature,
and those sinful propensities, we are now born with into
the world." Joseph Smith, "The Character, Preaching, &c.
of the Rev. George Whitefield, in a Sermon Preached at
Charlestown, South Carolina, March 26th, 1740, by Joseph
Smith, V.D.M.," in *SIS*, 792.

225 Whitefield, "A Letter to Wesley," in *TWRGW*, 4:67; idem,
Journals, 583.

226 Whitefield, "Of Justification By Christ," in *TWRGW*, 6:214;
idem, "Of Justification By Christ," in *SIS*, 520.

227 Whitefield, "All Men's Place," in *SIS*, 757. Whitefield
preached, "You are a moral man, but do not love God. You
do not get drunk, because it will make your head ache; you
do not commit fornication and adultery, which is common
among the great, and therefore they think God will not
punish them for it; perhaps you are not a fornicator, lest
you should stand in a sheet, though we have no discipline
among us now; you do not do these things, for fear of maintaining the bastard, or being taken up; but does your obedience proceed from love to God, to Christ? If not, may God
convince you of your miserable state before you go hence!"
Idem, "On Regeneration," in *TWRGW*, 6:267; idem, "On
Regeneration," in *SIS*, 550.

228 I address moral inability in the next subsection.

229 In his sermon "Marks of a True Conversion," Whitefield
stated, "What is the reason your children are so averse to

instruction, but because they bring enmity into the world with them, against a good and gracious God? So then, it is plain from scripture and fact, that children are born in sin, and consequently that they are children of wrath. And for my part, I think, that the death of every child is a plain proof of original sin; sickness and death came into the world by sin, and it seems not consistent with God's goodness and justice, to let a little child be sick or die, unless Adam's first sin was imputed to him." Whitefield, "Marks of a True Conversion," in *TWRGW*, 5:340-41; idem, "Marks of a True Conversion," in *SIS*, 271.

230 Whitefield, "The Seed of the Woman," in *TWRGW*, 5:7; idem, "The Seed of the Woman," in *SIS*, 35.

231 George Whitefield, "The Method of Grace," in *Select Sermons of George Whitefield* (Carlisle, PA: The Banner of Truth Trust, 1997), 79-80. In another sermon, Whitefield declared, "Though every thing in the earth, air, and water; every thing both without and within, concur to prove the truth of the assertion in the scripture, 'in *Adam* we all have died;' yet most are so hardened, through the deceitfulness of sin, that notwithstanding they may give an assent to the truth of the proposition in their heads, yet they never felt it really in their hearts. Nay, some in words professedly deny it, though their works too, too plainly prove them to be degenerate sons of a degenerate father. But when the Comforter, the Spirit of God, arrests a sinner, and convinces him of sin, all carnal reasoning against original corruption, every proud and high imagination, which exalteth itself against that doctrine, is immediately thrown down; and he is made to cry out, 'Who shall deliver me from the body of this death?' He now finds that concupiscence is sin; and does not so much bewail his actual sins, as the inward perverseness of his heart, which he now finds not only to be an enemy to, but also direct enmity against, God." Idem, "The Holy Spirit Convincing the World of Sin, Righteousness, and Judgment," in *TWRGW*, 6:130-31; idem, "The Holy Spirit Convincing the World of Sin, Righteousness, and Judgment," in *SIS*, 460-61.

232 George Whitefield, "Of Justification by Christ," in *TWRGW*, 6:218; idem, "Of Justification by Christ," in *SIS*, 520.

233 Whitefield, *Letters*, 500.

234 Whitefield, "Neglect of Christ, the Killing Sin," in *SIS*, 740.

235 Whitefield, "The Resurrection of Lazarus," in *TWRGW*, 6:123-24; idem, "The Resurrection of Lazarus," in *SIS*, 456. Regarding the deadness of the unregenerate and the need for the Holy Spirit to awaken them, the English itinerant preached, "But at the same time, I would as soon go to yonder church- yard, and attempt to raise the dead carcasses, with a 'come forth,' as to preach to dead souls, did I not hope for some superior power to make the word effectual to the designed end." Idem, "The Potter and the Clay," *TWRGW*, 5:211; idem, "The Potter and the Clay," in *SIS*, 181.

236 Whitefield, "The Method of Grace," in *Select Sermons*, 82.

237 To hearers who believed their religious activity would save them, Whitefield admonished, "Do not flatter yourselves of being good enough because you are morally so; because you go to church, say the prayers, and take the sacrament, therefore you think no more is required: alas! You are deceiving your own souls; and if God, in his free grace and mercy, does not shew you your error, it will only be leading you a softer way to your eternal ruin; but God forbid that any of you, to whom I am now speaking, should imagine this; no, you must be abased, and God must be exalted, or you will never begin at the right end; you will never see Jesus with comfort or satisfaction, unless you go to him only on the account on what he has done and suffered."

In the same message he also stated, "I speak the truth in Christ Jesus, I lie not, there is no fitness in you, but a fitness for eternal damnation; for what are you by nature but children of wrath, and your hearts are Satan's garrison. Because you have gone to church, said the prayers, gone to the sacrament, and done no one any harm, you speak peace to your souls; and all is in peace you think, and your case is good enough; but indeed all is a false peace, and if you have no other peace than this, you must shortly lie down in everlasting flames; this is an undergrounded self-created peace, and if you trust in this peace, you will perish." Whitefield, "The Folly and Danger of Parting With Christ For the Pleasures and Profits of Life," in *TWRGW*, 5:320, 325; idem, "The Folly and Danger of Parting With Christ For the Pleasures and Profits of Life," in *SIS*, 257, 260.

238 Whitefield, "Letter XCIV," in *TWRGW*, 1:90; idem, *Letters*, 90. In another reference regarding the issue of free will, Whitefield lamented, "Human nature, what is it without Christ, the bread of life! We will not come to him, that we may have life, though we may have it for asking; no, not for life eternal, as a free gift: we will not come to Christ, and accept it at his hand; we will not: it is not said, we shall not, but we will not. Pray why will not people come to Christ to have life? . . . We do not choose to come to Christ, because we do not choose to have him as a free gift; we do not like to come to him as poor and needy." Idem, "Neglect of Christ, the Killing Sin," in *SIS*, 745-46.

239 Whitefield, "Walking with God," in *TWRGW*, 5:24; idem, "Walking with God," in *SIS*, 48.

240 Whitefield, "The Potter and the Clay," in *TWRGW*, 5:202; idem, "The Potter and the Clay," in *SIS*, 174. In a similar statement preached to a religious society, the evangelist said that natural man is "no more able to see his way wherein he should go, than a blind man to describe the sun; that notwithstanding this, he must receive his sight ere he can see God: and that if he never sees him, he never can be happy. . . . A divine revelation we find is absolutely necessary, we being by nature as unable to know as we are to do our duty." Idem, "The Necessity and Benefits of Religious Society," in *TWRGW*, 5:110; idem, "The Necessity and Benefits of Religious Society," in *SIS*, 109.

241 Whitefield, "The Lord Our Righteousness," in *TWRGW*, 5:219; idem, "The Lord Our Righteousness," in *SIS*, 186.

242 Whitefield, "The Seed of the Woman," in *TWRGW*, 5:11-12; idem, "The Seed of the Woman," in *SIS*, 39.

243 Regarding the plight of unregenerate men and their need of such revelation of their depravity, Whitefield preached, "But when once you are sensible of your being lost damned creatures, and see hell gaping ready to receive you: if God was but to cut the thread of life, O then, then you would cry earnestly unto the Lord to receive, to open the door of mercy unto you; your bones would then be changed, you would no more flatter yourselves with your abilities good wishes; no, you would see how unable you were, how incapable to save yourselves; that there is no fitness, no free will in you; no fitness, but for eternal damnation, no free will but that

of doing evil; and that when you would do good, evil is present with you, and the thing that ye would not, that do ye." Whitefield, "Christ the Only Rest for the Weary and Heavy-Laden," in *TWRGW*, 5:310-11; idem, "Christ the Only Rest for the Weary and Heavy-Laden," in *SIS*, 250.

244 Whitefield referred to this doctrine as the "doctrine of election." I use the term "unconditional election" because it is more familiar to modern readers and is an accurate identification of the itinerant's view of the doctrine.

245 Darius Salter, *American Evangelism: Its Theology and Practice* (Grand Rapids: Baker Books, 1996), 41.

246 Whitefield, "Letter CCXIV," in *TWRGW*, 1:205; idem, *Letters*, 205.

247 In a letter to John Hutton, Whitefield said of election, "Oh the excellency of the doctrine of election and of the saints final perseverance, to those who are truly sealed by the spirit of promise! I am persuaded, till a man comes to believe and feel these important truths, he cannot come out of himself; but when convinced of these, and assured of the application of them to his own heart, he then walks by faith indeed, not in himself, but in the Son of God who died and gave himself for him. Love, not fear, constrains him to obedience." Whitefield, "Letter CVI," in *TWRGW*, 1:101; idem, *Letters*, 101.

248 The written debate between the two evangelists began as an issue of private correspondence. Whitefield admonished Wesley to keep the theological disagreement between them out of the public arena. The next chapter will present more information regarding this debate between Whitefield and Wesley and its impact upon Whitefield's preaching. For evidence of the debate, see Whitefield, "Letter CXCIX," in *TWRGW*, 189, 219; idem, *Letters*, 509.

249 John Wesley, "Free Grace," in *The SAGE Digital Library* [CD-ROM] (Albany, OR: Ages Software, 1996), 422.

250 Whitefield, "A Letter to Wesley," in *TWRGW*, 4:70.

251 Whitefield, "The Potter and the Clay," in *TWRGW*, 5:199; idem, "The Potter and the Clay," in *SIS*, 172. In a similar comment, Whitefield preached, "And as God is a sovereign agent, and his sacred Spirit bloweth when and where it listeth, surely he may reveal and make known his will to his creatures, when, where, and how he pleases; 'and who

shall say to him, what doest thou?'" Whitefield, "A Caution Against Despising the Day of Small Things," in *TWRGW*, 6:369; idem, "A Caution Against Despising the Day of Small Things," in *SIS*, 608.

252 Whitefield preached, "Are you not ready to say, Not unto us, not unto us, but unto thy free, thy unmerited, thy sovereign, distinguishing love and mercy, O Lord, be all the glory. It is this, and this alone, hath made the difference between us and others. We have nothing but what is freely given us from above: if we love God, it is because God first loved us." Whitefield, "Christians, Temples of the Living God," in *TWRGW*, 6:281; idem, "Christians, Temples of the Living God," in *SIS*, 558.

253 Preaching to a Christian women's society, Whitefield declared, "The Lord Jesus Christ, my dear sisters, doth choose you merely by his free grace; it is freely of his own mercy, that he brings you into the marriage covenant; you who have so grievously offended him, yet the Lord Jesus Christ hath chosen you: you did not, you would not, have chosen him; but when once, my dear sisters, he hath chosen you, then, and not till then, you make a choice of him for your Lord and Husband." Whitefield, "Christ the Best Husband: Or an Earnest Invitation to Young Women to Come and See Christ," in *TWRGW*, 5:66; idem, "Christ the Best Husband: Or an Earnest Invitation to Young Women to Come and See Christ," in *SIS*, 78.

254 Whitefield, "The Conversion of Zaccheus," in *TWRGW*, 6:49; idem, "The Conversion of Zaccheus," in *SIS*, 401.

255 Whitefield, "The Seed of the Woman," in *TWRGW*, 5:15; idem, "The Seed of the Woman," in *SIS*, 41. Regarding the relationship between election and Christ, Whitefield asserted, "We are his by eternal election: 'the sheep which thou hast given me,' says Christ. They were given by God the Father to Christ Jesus, in the covenant made between the Father and the Son from all eternity." Idem, "The Good Shepherd," in *SIS*, 784.

256 Whitefield, "The Furnace of Affliction," 688-89.

257 Ibid. In the same sermon, Whitefield said of election, "For my own part, I know no other doctrine that can truly humble the man: for either God must choose us, or we must choose God; either God must be the first mover, or man

must be the first mover; either God must choose them on account of some goodness, on account of some purity, or acts of piety, or God must choose them merely of his grace, for his own name's sake, and to let us know that we have not chosen him, but he has chosen us. I verily believe, that the grand reason why such doctrine is so spurned at and hated by carnal people, is, that it strikes at the very root of human pride, cuts the sinews of freewill all to pieces, and brings the poor sinner to lie down at the foot of sovereign grace; and, let his attainments in the school of Christ be ever so great, it constrains him to cry out, Lord, why me? Why me?" Ibid., 688.

258 Whitefield claimed that Zaccheus "was one of those whom the Father had given him from all eternity: therefore he must abide at his house that day. 'For whom he did predestinate, them he also called.'

. . . And if we do God justice, and are effectually wrought upon, we must acknowledge there was no more fitness in us than in Zaccheus; and, had not Christ prevented us by his call, we had remained dead in trespasses and sins, and alienated from the divine life, even as others." Whitefield, "The Conversion of Zaccheus," in *TWRGW*, 6:54; idem, "The Conversion of Zaccheus," in *SIS*, 404-05.

259 Speaking of Ananias' hesitancy, the English evangelist declared, "Here God stops his mouth immediately, by asserting his sovereignty, and preaching to him the doctrine of election. And the frequent conversation of notorious sinners to God, to me is one great proof amongst a thousand others, of that precious, but too much exploded and sadly misrepresented, doctrine of God's electing love; for whence is it that such are taken, whilst thousands, not near so vile, die senseless and stupid? All the answer that can be given, is, *they are chosen vessels*; 'Go thy way, (says God) for he is a chosen vessel unto me, to bear my name before the *Gentiles*, and kings, and the children of *Israel*. For I will show him how great things he must suffer for my name's sake.'" Whitefield, "Saul's Conversion," in *TWRGW*, 6:152; idem, "Saul's Conversion," in *SIS*, 476.

260 Wesley, "Free Grace," 423.

261 Whitefield, "A Letter to Wesley," in *TWRGW*, 4:70.

262 Whitefield, "Letter XCV," in *TWRGW*, 1:90. Relating the issue of Christ's righteousness to the election, the itinerant stated, "For, if the whole personal righteousness of Jesus Christ be not the sole cause of my acceptance with God, if any work done by or foreseen in me, was the least to be joined with it, or looked upon by God as an inducing, impulsive case of acquitting my soul from guilt, then I have somewhat whereof I may glory in myself." Idem, "The Lord Our Righteousness," in *TWRGW*, 5:226; idem, "The Lord Our Righteousness," in *SIS*, 191.

263 Whitefield, "A Faithful Minister's Parting Blessing," in *SIS*, 622.

264 Wesley, "Free Grace," 419; Whitefield, "A Letter to Wesley," in *TWRGW*, 4:64-65.

265 Whitefield, "A Letter to Wesley," in *TWRGW*, 4:64-65.

266 Ibid.

267 Ibid.

268 Regarding his definition of the doctrine of reprobation, Whitefield stated, "I believe the doctrine of reprobation, in this view, that God intends to give saving grace, through Jesus Christ, only to a certain number, and that the rest of mankind, after the fall of Adam, being justly left of God to continue in sin, will at last suffer that eternal death, which is its proper wages." Whitefield, "A Letter to Wesley," in *TWRGW*, 4:58.

269 Wesley, "Free Grace," 421; Whitefield, "A Letter to Wesley," in *TWRGW*, 4:67. Regarding divine justice in reprobation, Whitefield stated that "God may justly damn any man for omitting the least duty of the moral law, and yet in himself is not obliged to give any one any reward supposing he has done all he can." Whitefield, "The Lord Our Righteousness, in *TWRGW*, 5:225-26; idem, "The Lord Our Righteousness," in *SIS*, 191.

270 Wesley, "Free Grace," 423.

271 Whitefield, "A Letter to Wesley," in *TWRGW*, 4:71.

272 Ibid.

273 Ibid., 4:58.

274 Wesley, "Free Grace," 418.

275 Whitefield, "A Letter to Wesley," in *TWRGW*, 4:59. The concluding sections of this chapter will present a more thorough discussion regarding Whitefield's understanding

concerning the relationship between the doctrines of grace and the use of means.

276 Wesley cited a number of texts he claimed are "clear proof that Christ died, not only for those that are saved, but also them that perish." See paragraph 21, in Wesley's sermon "Free Grace," found in the second appendix of this book. Wesley, "Free Grace," 423.

277 In the same section as the quote above, the itinerant wrote that this covenant was "God's design of saving his church by the death of his Son." Whitefield, "A Letter to Wesley," in *TWRGW*, 4:68.

278 Whitefield, "The Good Shepherd," in *SIS*, 784.

279 Whitefield, "The Righteousness of Christ, An Everlasting Righteousness," in *TWRGW*, 5:243-44; idem, "The Righteousness of Christ, An Everlasting Righteousness," in *SIS*, 203-4.

280 For the biblical passages Wesley cited, see Wesley, "Free Grace," 423.

281 Whitefield, "The Beloved of God," in *SIS*, 680. The identity of the "young man" to whom Whitefield referred is not clear. Perhaps he is the man mentioned in Mark's Gospel (Mark 10:17-23).

In another message, the English itinerant stated that "though Jesus Christ in one respect is the Saviour of all, and are to offer (preach) Jesus Christ universally to all, yet he is said in a special manner to be the Saviour of them that believe." Idem, "A Faithful Minister's Parting Blessing," in *SIS*, 620.

282 Whitefield, "A Letter to Wesley," in *TWRGW*, 4:71.

283 Regarding the substitutionary nature of Christ's atonement, Whitefield stated, "In that nature he obeyed, and thereby fulfilled the whole moral law in our stead; and also died a painful death upon the cross, and thereby became a curse for, or instead of, those whom the Father had given to him." Whitefield, "The Lord Our Righteousness," in *TWRGW*, 5:219; idem, "The Lord Our Righteousness," in *SIS*, 186.

284 Whitefield, "A Letter to Wesley," in *TWRGW*, 4:71. In another letter to Wesley, Whitefield stated, "Judge whether it is not a greater blasphemy to say, 'Christ died for souls now in hell.' Surely, dear Sir, you do not believe there will be a

general gaol delivery of damned souls hereafter. O that you would study the covenant of grace! O that you were truly convinced of sin, and brought to the foot of sovereign grace!" Idem, "Letter CCXXI," in *TWRGW*, 1:212; idem, *Letters*, 212.

285 Whitefield believed that the Holy Spirit is "the third Person in the ever-blessed Trinity, consubstantial and coeternal with the Father and the Son, proceeding from, yet equal to them both. He is emphatically called Holy, because infinitely holy in himself, and the author and finisher of holiness in us." Whitefield, "Marks of Having Received the Holy Ghost," in *TWRGW*, 6:162; idem, "Marks of Having Received the Holy Ghost," in *SIS*, 482.

286 Whitefield, "Letter CXXXIII," in *TWRGW*, 1:125; idem, *Letters*, 125.

287 Whitefield, "The Extent and Reasonableness of Self-Denial," in *TWRGW*, 5:433; idem, "The Extent and Reasonableness of Self-Denial," in *SIS*, 337.

288 I will present Whitefield's theological views regarding universal invitations to the gospel in a later section of this chapter.

289 Whitefield, "Christians, Temples of the Living God," in *TWRGW*, 6:274; idem, "Christians, Temples of the Living God," in *SIS*, 553.

290 Whitefield, "The Beloved of God," in *SIS*, 681.

291 Whitefield, "The Holy Spirit Convincing the World of Sin, Righteousness, and Judgment," in *TWRGW*, 6:130; Idem, "The Holy Spirit Convincing the World of Sin, Righteousness, and Judgment," in *SIS*, 460. Also idem, "The Method of Grace," in *Select Sermons*, 79.

Whitefield by no means meant to limit God's sovereignty in mentioning the method of conviction. He stated, "I say, generally: For, as God is the sovereign agent, his sacred Spirit bloweth not only on whom, but when and how it listeth. Therefore, far be it from me to confine the Almighty to one way of acting, or say that all undergo an equal degree of conviction: no, there is a holy variety in God's methods of calling home his elect. But this we may affirm assuredly, that, wherever there is a work of true conviction and conversion wrought upon a sinner's heart, the Holy Ghost, whether by a greater or less degree of inward soul-trouble, does that which our Lord Jesus told the disciples, in the words of the text, that he should do when he came." Idem, "The Holy Spirit Convincing," in *TWRGW*, 6:128-29; idem, "The Holy Spirit Convincing," in *SIS*, 459.

292 Whitefield, "The Method of Grace," 80-81. Also idem, "The Holy Spirit Convincing," in *TWRGW*, 6:131-34; idem, "The Holy Spirit Convincing," in *SIS*, 460-63; idem, "Of Justification By Christ," in *TWRGW*, 6:218-19; idem, "Of Justification By Christ," in *SIS*, 520-21; idem, "Saul's Conversion," in *TWRGW*, 6:147; idem, "Saul's Conversion," in *SIS*, 472.

293 Whitefield, "The Holy Spirit Convincing," in *TWRGW*, 6:131; idem, "The Holy Spirit Convincing," in *SIS*, 461. Also idem, "The Method of Grace," in *Select Sermons*, 82; idem, "Christ the Only Rest for the Weary and Heavy-Laden," in *TWRGW*, 5:315-16; idem, "Christ the Only Rest for the Weary and Heavy-Laden," in *SIS*, 253-54.

294 In his sermon "Self-Inquiry Concerning the Work of God," Whitefield asserted, "We think we can believe when we will, but the Spirit alone can convince us we have no faith, the Spirit alone can convince us of our want of faith, and can alone impart it to the poor awakened sinner; consequently, you may ask yourselves whether God has wrought in you, not only a sense of your own misery, but also a sense of your remedy; set you upon hungering and thirsting, such a hungering and thirsting as has never been satisfied but by an application of the blood of Christ imputed to you." Whitefield, "Self-Inquiry Concerning the Work of God," in *SIS*, 709.

295 Whitefield, "Christ the Best Husband, or An Earnest Invitation to Young Women to Come and See Christ," in *TWRGW*, 5:70; idem, "Christ the Best Husband," in *SIS*, 81. In another sermon, Whitefield stated, "Before we are actually married, or united to him by faith, or, to keep to the terms of the text, before we assuredly can say, that, 'our Maker is our husband,' we must be made willing people in the day of God's power; we must be sweetly and effectually persuaded by the holy Spirit of God, that the glorious Emmanuel is willing to accept of us just as we are, and also that we are willing to accept of him upon his own terms, yea, upon any terms." Idem, "Christ the Believer's Husband," in

TWRGW, 5:176; idem, Christ the Believer's Husband," in *SIS*, 155.

296 Whitefield, "The Conversion of Zaccheus," in *TWRGW*, 6:54; idem, "The Conversion of Zaccheus," in *SIS*, 405.

297 In his sermon "Blind Bartimeus," the itinerant prayed that God would make the gospel "effectual to the quickening and raising" of his hearers. He also prayed that God would "effectually now strike" his hearers. Whitefield, "Blind Bartimeus," in *TWRGW*, 5:411; idem, "Blind Bartimeus," in *SIS*, 322; idem, "Saul's Conversion," in *TWRGW*, 6:147; idem, "Saul's Conversion," in *SIS*, 472.

298 Whitefield, "A Letter to Wesley," in *TWRGW*, 4:62. Regarding his eternal security, Whitefield wrote in his journals, "But God, whose gifts and callings are without repentance, would let nothing pluck me out of His hands, though I was continually doing despite to the Spirit of God." Idem, *Journals*, 42. Also idem, "The Good Shepherd," in *SIS*, 787.

299 Whitefield, "Christ the Believer's Husband," in *TWRGW*, 5:182; idem, "Christ the Believer's Husband," in *SIS*, 160. In his letter to Wesley, Whitefield wrote, "But, without the belief of the doctrine of election, and the immutability of the free love of GOD, I cannot see how it is possible that any should have a comfortable assurance of eternal salvation." Idem, "A Letter to Wesley," in *TWRGW*, 4:64.

300 Whitefield, "The Resurrection of Lazarus," in *TWRGW*, 6:115; idem, "The Resurrection of Lazarus," in *SIS*, 450.

301 Whitefield, "Christians, Temples of the Living God," in *TWRGW*, 6:280; idem, "Christians, Temples of the Living God," in *SIS*, 557. In another sermon, Whitefield contended, "As the obedience of Christ is imputed to believers, so his perseverance in that obedience is to be imputed to them also; and it argues great ignorance of the covenant of grace and redemption, to object against it.

By the word *redemption*, we are to understand, not only a complete deliverance from all evil, but also a full enjoyment of all good both in body and soul: I say, both in body and soul; for the Lord is also for the body; the bodies of the saints in this life are temples of the Holy Ghost; God makes a covenant with the dust of believers; after death, though worms destroy them, yet, even in their flesh shall they see

God." Idem, "Christ the Believer's Wisdom," in *TWRGW*, 6:196; idem, "Christ the Believer's Wisdom," in *SIS*, 506.

302 Whitefield, "Christ the Believer's Husband," in *TWRGW*, 5:195; idem, "Christ the Believer's Husband," in *SIS*, 169.

303 Whitefield, "The Righteousness of Christ," in *TWRGW*, 5:245; idem, "The Righteousness of Christ," in *SIS*, 205. In a letter written to his brother, Whitefield stated, "I fear not falling finally; for God I believe chose me in Christ before ever the earth and the world were made, as a vessel of his saving mercy; but I fear I shall provoke him to let me fall foully, and then how will the Philistines rejoice?" Idem, "Letter LXXXI," in *TWRGW*, 1:78. Also idem, "The Seed of the Woman," in *TWRGW*, 1:19; idem, "The Seed of the Woman," in *SIS*, 44; idem, "Christ the Believer's Husband," in *TWRGW*, 1:190; idem, "Christ the Believer's Husband," in *SIS*, 166.

304 Whitefield, "Christ the Best Husband," in *TWRGW*, 1:67; idem, "Christ the Best Husband," in *SIS*, 79. Also idem, "The Folly and Danger of Parting With Christ for the Pleasures and Profits of Life," in *TWRGW*, 5:332; idem, "The Folly and Danger of Parting With Christ for the Pleasures and Profits of Life," in *SIS*, 265.

305 Kidd, *George Whitefield*, 48.

306 The *ordo salutis* refers to the order of salvation. Referring to the view of "great majority of Reformed theologians" regarding the order of salvation, Louis Berkhof stated, "They begin the *ordo salutis* with regeneration or with calling, and thus emphasize the fact that the application of the redemptive work of Christ is in its incipiency a work of God. This is followed by a discussion of conversion, in which the work of regeneration penetrates to the conscious life of the sinner, and he turns from self, the world, and Satan, to God. Conversion includes repentance and faith, but because of its great importance the latter is generally treated separately. The discussion of faith naturally leads to that of justification, inasmuch as this is mediated to us by faith. And because justification places man in a new relation to God, which carries with it the gift of adoption, and which obliges man to a new obedience and also enables him to do the will of God from the heart, the work of sanctification next comes into consideration. Finally the order of salva-

tion is concluded with the doctrine of perseverance of the saints and their final glorification." Berkhof also stated that the Reformed view maintains that regeneration logically precedes conversion. Louis Berkhof, *Systematic Theology* (Grand Rapids: Wm. B. Eerdmans Publishing Co., 1941), 418-20. This section will present information regarding whether Whitefield separated regeneration from conversion; however, this writer's intent is not to grant a detailed analysis of the itinerant's adherence or lack of adherence to each element of the *ordo salutis*.

307 Whitefield, "The Potter and the Clay," in *TWRGW*, 5:210. In his message "On Regeneration," Whitefield stated, " Now, what can be understood by al these different terms of being *born again*, of *putting off the old man*, and *putting on the new*, of being *renewed in the spirit of our minds*, and becoming *new creatures;* but that Christianity requires a thorough, real, inward change of heart?" Whitefield, "On Regeneration," in *TWRGW, 6:262;* idem, "On Regeneration," in *SIS,* 546.

308 Whitefield, "What Think Ye of Christ?," in *TWRGW*, 5:368; idem, "What Think Ye of Christ?," in *SIS*, 290; idem, "On Regeneration," in *TWRGW*, 6:257; idem, "On Regeneration," in *SIS*, 543; idem, "A Penitent Heart, the Best New Year's Gift," in *TWRGW*, 6:4; idem, "A Penitent Hear, the Best New Year's Gift," in *SIS*, 368.

309 Whitefield, "On Regeneration," in *TWRGW*, 6:257; idem, "On Regeneration," in *SIS*, 543.

310 In his sermon "All Men's Place," Whitefield referred to the "unregenerate" as "those that are not born of God." Whitefield, "All Men's Place," in *SIS*, 751.

311 Whitefield, "A Penitent Heart," in *TWRGW*, 6:4; idem, "A Penitent Heart," in *SIS*, 368.

312 In Reformed theology, repentance is traditionally a part of conversion in the *ordo salutis*. Berkhof stated that "conversion comprises two elements, namely, repentance and faith." Berkhof, *Systematic Theology*, 486.

313 In this section, I will present clarification regarding Whitefield's understanding of repentance, while I will offer a more thorough treatment of his view of conversion in a subsequent part of this chapter.

314 J. I. Packer, "The Spirit with the Word: the Reformational Revivalism of George Whitefield," in *The Bible, the Reformation, and the Church*, ed. W. P. Stephens (Sheffield, UK: Sheffield Academic Press, 1995), 183-84.

315 Whitefield, "A Penitent Heart," in *TWRGW*, 6:4; idem, "A Penitent Heart," in *SIS*, 368.

316 Whitefield, *Journals*, 212.

317 Whitefield, "A Penitent Heart," in *TWRGW*, 6:19; idem, "A Penitent Heart," in *SIS*, 380.

318 Ibid.

319 Whitefield, "A Penitent Heart," in *TWRGW*, 6:5; idem, "A Penitent Heart," in *SIS*, 369.

320 Whitefield, "A Penitent Heart," in *TWRGW*, 6:7-8; idem, "A Penitent Heart," in *SIS*, 371. Whitefield stated, "Resolve this day to have done with your sins for ever; let your old ways and you be separated; you must resolve against it, for there can be no true repentance without a resolution to forsake it.

. . . Resolve to cast thyself at the feet of Christ in subjection to him, and throw thyself into the arms of Christ for salvation by him." Ibid.

321 Whitefield, "Letter 6," in *Letters*, 491.

322 Whitefield, "Repentance and Conversion," in *SIS*, 661.

323 I will present a more thorough discussion of Whitefield's understanding of conversion in a later section of this chapter.

324 Whitefield's understanding of this aspect of repentance is consistent with John Flavel and David Clarkson's comments regarding the subject. In response to the question, "Who is the author of saving repentance?," John Flavel presented the following answer: "The Spirit of God is the author of it; the heart by nature is so hard, that none but the Spirit can break it; Ezek. xxxvi. 26, 27. A new heart also will I give you, and a new spirit will I put within you: And I will take away the stony heart out of your flesh, and I will give you a heart of flesh. And I will put my Spirit within you, &c." John Flavel, "An Exposition of the Assembly's Shorter Catechism," in *The Works of John Flavel* (Edinburgh: The Banner of Truth Trust, 1968), 6:266. David Clarkson presented a similar understanding in his work "Of Repentance." He stated, "We want both habits and acts before we

can repent; Christ must both give us soft hearts, hearts that can repent, and must teach them by his Spirit before they will repent. Except he smite those rocks, they will yield no water; no tears for sin; except he break these hearts, they will not bleed." David Clarkson, "Of Repentance," in *The Works of David Clarkson* (Edinburgh: The Banner of Truth Trust, 1988), 1:21.

325 Whitefield, "All Men's Place," in *SIS*, 754.

326 Ibid.

327 Regarding his avoidance of debates over baptism, Whitefield stated, "I cannot make sport for the devil by railing against infant or adult baptism: it is a strange thing how the bigots can set a world on fire by throwing water at one another, and that people cannot be baptized, or sprinkled as others call it, without bespattering one another, and shew that the chief thing they have been baptized into, are the waters of strife; this is catching at shadows, and making sport for the devil, while the combatants on both sides, being thus engaged in throwing the shadowy water at one another, lose the substantials of religion, while they are defending the outside of it. For my part, I do not enter into the debate about infant or adult baptism: . . . Would it not be better for us to take care not to offend our brethren, not to raise one another's spirits and corruptions, but rather, when we come together, talk of the heart, and inquire whether, when we received the outward sign by sprinkling or dipping, we really received the thing signified in our hearts, and exemplify that thing signified in our lives." Whitefield, "Spiritual Baptism," in *SIS*, 731-32.

328 While Whitefield voiced opposition to the concept of baptismal regeneration, he did not present a formal treatment of Article 28, the section of the Thirty-Nine Articles upon which most Anglican proponents based their belief in the idea; however, the itinerant did make some statements which shed light upon his personal understanding of baptism. In his sermon "Christians, Temples of the Living God," the itinerant refers to baptism as "an external formal dedication." Whitefield, "Christians, Temples," in *TWRGW*, 6:274; idem, "Christians, Temples," in *TWRGW*, 553. Whitefield also spoke of Christians being "devoted to God at baptism." Idem, "Law Gospelized; or, an Address to

all Christians Concerning Holiness of Heart and Life: Being an Attempt to Render Mr. Law's Serious Call More Useful to the Children of God, by Excluding Whatever is Not Truly Evangelical, and Illustrating the Subject More Fully From the Scriptures," in *TWRGW*, 4:378. In his Journals, the itinerant speaks of his baptism as an infant being sealed later in his life "with my Saviour's most blessed Body and Blood." Idem, *Journals*, 195. He preached that, if parents were convinced of original sin, they would not make baptism a "matter of form," but would pray for their children's conversions and lead them to that end. Idem, "Marks of a True Conversion," in *TWRGW*, 5:341; idem, "Marks of a True Conversion," in *SIS*, 272. All of these statements from Whitefield suggest that the itinerant saw baptism as a dedication of the infant to Christ and a covenant made by the parents to raise the child within the Church of England and in the knowledge of the gospel, looking forward to his future conversion.

One may also deduce from Whitefield's actions that he did not oppose infant baptism. In his Journals, he mentions baptizing infants on at least three occasions. Idem, *Journals*, 151, 422. In a letter written to a friend, the English itinerant mentioned baptizing his own infant. Idem, "Letter DXXXV," in *TWRGW*, 2:40. Whitefield even composed a hymn for infant baptism which speaks of the parents setting the infant apart for God. Idem, "Hymn CXXV," in *A Collection of Hymns for Social Worship, More Particularly Designed for the Use of the Tabernacle and Chapel Congregations in London* (London: Henry Cock, 1777), in *The Works of George Whitefield* [CD-ROM] (Shropshire, UK: Quinta Press, 2000), 99-100. It would be difficult to conclude, from Whitefield's actions and from his composition of such a hymn, that the itinerant opposed infant baptism.

329 Whitefield, "An Answer to the Second Part of an Anonymous Pamphlet, Entitled, 'Observations Upon the Conduct and Behaviour of a Certain Sect, Usually Distinguished by the Name of Methodists:' in a Second Letter to the Right Reverend the Bishop of London, and the Other Right Reverend Bishops Concerning the Publication Thereof," in *TWRGW*, 4:162; idem, "Remarks on a Pamphlet, Entitled,

The Enthusiasm of Methodists and Papists Compared; Wherein Several Mistakes in Some Parts of My Past Writings and Conduct are Acknowledged, and My Present Sentiments Concerning Methodists Explained. In a Letter to the Author," in *TWRGW*, 4:241.

330 Whitefield queried, "And do not the greatest part of the poor souls now in *England*, go on secure that they shall be eternally happy, and yet have no better foundation of comfort and assurance of the gospel new-birth, than that which is founded on the doctrine of a sudden and instantaneous change wrought upon them in baptism?" Whitefield, "An Answer to the Second Part," in *TWRGW*, 4:162.

331 Whitefield, "On Regeneration," in *TWRGW*, 6:259-260; idem, "On Regeneration," in *SIS*, 545.

332 Whitefield, "All Men's Place," in *SIS*, 752. In his sermon "The Wise and Foolish Virgins," Whitefield stated, "It is not merely being baptized by water, but being born again of the Holy Ghost, that must qualify you for salvation; and it will do no service at that great day, to say unto Christ, Lord, my name is in the register of such an such a parish." Idem, "The Wise and Foolish Virgins," in *TWRGW*, 5:384; idem, "The Wise and Foolish Virgins," in *SIS*, 303. For more comments from Whitefield regarding the relationship between the new birth and baptism, see Whitefield, "An Answer to the Second Part," in *TWRGW*, 4:162-163; and idem, "Spiritual Baptism," in *SIS*, 732-33.

333 Whitefield, "Marks of a True Conversion," in *TWRGW*, 5:337; idem, "Marks of a True Conversion," in *SIS*, 268.

334 Whitefield, "All Men's Place," in *SIS*, 752.

335 Whitefield, "On Regeneration," in *TWRGW*, 6:267; idem, "On Regeneration," in *SIS*, 550.

336 See Whitefield, "Christ the Only Rest for the Weary and Heavy-Laden," in *TWRGW*, 5:308- 9; idem, "Christ the Only Rest for the Weary and Heavy-Laden," in *SIS*, 248-49; idem, "The Almost Christian," in *TWRGW*, 6:179; idem, "The Almost Christian," in *SIS*, 494; idem, "On Regeneration," in *TWRGW*, 6:266; and idem, "On Regeneration," in *SIS*, 549.

337 Whitefield, "What Think Ye of Christ?," in *TWRGW*, 5:369; idem, "What Think Ye of Christ?," in *SIS*, 292. In another sermon, Whitefield preached, "Now till the Spirit of God is

felt on our souls as the wind in our bodies, indeed, my dear
brethren, you have no interest in him: religion consists not
in external performance, it must be in the heart, or else it is
only a name, which cannot profit us, a name to live whilst
we are dead." Whitefield, "The Folly and Danger of Being
Not Righteous Enough," in *TWRGW*, 5:126; idem, "The
Folly and Danger of Being Not Righteous Enough," in *SIS*,
120.

338 Louis Berkhof's comments regarding conversion present a
helpful framework for this section on Whitefield's understanding of conversion. Berkhof stated, "True conversion
is born of godly sorrow, and issues in a life of devotion to
God, II Cor. 7:10. It is a change that is rooted in the work
of regeneration, and that is effected in the conscious life
of the sinner by the Spirit of God; a change of thoughts
and opinions, of desires and volitions, which involves the
conviction that the former direction of life was unwise and
wrong and alters the entire course of life. There are two
sides to this conversion, the one active and the other passive; the former being the act of God, by which He changes
the conscious course of man's life, and the latter, the result of this action as seen in man's changing his course of
life and turning to God. Consequently, a twofold definition
must be given of conversion: (a) Active conversion is *that
act of God whereby he causes the regenerated sinner, in
His conscious life, to turn to Him in repentance and faith.*
(b) Passive conversion is *the resulting conscious act of the
regenerated sinner whereby he, through the grace of God,
turns to God in repentance and faith.*" Berkhof, *Systematic
Theology*, 483.

339 Whitefield, "The Seed of the Woman," in *TWRGW*, 5:15-16;
idem, "The Seed of the Woman," in *SIS*, 42.

340 Whitefield, "The Resurrection of Lazarus," in *TWRGW*,
6:123; idem, "The Resurrection of Lazarus," in *SIS*, 456.
In his sermon "The Conversion of Zaccheus," the itinerant
stated, "The righteousness of Jesus Christ is the sole cause
of our finding favour in God's sight: this righteousness apprehended by faith (which is also the gift of God) makes
it our own; and this faith, if true will work by love." Idem,
"The Conversion of Zaccheus," in *TWRGW*, 6:49; idem,
"The Conversion of Zaccheus," in *SIS*, 401.

341 Whitefield, "The Lord Our Righteousness," in *TWRGW*, 5:232; idem, "The Lord Our Righteousness," in *SIS*, 195.

342 Whitefield, *Journals*, 212.

343 Whitefield, "A Penitent Heart," in *TWRGW*, 6:19; idem, "A Penitent Heart," in *SIS*, 380.

344 Whitefield, "A Penitent Heart," in *TWRGW*, 6:4; idem, "A Penitent Heart," in *SIS*, 368.

345 Whitefield, "The Care of the Soul Urged as the One Thing Needful," in *TWRGW*, 5:458; idem, "The Care of the Soul Urged as the One Thing Needful," in *SIS*, 355.

346 Whitefield, "Self-Inquiry Concerning the Work of God," in *SIS*, 707.

347 Refer to the previous section on effectual calling for a more thorough discussion of the convicting work of the Holy Spirit.

348 Describing this process of conviction over sin, particularly original sin, Whitefield stated, "But when the Comforter, the Spirit of God, arrests a sinner, and convinces him of sin, all carnal reasoning against original corruption, every proud and high imagination, which exalteth itself against that doctrine, is immediately thrown down; and he is made to cry out, 'Who shall deliver me from the body of this death?'" Whitefield, "The Holy Spirit Convincing," in *TWRGW*, 6:130-31; idem, "The Holy Spirit Convincing," in *SIS*, 460-61.

349 Whitefield, "The Holy Spirit Convincing," in *TWRGW*, 6:136; idem, "The Holy Spirit Convincing," in *SIS*, 463.

350 Whitefield, "A Penitent Heart," in *TWRGW*, 6:7; and idem, "A Penitent Heart," in *SIS*, 370.

351 Whitefield, "Letter XIX," in *TWRGW*, 1:24; idem, *Letters*, 24.

352 Whitefield, "The Holy Spirit Convincing," in *TWRGW*, 6:132; idem, "The Holy Spirit Convincing," in *SIS*, 461.

353 Whitefield, "Repentance and Conversion," in *SIS*, 663.

354 Whitefield, "A Penitent Heart," in *TWRGW*, 6:7-8; idem, "A Penitent Heart," in *SIS*, 371. This sermon is one of the best resources for gaining insight into Whitefield's understanding of repentance.

355 Whitefield, "The Power of Christ's Resurrection," in *TWRGW*, 6:326; idem, "The Power of Christ's Resurrection," in *SIS*, 584. Referring to accepting the righteousness

of Christ by faith, Whitefield stated, "For entertaining this doctrine in your heads, without receiving the Lord Jesus Christ savingly by a lively faith into your hearts, will but increase your damnation." Whitefield, "The Lord Our Righteousness," in *TWRGW*, 5:229; idem, "The Lord Our Righteousness," in *SIS*, 193.

356 Whitefield, "The Folly and Danger of Not Being Righteous Enough," in *TWRGW*, 5:137; idem, "The Folly and Danger of Not Being Righteous Enough," in *SIS*, 128-29.

357 Whitefield, "Satan's Devices," in *TWRGW*, 6:246; idem, "Satan's Devices," in *SIS*, 537. For more comments from the itinerant regarding faith in the blood of Christ see Whitefield, "The Danger of Parting With Christ For the Pleasures and Profits of Life," in *TWRGW*, 5:334; idem, "The Danger of Parting With Christ For the Pleasures and Profits of Life," in *SIS*, 267; idem, "Christ the Believer's Wisdom," in *TWRGW*, 6:191; idem, "Christ the Believer's Wisdom," in *SIS*, 502-03.

358 Whitefield, "The Seed of the Woman," in *TWRGW*, 5:15; idem, "The Seed of the Woman," in *SIS*, 42.

359 Whitefield, "The Gospel a Dying Saint's Triumph," in *SIS*, 652-53. In a letter written to religious societies, the itinerant admonished them to "be very cautious, my brethren, whom you admit into fellowship with you. Examine them again and again, not barely whether they receive the sacrament, and go to church; but whether they be in the faith. Set them upon proving their own selves; and by no means receive them into your brotherhood, unless they can produce sufficient evidences of their having tasted the good word of life, and felt the powers of the world to come. This, some may object, is not a very good way to increase and multiply you as to number; but it is the best, the only way, to establish and increase a communion of true saints." Idem, "A Letter to the Religious Societies of England," in *TWRGW*, 4:26.

360 Whitefield, "Of Justification By Christ," in *TWRGW*, 6:216; idem, "Of Justification By Christ," in *SIS*, 519.

361 Whitefield, "What Think Ye of Christ?," in *TWRGW*, 5:366; idem, "What Think Ye of Christ?," in *SIS*, 290.

362 Whitefield, "The Extent and Reasonableness of Self-Denial," in *TWRGW*, 5:432; idem, "The Extent and Reasonable-

No Better Gospel

ness of Self-Denial," in *SIS*, 337. See also Whitefield, "The Pharisee and the Publican," in *TWRGW*, 6:46; idem, "The Pharisee and the Publican," in *SIS*, 399; idem, "Of Justification," in *TWRGW*, 6:221; idem, "Of Justification," in *SIS*, 522.

363 Whitefield, "Abraham's Offering Up His Son Isaac," in *TWRGW*, 5:49; idem, "Abraham's Offering Up His Son Isaac," in *SIS*, 66. See also Whitefield, "Answer to the Bishop," in *TWRGW*, 4:7-8.

364 Whitefield stated, "You may, perhaps, live honest and outwardly moral lives, but if you depend on that morality, or join works with your faith, in order to justify you before God, you have no lot or share in Christ's redemption: For what is this but to deny the Lord that has bought you? What is this but making yourselves your own saviours? taking the crown from Jesus Christ, and putting it on your own heads?" Whitefield, "The Wise and Foolish Virgins," in *TWRGW*, 5:389; idem, "The Wise and Foolish Virgins," in *SIS*, 307.

365 Whitefield, "The Lord Our Righteousness," in *TWRGW*, 5:228; idem, "The Lord Our Righteousness," in *SIS*, 192-93.

366 Whitefield, "What Think Ye of Christ?," in *TWRGW*, 5:358; idem, "What Think Ye of Christ?," in *SIS*, 284. See also Whitefield, "The Lord Our Righteousness," in *TWRGW*, 5:218; Idem, "The Lord Our Righteousness," in *SIS*, 185; idem, "The Seed of the Woman," in *TWRGW*, 5:16; idem, "The Seed of the Woman," in *SIS*, 42.

367 Peter Toon claimed that Flavius Illyricus and Nicolaus Hemmingius originally made the distinction between passive and active obedience. He contended that Beza popularized these concepts and their relationship to justification among Reformed theologians. Peter Toon, *The Emergence of Hyper- Calvinism in English Nonconformity 1689-1765* (London: The Olive Tree, 1967), 15-16.

368 Whitefield, "The Lord Our Righteousness," in *TWRGW*, 5:219-20; idem, "The Lord Our Righteousness," in *SIS*, 186. In his sermon "What Think Ye of Christ?," Whitefield stated, "In this body he formed a complete obedience to the law of God; whereby he in our stead fulfilled the covenant of works, and at last became subject to death; even

death upon the cross; that as God he might satisfy, as man he might obey and suffer; and being God and man in one person, might once more procure a union between God and our souls." Idem, "What Think Ye of Christ?," in *TWRGW*, 5:359; idem, "What Think Ye of Christ?," in *SIS*, 285. See also Whitefield, "Christ the Only Preservative Against a Reprobate Spirit," in *TWRGW*, 6:294; idem, "Christ the Only Preservative Against a Reprobate Spirit," in *SIS*, 566; idem, "What Think Ye of Christ?," in *TWRGW*, 5:361; idem, "What Think Ye of Christ?," in *SIS*, 286.

369 Whitefield, "What Think Ye of Christ?," in *TWRGW*, 5:366; idem, "What Think Ye of Christ?," in *SIS*, 290.

370 Whitefield, "What Think Ye of Christ?," in *TWRGW*, 5:362; idem, "What Think Ye of Christ?," in *SIS*, 287.

371 Whitefield, "The Conversion of Zaccheus," in *TWRGW*, 6:56; idem, "The Conversion of Zaccheus," in *SIS*, 406.

372 Whitefield, "The Folly and Danger," in *TWRGW*, 5:137; idem, "The Folly and Danger," in *SIS*, 129.

373 Whitefield stated, "In one sense, God now sees no sin in them; the whole covenant of works is fulfilled in them; they are actually justified, acquitted, and looked upon as righteous in the sight of God; they are perfectly accepted in the beloved; they are complete in him; the flaming sword of God's wrath, which before moved every way, is now re-moved, and free access given to the tree of life; they are en-abled to reach out the arm of faith, and pluck, and live for evermore." Whitefield, "Christ the Believer's Wisdom," in *TWRGW*, 6:190-91; idem, "Christ the Believer's Wisdom," in *SIS*, 502.

374 Whitefield, "The Method of Grace," in *Select Sermons*, 86.

375 Whitefield, "The Lord Our Righteousness," in *TWRGW*, 5:221; idem, "The Lord Our Righteousness," in *SIS*, 187-88. Speaking of Paul and James' comments in Scripture regarding works, Whitefield stated that "it is plain, that St. James is talking of declarative justification before men; shew me, demonstrate, evidence to me, that thou hast a true faith, by thy works: whereas St. Paul is talking only of our being justified in the sight of God; and thus he proves that Abraham, as we also are to be, was justified before ever the moral or ceremonial law was given to the Jews: for it is written, "Abraham believed in the Lord, and it was ac-

counted to him for righteousness." Idem, "What Think Ye of Christ?," in *TWRGW*, 5:365; idem, "What Think Ye of Christ?," in *SIS*, 289.

376 Regarding Zaccheus, Whitefield preached, "See an instance of this convert Zaccheus: no sooner had he received Jesus Christ by faith into his heart, but he evidences it by his works; for, ver. 8. We are told, 'Zaccheus stood forth, and said unto the Lord, Behold, Lord the half of my goods I give unto the poor; and if I have taken any thing from any man by false accusation, I restore him four-fold.'" Whitefield, "The Conversion of Zaccheus," in *TWRGW*, 6:56; idem, "The Conversion of Zaccheus," in *SIS*, 406-7.

377 Whitefield, "Christ the Believer's Husband," in *TWRGW*, 5:187; idem, "Christ the Believer's Husband," in *SIS*, 163.

378 Whitefield, "Christ the Believer's Wisdom," in *TWRGW*, 6:192

379 Whitefield, "Christ the Believer's Wisdom," in *TWRGW*, 6:202; idem, "Christ the Believer's Wisdom," in *SIS*, 511. See also Whitefield, "A Letter to the Religious Societies," in *TWRGW*, 4:33.

380 Whitefield, "Walking with God," in *TWRGW*, 5:25; idem, "Walking with God," in *SIS*, 48. In a letter to a fellow believer, Whitefield stated that such progressive sanctification is "the privilege of a real Christian, always growing, and making perpetual advances in the divine life. The path of the just shines more and more until the perfect day." Idem, "Letter DCCLII," in *TWRGW*, 2:253. See also Whitefield, "Letter DCCCXLI," in *TWRGW*, 2:355.

381 Whitefield, "A Prayer for One Newly Awakened With a Sense of the Divine Life," in *TWRGW*, 4:450. In another example, Whitefield encourages a believer stating, "What have you to do now, but daily to sit at the dear Redeemer's feet and hear his word; I mean, search the scriptures, which testify of him: and for His great name's sake, let your remaining life be one continued sacrifice of love to God and man. This is true faith, even a faith that works by love, and overcomes this wicked world. Well may it be styled precious faith. It is precious in itself, and precious in its fruits. It lays hold on, and unites to Christ, and carries out the soul day by day after a nearer conformity to him. It goes on from strength to strength, and conducts the soul at length to the

perfect and uninterrupted vision of the ever-blessed God."
Whitefield, "Letter DCCCXX," in *TWRGW*, 2:332.

382 Whitefield, "A Letter to Wesley," in *TWRGW*, 4:66; Idem,
Journals, 582. See also Whitefield, "Letter CCXXI," in
TWRGW, 1:210-12; idem, Letters, 210-12; idem, "Letter
CCXXIX," in *TWRGW*, 219; idem, Letters, 219; idem, "Letter DCXXII," in *TWRGW*, 2:126-27. In a letter to the Bishop of London, Whitefield stated, "I am so far from thinking that an imagination that we are already in a state of
perfection, is only apt to lead men into spiritual pride, that
I condemn it as the very quintessence and the highest degree of it." Whitefield, "An Answer to the Second Part," in
TWRGW, 4:151.

383 Whitefield, "Walking with God," in *TWRGW*, 5:24; idem,
"Walking with God," in *SIS*, 48.

384 Whitefield stated, "I know some people cannot look
back to see how many sins they have been guilty of; but
if grace help us to a sight of our inherent corruptions, it
will make us weary of it, and lead us to the blood of Christ,
to cleanse us from it; consequently, if your souls prosper,
the more you will fall in love with the glorious Redeemer,
and with his righteousness. I never knew a person in my
life that diligently used the word, and other means, but as
they improved in grace, saw more and more the necessity
of depending upon a better righteousness than our own."
Whitefield, "Soul Prosperity," in *SIS*, 646.

385 Whitefield, "Blind Bartimeus," in *TWRGW*, 5:411; idem,
"Blind Bartimeus," in *SIS*, 322; idem, "The Gospel Supper,"
in *TWRGW*, 6:29; idem, "The Gospel Supper," in *SIS*, 387;
idem, "The Gospel a Dying Saint's," in *SIS*, 653.

386 Whitefield, "The Marriage of Cana," in *TWRGW*, 6:75;
idem, "The Marriage of Cana," in *SIS*, 420. See also Whitefield, "Christ the Best Husband," in *TWRGW*, 5:68, 74;
idem, "Christ the Best Husband," in *SIS*, 79, 84.

387 Whitefield, "Observations on Some Fatal Mistakes, in
a Book Lately Published, and Intitled, 'The Doctrine of
Grace; or The Office and Operations of the Holy Spirit Vindicated from the Insults of Infidelity, and the Abuses of Fanaticism," in *TWRGW*, 4:287.

388 John Hussey, God's Operations of Grace but No Offers of
Grace (Elon, NC: Primitive Publications, 1973), 72. Refer to

the end of the first chapter of this book for a review of the discussion regarding Hyper-Calvinism in the eighteenth century.

389 Whitefield, "Letter CLXIX," in *TWRGW*, 1:156; idem, "Letter CLXIX," in Letters, 156. See also Idem, "Letter DCXXII," in *TWRGW*, 2:127. Regarding a preaching engagement in which he preached to twenty thousand people in Kennington, England, Whitefield stated, "I offered Jesus Christ to all who could apply Him to their hearts by faith. Oh that all would embrace Him! The Lord make them willing in the day of His power." Whitefield, *Journals*, 264.

390 Whitefield, "Christ the Best Husband," in *TWRGW*, 5:74-75; idem, "Christ the Best Husband," in *SIS*, 84. See also Whitefield, "The Gospel Supper," in *TWRGW*, 6:30; idem, "The Gospel Supper," in *SIS*, 387; idem, "Christ the Best Husband," in *TWRGW*, 5:68; idem, "Christ the Best Husband," in *SIS*, 79.

391 John Gill, "Answer to the Birmingham Dialogue-Writer, Part II," in *A Collection of Sermons and Tracts: in Two Volumes* (London: George Keith, 1773), 2:146.

392 Whitefield, "The Gospel a Dying Saint's," in *SIS*, 653.

393 In his sermon "A Penitent Heart, the Best New Year's Gift," Whitefield stated, "I am, Fourthly, to exhort you all, high and low, rich and poor, one with another, to repent of all your sins, and turn unto the Lord. And I shall speak to each of you; for you have either repented, or you have not, you are believers in Christ Jesus, or unbelievers." Whitefield, "A Penitent Heart," in *TWRGW*, 6:10; idem, "A Penitent Heart," in *SIS*, 373.

394 *The Canons of the Synod of Dort*, in *A History of the Creeds of Christendom*, ed. Philip Schaff (Grand Rapids: Baker Books, 1998), 1:522.

395 Whitefield, "A Letter to Wesley," in *TWRGW*, 4:59; idem, *Journals*, 575.

396 Whitefield, "Blind Bartimeus," in *TWRGW*, 5:411; idem, "Blind Bartimeus," in *SIS*, 322.

397 Luke Tyerman, *The Life of the Reverend George Whitefield* (London: Hodder and Stoughton, 1876-1877; reprint, Azle, TX: Need of the Times Publishers, 1995), 2:610.

Chapter 3

398 John Gillies, *Memoirs of Rev. George Whitefield* (New Haven: Whitmore & Buckingham and H. Mansfield, 1834), 284.

399 Kevin A. Miller, "Did You Know?" *Christian History* 38, no.2 (1993): 2.

400 Samuel Drew, "Memoirs," in *SIS* (London: Henry Fisher, Son, & P. Jackson, 1828), vii.

401 Albert D. Belden, "What America Owes to George Whitefield," *Religion and Life* 20, no. 3 (Summer 1951): 446.

402 Charles Chauncy, *Seasonable Thoughts on the State of Religion in New England* (Hicksville, NY: The Regina Press, 1975), 126-27.

403 Regarding Whitefield's motives for itinerant preaching, Chauncy queried, "And when he had got into this Way, might he not be too much encouraged to go on in it, from the *popular applauses*, every where, so liberally heaped on him? If he had not been under so strong a bias from something or other of this nature, why so fond of preaching always himself, to the exclusion, not of his *brethren* only, but his *fathers*, in *grace* and *gifts* and *learning*, as well as *age*?" Ibid., 36.

404 Ibid.

405 The President of Harvard wrote a letter to Whitefield stating, "It seems to us strange preposterous management, for any man to go about from one province and colony to another, year after year, acting as an extraordinary officer of Christ, and never shew all the while, what warrant he hath from the Word of God to so do, . . . Is not this just such conduct, as might be expected from any bold deceiver, who was conscious to himself, that he could give no account of his present way of acting, which would bear examination?" Edward Wigglesworth, *A Letter to the Reverend George Whitefield, by Way of Reply to His Answer to the College Testimony Against Him and His Conduct* (Boston: T. Fleet, 1745), 13.

406 *The Testimony of the President, Professors, Tutors, and Hebrew Instructor of Harvard College, against George Whitefield*, in *The Great Awakening*, ed. Alan Heimert and Perry Miller (Boston: n.p., 1744; reprint, Indianapolis:

Bobbs-Merrill Educational Publishing, 1967), 351 (page citations are to the reprint edition).

407 George Whitefield, "A Letter to the Reverend the President, and Professors, Tutors, and Hebrew Instructor, of Harvard-College in Cambridge; in Answer to A Testimony Published by Them Against the Reverend Mr. George Whitefield, and His Conduct," in *TWRGW*, 4:218.

408 George Whitefield, *A Letter to the Reverend Dr. Chauncy, on Account of Some Passages Relating to the Rev. Mr. Whitefield, in His Book Intitled Seasonable Thoughts on the State of Religion in New-England* (Boston: S. Kneeland and T. Green, 1745), 4-5.

409 George Whitefield, "Blind Bartimeus," in *TWRGW* (London: Printed for Edward and Charles Dilly, in the Poultry; and Messrs. Kincaid and Bell, at Edinburgh, 1771-1772), 5:405; idem, "Blind Bartimeus," in *SIS* (London: Henry Fisher, Son, & P. Jackson, 1828), 318.

410 Whitefield, *A Letter to the Reverend Dr. Chauncy*, 5.

411 Frank Lambert, *Inventing the "Great Awakening"* (Princeton: Princeton University Press, 1999), 90. Referring to Whitefield's supposed strategy for marketing and orchestrating revival in the colonies, Lambert writes, "The itinerant, whose English successes had inspired American evangelicals, connected the local awakenings, fashioning them into an intercolonial movement—crafting a national event before the existence of a nation." Frank Lambert, *"Pedlar in Divinity"* (Princeton: Princeton University Press, 1994), 95.

412 Lambert, *Inventing the "Great Awakening"*, 91. Speaking of both Whitefield's supposed self-promotion efforts and his strategy to create and market the Great Awakening, Lambert asserts, "Having worked out in England a set of techniques and strategies to promote revival, Whitefield introduced them to Americans. And he exploited the colonial press as he had the English print trade to publicize his successes and prime distant audiences to expect similar experiences when he preached among them." Ibid.

413 Lambert, *"Pedlar in Divinity,"* 105.

414 Lambert, *Inventing the "Great Awakening"*, 254.

415 Lambert, *"Pedlar in Divinity,"* 96.

416 Refer to the previous chapter of this book for Whitefield's understanding of the Great Commission.

417 Whitefield, "Letter DCXCVIII," in *TWRGW*, 2:193. Whitefield also stated, "No, let the name of Whitefield die, so that the cause of Jesus Christ may live." Idem, "Letter DCCXL-VII," in *TWRGW*, 2:248.

418 Harry S. Stout, *The Divine Dramatist: George Whitefield and the Rise of Modern Evangelicalism* (Grand Rapids: Eerdmans, 1991), xxi.

419 Ibid., 37. Regarding Whitefield's motivation to preach, Stout asserts, "Preaching could do what missions and charity could not: it could make him an unrivaled somebody in the cause of Christ." Ibid.

420 Ibid., 40.

421 George Whitefield, *George Whitefield's Journals* (London: The Banner of Truth Trust, 1960), 89.

422 Whitefield, "Letter CXI," in *TWRGW*, 1:106-07; idem, *George Whitefield's Letters* (Carlisle, PA: The Banner of Truth Trust, 1976), 106-07. In another letter, the itinerant told its recipient "how difficult it is to meet with success, and not be puffed up with it, and therefore if any such thing was discernible in my conduct, oh pity me, and pray to the Lord to heal my pride." Idem, "Letter CXXX," in *TWRGW*, 1:122-23; idem, *Letters*, 122-23. For other letters where he reveals his struggle with popularity and pride, see Whitefield, "Letter LXX," in *TWRGW*, 1:68; idem, *Letters*, 68; idem, "Letter LXI," in *TWRGW*, 1:60; idem, *Letters*, 60.

423 Sarah Edwards quoted in J. B. Wakeley, *Anecdotes of the Rev. George Whitefield* (London: Hodder and Stoughton, 1879), 277. To Stout's credit, he does mention this quotation in his biography; however, he does not reply to her claim that anyone who knew Whitefield would not think his preaching "all theatrical artifice and display." Stout, *The Divine Dramatist*, 127.

424 Joseph Smith, "The Character, Preaching, &c. of the Rev. George Whitefield," in *SIS*, 797.

425 To the Georgia Assembly, Benjamin Franklin said of Whitefield, "I knew him intimately upwards of 30 years: his integrity, disinterestedness, and indefatigable zeal in prosecuting every good work, I have never seen equalled, I shall never see excelled." Benjamin Franklin, quoted in Arnold

A. Dallimore, *George Whitefield* (Carlisle, PA: The Banner of Truth Trust, 1980), 2:453. It is interesting that Stout includes the same quote in his biography. Stout, *The Divine Dramatist*, 286-87.

426 Because I present numerous examples from Whitefield's preaching regarding the "five points" of Calvinism in the previous chapter, to avoid redundancy, here I will only present a few examples from his preaching and will cite additional pertinent references. Readers should view this section in conjunction with the numerous examples in the last chapter regarding the itinerant's incorporation of Calvinistic doctrine in his preaching.

427 Whitefield, "The Seed of the Woman, and the Seed of the Serpent," in *TWRGW*, 5:13; idem, "The Seed of the Woman, and the Seed of the Serpent," in *SIS*, 40.

428 Whitefield, "A Penitent Heart, the Best New Year's Gift," in *TWRGW*, 6:6; idem, "A Penitent Heart, the Best New Year's Gift," in *SIS*, 370.

429 Whitefield, "The Indwelling of the Spirit, the Privilege of All Believers," in *TWRGW*, 6:98; idem, "The Indwelling of the Spirit, the Privilege of All Believers," in *SIS*, 437. In his sermon "Walking with God," Whitefield told his hearers that "the carnal mind, the mind of the unconverted natural man, nay, the mind of the regenerate, so far as any part of him remains unrenewed, is enmity, not only an enemy, but 'enmity itself, against God; so that it is not subject to the law of God, neither indeed can it be.'" Idem, "Walking with God," in *TWRGW*, 5:23; idem, "Walking with God," in *SIS*, 47. For more of Whitefield's comments regarding original sin and its effects, see Whitefield, "Christ the Believer's Husband," in *TWRGW*, 5:191-92; idem, "Christ the Believer's Husband," in *SIS*, 166-67; idem, "The Seed of the Woman," in *TWRGW*, 5:10, 12; idem, "The Seed of the Woman," in *SIS*, 38-39.

430 Whitefield, "Christ the Only Rest for the Weary and Heavy-Laden," in *TWRGW*, 5:311; idem, "Christ the Only Rest for the Weary and Heavy-Laden," in *SIS*, 250. For more comments from Whitefield regarding moral inability, see also Whitefield, "What Think Ye of Christ?," in *TWRGW*, 5:367; idem, "What Think Ye of Christ?," in *SIS*,

291; idem, "Blind Bartimeus," in *TWRGW*, 5:411; idem, "Blind Bartimeus," in *SIS*, 322.

431 Whitefield, "The Potter and the Clay," in *TWRGW*, 5:201-2; idem, "The Potter and the Clay," in *SIS*, 173-74.

432 Whitefield, "The Conversion of Zaccheus," in *TWRGW*, 6:54; idem, "The Conversion of Zaccheus," in *SIS*, 405.

433 Whitefield, "The Seed of the Woman," in *TWRGW*, 5:20; idem, "The Seed of the Woman," in *SIS*, 45.

434 Whitefield, "Christ the Only Rest," in *TWRGW*, 5:310; idem, "Christ the Only Rest," in *SIS*, 250.

435 Whitefield, "Christ the Support of the Tempted," in *TWRGW*, 5:289-90; idem, "Christ the Support of the Tempted," in *SIS*, 236.

436 Whitefield, "Letter CXCIX," in *TWRGW*, 1:189; idem, *George Whitefield's Letters* (Carlisle, PA: The Banner of Truth Trust, 1976), 189.

437 Whitefield, *Letters*, 509. Whitefield wrote this letter on February 1, 1741.

438 For confirmation of the date the itinerant preached this message, see Richard Owen Roberts, *Whitefield in Print* (Wheaton: Richard Owen Roberts Publishers, 1988), 44.

439 Whitefield, "The Seed of the Woman," in *TWRGW*, 5:15; idem, "The Seed of the Woman," in *SIS*, 41. In this message, the English evangelist asserted, "God the Father and God the Son had entered in to a covenant concerning salvation of the elect from all eternity, wherein God the Father promised, that, if the Son would offer his soul a sacrifice for sin, he should see his seed." Ibid.

440 Whitefield, "The Conversion of Zaccheus," in *TWRGW*, 6:54; idem, "The Conversion of Zaccheus," in *SIS*, 404-05. The itinerant stated that Zaccheus was "one of those whom the Father had given him from all eternity: therefore he must abide at his house that day. 'For whom he did predestinate, them he also called.'... And if we do God justice, and are effectually wrought upon, we must acknowledge there was no more fitness in us than in Zaccheus; and, had not Christ prevented us by his call, we had remained dead in trespasses and sins, and alienated from the divine life, even as others." Ibid.

441 This letter appeared in the revival publication *The Weekly History*. In the letter, Whitefield wrote, "What was there

in you and me, Mr. O, that should move God to chuse us before the foundation of the world? Why are we taken and others left? Was there any fitness foreseen in us, except a fitness for damnation? I believe not; no, God chose us from eternity, he called us in time, and I am perswaded will keep us from falling finally 'till time shall be no more." George Whitefield, "An Abstract of a Letter from the Rev. Mr. Whitefield," *The Weekly History* 4 (1741): 4. This letter is also available in Whitefield, "Letter XCV," in *TWRGW*, 1:90; idem, Letters, 90.

442 One might speculate regarding the reasons behind Whitefield's inaccurate statement to Wesley. Perhaps the itinerant intended that he had not disputed over the doctrine of election in his preaching or publications. In his letter written on February 1, 1741, in response to Wesley's sermon "Free Grace," Whitefield asked his friend, "Why did you throw out a bone of contention?" Whitefield, *Letters*, 509. Maybe the English itinerant believed it contentious to preach against a particular doctrine. Perhaps he merely meant that the doctrine of election was not a focus of his preaching, but he would now grant it more attention. Regardless of the speculations one might offer as an explanation for Whitefield's inaccuracy, it remains an inaccuracy.

443 Whitefield, "Christ the Believer's Wisdom, Righteousness, Sanctification, and Redemption," in *TWRGW*, 6:202; idem, "Christ the Believer's Wisdom, Righteousness, Sanctification, and Redemption," in *SIS*, 510-11.

444 Whitefield, "A Penitent Heart," in *TWRGW*, 6:8; idem, "A Penitent Heart," in *SIS*, 372.

445 Whitefield, "Satan's Devices," in *TWRGW*, 6:247; idem, "Satan's Devices," in *SIS*, 537-38.

446 Whitefield, "Christ the Believer's Wisdom," in *TWRGW*, 6:188-89; idem, "Christ the Believer's Wisdom," in *SIS*, 501.

447 Whitefield, "The Righteousness of Christ, an Everlasting Righteousness," in *TWRGW*, 6:246; idem, "The Righteousness of Christ, an Everlasting Righteousness," in *SIS*, 205-06.

448 Whitefield, "The Holy Spirit Convincing the World of Sin, Righteousness, and Judgment," in *TWRGW*, 6:140; idem, "The Holy Spirit Convincing the World of Sin, Righteous-

ness, and Judgment," in *SIS*, 467-68. In his sermon "The Beloved of God," Whitefield instructed his hearers not "to examine whether they were elected or rejected, or no: they should do as a good woman once did, when Satan tempted her, and wanted to distress her, that there were but few to be saved; she said, if there were but two to be saved, she would strive to be one of them." Whitefield, "The Beloved of God," in *SIS*, 681.

449 George Whitefield, *George Whitefield's Journals* (London: The Banner of Truth Trust, 1960), 491. Whitefield wrote this entry in his journal on November 9, 1740.

450 Seth N. Polk, "The Theology and Methods of George White-field," *Journal of the American Society for Church Growth* 14 (Spring 2003): 7.

451 Whitefield, "The Righteousness of Christ, an Everlasting Righteousness," in *TWRGW*, 5:243; idem, "The Righteousness of Christ, an Everlasting Righteousness," in *SIS*, 203.

452 Whitefield, "The Indwelling of the Spirit," in *TWRGW*, 6:92; idem, "The Indwelling of the Spirit," in *SIS*, 433.

453 Whitefield, "The Furnace of Affliction," in *SIS*, 689.

454 Whitefield, "The Conversion of Zaccheus," in *TWRGW*, 6:62; idem, "The Conversion of Zaccheus," in *SIS*, 411. For more of Whitefield's references to Christ's death applying to believers, see Whitefield, "Christ the Believer's Husband," in *TWRGW*, 5:196; idem, "Christ the Believer's Husband," in *SIS*, 169-70; idem, "The Folly and Danger of Parting With Christ for the Pleasures and Profits of Life," in *TWRGW*, 5:330; idem, "The Folly and Danger of Parting With Christ for the Pleasures and Profits of Life," in *SIS*, 264; idem, "Christ the Only Preservative Against a Reprobate Spirit," in *TWRGW*, 6:290; idem, "Christ the Only Preservative Against a Reprobate Spirit," in *SIS*, 563.

455 The only exception I could find where Whitefield told a group, other than the elect, believers, or "brethren," that Christ died for them was when he addressed some hearers he believed were spiritually affected by his sermon on the resurrection of Lazarus. To this group of affected hearers, the itinerant stated, "You do not know how you grieve the heart of Jesus. I beseech you give him no fresh cause to weep over you upon account of your unbelief: let him not again groan in his spirit, and be troubled. Behold how he

has loved you, even so as to lay down his life for you. What could he do more? I pray you therefore, dead sinners, come forth; arise, and sup with Jesus." Whitefield, "The Resurrection of Lazarus," in *TWRGW*, 6:125; idem, "The Resurrection of Lazarus," in *SIS*, 457.

456 Whitefield, "Christ the Only Preservative," in *TWRGW*, 6:299-300; idem, "Christ the Only Preservative," in *SIS*, 569-70.

457 Whitefield, "Christ the Support of the Tempted," in *TWRGW*, 5:295; idem, "Christ the Support of the Tempted," in *SIS*, 238.

458 Whitefield, "Christ the Only Preservative," in *TWRGW*, 6:294; idem, "Christ the Only Preservative," in *SIS*, 566.

459 Whitefield, "Saul's Conversion," in *TWRGW*, 6:153-54; idem, "Saul's Conversion," in *SIS*, 476-77. In this sermon, the evangelist noted that Ananias referred to Paul as "brother" prior to the scales falling from the Apostle's eyes and before his justification and adoption by the Holy Spirit. It seems that the English itinerant implied that Ananias referred to Paul as "brother" even though, as Whitefield claimed in the sermon, the process of Paul's conversion had not yet been completed. Ibid.

460 Whitefield, "The Folly and Danger," in *TWRGW*, 5:328; idem, "The Folly and Danger," in *SIS*, 262-63.

461 Whitefield, "What Think Ye of Christ?," in *TWRGW*, 5:370; idem, "What Think Ye of Christ?," in *SIS*, 292-93.

462 Whitefield, "Christ the Support of the Tempted," in *TWRGW*, 5:295; idem, "Christ the Support of the Tempted," in *SIS*, 238; idem, "Christ the Only Preservative," in *TWRGW*, 6:294; idem, "Christ the Only Preservative," in *SIS*, 566.

463 Whitefield, "The Resurrection of Lazarus," in *TWRGW*, 6:123-24; idem, "The Resurrection of Lazarus," in *SIS*, 456.

464 Whitefield, "The Good Shepherd," in *SIS*, 784.

465 Whitefield, "The Duty of Searching the Scriptures," in *TWRGW*, 6:86; idem, "The Duty of Searching the Scriptures," in *SIS*, 428.

466 Whitefield, "The Seed of the Woman," in *TWRGW*, 5:11; idem, "The Seed of the Woman," in *SIS*, 38.

467 Whitefield, "What Think Ye of Christ?," in *TWRGW*, 5:366; idem, "What Think Ye of Christ?," in *SIS*, 290. See also

Whitefield, "The Gospel Supper," in *TWRGW*, 6:31; idem, "The Gospel Supper," in *SIS*, 388.

468 Whitefield, "Christ the Believer's Wisdom," in *TWRGW*, 6:190; idem, "Christ the Believer's Wisdom," in *SIS*, 502.

469 Whitefield, "The Wise and Foolish Virgins," in *TWRGW*, 5:382; idem, "The Wise and Foolish Virgins," in *SIS*, 302.

470 Whitefield, "The Good Shepherd," in *SIS*, 788.

471 Whitefield, "Christ the Believer's Wisdom," in *TWRGW*, 6:190-91; Idem, "Christ the Believer's Wisdom," in *SIS*, 502-03. For more references to the relationship between Christ and the doctrine of the perseverance of the saints, see Whitefield, "Soul Dejection," in *SIS*, 728; idem, "Christ the Believer's Husband," in *TWRGW*, 5:190-91; and idem, "Christ the Believer's Husband," in *SIS*, 166.

472 Whitefield, "Christ the Best Husband: Or an Earnest Invitation to Young Women to Come and See Christ," in *TWRGW*, 5:71-72; idem, "Christ the Best Husband: Or an Earnest Invitation to Young Women to Come and See Christ," in *SIS*, 82. In another sermon, Whitefield admonished believers regarding evil men, "And, therefore, be not afraid of their wrath, though it is cruel, and of their anger, though it be fierce: let them shoot their arrows, even bitter words, against us, blessed be God, the shield of faith will be a preservative against them all." Idem, "The Folly and Danger," in *TWRGW*, 5:332; idem, "The Folly and Danger," in *SIS*, 265. For more comments from Whitefield regarding God's protection and the perseverance of the saints, see Whitefield, "The Furnace of Affliction," in *SIS*, 693; idem, "The Beloved of God," in *SIS*, 685.

473 Whitefield, "An Exhortation to the People of God Not to be Discouraged in Their Way, By the Scoffs and Contempt of Wicked Men," in *TWRGW*, 6:362-63; idem, "An Exhortation to the People of God Not to be Discouraged in Their Way, By the Scoffs and Contempt of Wicked Men," in *SIS*, 605.

474 Whitefield, "Christ the Only Preservative Against a Reprobate Spirit," in *TWRGW*, 6:298-99; idem, "Christ the Only Preservative Against a Reprobate Spirit," in *SIS*, 569. To a group of Christian women, "I offer Jesus Christ to all of you; if you have been ever so notorious for sin, if you have been as great a harlot as Mary Magdalen was, when

No Better Gospel

once you are espoused to Christ, you shall be forgiven."
Idem, "Christ the Best Husband," in *TWRGW*, 5:70; idem,
"Christ the Best Husband," in *SIS*, 81. For another example of Whitefield addressing various categories of sin in an
invitation, see Whitefield, "What Think Ye of Christ?," in
TWRGW, 5:371; idem, "What Think Ye of Christ?," in *SIS*,
293.

475 Whitefield, "Christ the Only Preservative," in *TWRGW*,
6:295; idem, "Christ the Only Preservative," in *SIS*, 567.

476 Addressing the slaves in one audience, Whitefield preached,
"Here, then, I could conclude; but I must not forget the *poor
negroes*: no, I must not. Jesus Christ has died for them, as
well as for others. Nor do I mention you last, because I despise your souls, but because I would have what I shall say,
make the deeper impression upon your hearts. O that you
would seek the Lord to be your righteousness! Who knows
but he may be found of you? For in Jesus Christ there is neither male nor female, bond nor free; even you may be the
children of God, if you believe in Jesus. Did you never read
of the eunuch belonging to the queen of *Candace*? a negro,
like yourselves. He believed. The Lord was his righteousness. He was baptised. Do you also believe, and you shall
be saved. Christ Jesus is the same now as he was yesterday,
and will wash you in his own blood. Go home then, turn the
words of the text into a prayer, and entreat the Lord to be
your righteousness." Whitefield, "The Lord Our Righteousness," 5:234; idem, "The Lord Our Righteousness," in *SIS*,
197. I will address further the relationship between Whitefield and slavery in a later section of this chapter.

477 Whitefield, "The Eternity of Hell Torments," in *TWRGW*,
5:402-3; idem, "The Eternity of Hell Torments," in *SIS*,
316.

478 Whitefield, "The Care of the Soul Urged as the One Thing
Needful," in *TWRGW*, 5:471-72; idem, "The Care of the
Soul Urged as the One Thing Needful," in *SIS*, 365-66. For
more examples of Whitefield addressing groups of people
in various spiritual conditions, see Whitefield, "Walking
with God," in *TWRGW*, 5:35-37; idem, "Walking with God,"
in *SIS*, 56-58; idem, "The Folly and Danger," in *TWRGW*,
5:334; idem, "The Folly and Danger," in *SIS*, 267.

479 Whitefield, "Spiritual Baptism," in *SIS*, 738. In another sermon, Whitefield stated, "Methinks I hear you say, 'We have been dedicated to God in baptism, we go to church or meeting, we say our prayers, repeat our creeds, or have subscribed the articles, and the confession of faith; we are quite orthodox, and great friends to the doctrines of grace; we do nobody any harm, we are church members, we keep up family prayer, and constantly go to the table of the Lord.' All these things are good in their places. But thus far, nay, much farther may you go, and yet be far from the kingdom of God. . . . Awake ye outward court worshippers: ye are building on a sandy foundation;–take heed lest you also go to hell by the very door of heaven." Idem, "Christians, Temples of the Living God," in *TWRGW*, 6:284-85; idem, "Christians, Temples of the Living God," in *SIS*, 560-61. See also Whitefield, "On Regeneration," in *TWRGW*, 6:266- 67; idem, "On Regeneration," in *SIS*, 549.

480 Whitefield, "The Lord Our Righteousness," in *TWRGW*, 5:233; idem, "The Lord Our Righteousness," in *SIS*, 196-97.

481 Whitefield, "Repentance and Conversion," in *SIS*, 668.

482 In his sermon "All Men's Place," Whitefield preached, "Young people, young people, that are going to hell giddily, may God stop you this night: were I to talk to you seriously, you would say as a young gentleman did, when I desired he would not swear; he turned to me and said, Doctor, (I was no more a doctor then than now, and but young too,) it is very hard you will not let a man go to hell his own way: if any of you be of this stamp, God grant he may not let you go to hell your own way, but go to heaven in God's way, in Christ's way." Whitefield, "All Men's Place," in *SIS*, 758.

483 In his sermon "The Lord Our Righteousness," alluding to the biblical story of the prodigal son, Whitefield encouraged young people to "leave your swine's trough" and run to their heavenly Father. Whitefield, "The Lord Our Righteousness," in *TWRGW*, 5:232; idem, "The Lord Our Righteousness," in *SIS*, 195.

484 Whitefield, "The Lord Our Righteousness," in *TWRGW*, 5:233; idem, "The Lord Our Righteousness," in *SIS*, 196. For another example of Whitefield's references to mid-

dle-aged persons in his invitations, see Whitefield, "Repentance and Conversion," in *SIS*, 668, 670.

485 Whitefield, "The Lord Our Righteousness," in *TWRGW*, 5:233; idem, "The Lord Our Righteousness," in *SIS*, 196. For more examples of Whitefield's invitations to elderly hearers, see Whitefield, "The Care of the Soul Urged as the One Thing Needful," in *TWRGW*, 5:459-60; idem, "The Care of the Soul Urged as the One Thing Needful," in *SIS*, 356-57; and Idem, "Repentance and Conversion," in *SIS*, 670; and idem, "Soul Dejection," in *SIS*, 729.

486 Whitefield, "Self-Inquiry Concerning the Work of God," in *SIS*, 707.

487 Whitefield, "The Pharisee and the Publican," in *TWRGW*, 6:44; idem, "The Pharisee and the Publican," in *SIS*, 397-98. The itinerant based his message upon the biblical account found in Luke 18:9-17.

488 Whitefield, "The Lord Our Righteousness," in *TWRGW*, 5:229; idem, "The Lord Our Righteousness," in *SIS*, 193. In another sermon, Whitefield inquired, "Were you ever, with the great apostle of the Gentiles, made to abhor your own righteousness, which is by the law, and acknowledge that you deserve to be damned, though you should give all your goods to feed the poor." Idem, "The Holy Spirit Convincing the World of Sin, Righteousness, and Judgment," in *TWRGW*, 6:132; idem, "The Holy Spirit Convincing the World of Sin, Righteousness, and Judgment," in *SIS*, 461.

489 Whitefield, "Self-Inquiry," in *SIS*, 708.

490 Whitefield, "The Pharisee and the Publican," in *TWRGW*, 6:46-48; idem, "The Pharisee and the Publican," in *SIS*, 399-401.

491 Whitefield, "Marks of a True Conversion," in *TWRGW*, 5:346; idem, "Marks of a True Conversion," in *SIS*, 275.

492 Whitefield, "Abraham's Offering," in *TWRGW*, 5:50; idem, "Abraham's Offering," in *SIS*, 67. For another example of Whitefield's inquiries regarding the new birth, see Whitefield, "On Regeneration," in *TWRGW*, 6:269; idem, "On Regeneration," in *SIS*, 551.

493 Whitefield, "The Potter and the Clay," in *TWRGW*, 5:213; idem, "The Potter and the Clay," in *SIS*, 182.

494 Whitefield preached, "O do not put a slight on infinite love: what would you have Christ do more? Is it not enough for

him to come on purpose to save? Will you not serve God in your souls, as well as with your bodies? . . . O ye of little faith, why are ye fearful lest he should not accept of you? If you will not believe me, sure you will believe the Lord Jesus Christ; he has told you that he will receive you, then why tarry ye, and do not go to him directly?" Whitefield, "The Folly and Danger," in *TWRGW*, 5:326; idem, "The Folly and Danger," in *SIS*, 261.

495 Whitefield, "Christ the Believer's Wisdom," in *TWRGW*, 6:200-1; idem, "Christ the Believer's Wisdom," in *SIS*, 510.

496 Whitefield asked one audience, "You may think to put it off till the morning though before the morning you may be damned. Pray why will you not be converted now? If you were in prison, and a person would take you out, you would choose to be let out to-night before morning, that you might sleep better; why will you not do that for your soul, you would for your body?" Whitefield, "Repentance and Conversion," in *SIS*, 667. For more questions intended to cause hearers to come to Christ, see Whitefield, "What Think Ye of Christ?," in *TWRGW*, 5:359; idem, "What Think Ye of Christ?," in *SIS*, 285.

497 Whitefield, "Christ the Only Rest," in *TWRGW*, 5:314; idem, "Christ the Only Rest," in *SIS*, 252.

498 Whitefield, "Christ the Believer's Husband," in *TWRGW*, 5:192; idem, "Christ the Believer's Husband," in *SIS*, 167.

499 Regarding the eternal destiny of their souls, Whitefield stated, "You need to view that commodity on all sides, of which you do in effect say, For this will I sell my soul; for this will I give up heaven and venture hell, be heaven and hell whatever they may. In the name of God, brethren, is this the part of a man, of a rational creature–to go on with your eyes open towards a pit of eternal ruin, because there are a few gay flowers in the way? or what if you shut your eyes, will that prevent your fall? . . . It signifies little to say, I will not think of these things, I will not consider them: God has said, 'In the last days they shall consider it perfectly,' Jer. xxiii. 20. The revels of a drunken malefactor, will not prevent nor respite his execution." Whitefield, "The Care of the Soul," in *TWRGW*, 5:470-71; idem, "The Care of the Soul," in *SIS*, 365.

500 Whitefield, "A Penitent Heart," in *TWRGW*, 6:16; idem, "A Penitent Heart," in *SIS*, 378. In the same sermon, White-field preached, "Repent, repent therefore, my dear breth-ren, as John the Baptist, and our blessed Redeemer himself earnestly exhorted, and turn from your evil ways, and the Lord will have mercy on you." Idem, "A Penitent Heart," in *TWRGW*, 6:19; idem, "A Penitent Heart," in *SIS*, 380. In another sermon, the itinerant declared, "If he come to Christ, confess and forsake his sin, then Jesus will have mercy upon him: and if, my brethren, you are sensible of your sins, convinced of your iniquities, and feel yourselves lost, undone sinners, and come and tell Christ of your lost condition, you will soon find how ready he is to help you; he will give you his Spirit; and if you have his Spirit, you can-not be reprobates: you will find his Spirit to be quickening and refreshing; not like the spirit of the world, a spirit of re-proach, envy, and all uncharitableness." Idem, "Christ the Only Preservative," in *TWRGW*, 6:287-88; idem, "Christ the Only Preservative," in *SIS*, 562.

501 In his sermon "Marks of a True Conversion," Whitefield stated, "If ye confess your sins, and leave them, and lay hold on the Lord Jesus Christ, the Spirit of God shall be given you; if you will go and say, Turn me, O my God! thou knowest not, O man, what the return of God may be to thee." Whitefield, "Marks of a True Conversion," in *TWRGW*, 5:352; idem, "Marks of a True Conversion," in *SIS*, 280. The evangelist encouraged listeners to come to Christ for forgiveness,"to be acquitted; come to his blood to be pardoned; you must believe on him, not only with a bare speculative belief, (that the devil has, and all the damned in hell,) but to have his blood applied and brought home to the soul; we must come to him as the author and finisher of our faith." Whitefield, "Neglect of Christ, the Killing Sin," in *SIS*, 745. He admonished his listeners to "Come, put ye on the Lord Jesus. Come, haste ye away and walk with God, and make no longer provision for the flesh, to fulfill the lust thereof. Stop, stop, O sinner! turn ye, turn ye, O ye uncon-verted men, for the end of that way your are now walking in, however right it may seem in your blinded eyes, will be death, even eternal destruction both of the body and soul." Idem, "Walking with God,' in *TWRGW*, 5:35; idem, "Walk-

ing with God," in *SIS*, 56. For other directions from White-field regarding confession and repentance, see Whitefield, "A Penitent Heart," in *TWRGW*, 6:6-8; idem, "A Penitent Heart," in *SIS*, 370-71; idem, "Christ the Believer's Refuge," in *SIS*, 637.

502 Whitefield preached, "O then believe, repent! I beseech you, believe the gospel." Whitefield, "The Potter and the Clay," in *TWRGW*, 5:214; idem, "The Potter and the Clay," in *SIS*, 183.

503 Whitefield, "The Folly and Danger," in *TWRGW*, 5:137; idem, "The Folly and Danger," in *SIS*, 128-29. See also Whitefield, "Christ the Only Preservative," in *TWRGW*, 6:294; idem, "The Folly and Danger," in *SIS*, 566; idem, "The Lord Our Light," in *SIS*, 704.

504 Remember from the previous chapter that George White-field believed conversion involved individuals exercising repentance and faith in Christ. Such instructions are con-sistent with his theological understanding of conversion.

505 Whitefield, "Christ the Only Rest," in *TWRGW*, 5:316; idem, "Christ the Only Rest," in *SIS*, 254. Whitefield in-structed an assemblage of women to "put off all your good works, for they will be but a means to keep you from Christ; no, you must come as not having your own righteousness, which is of the law, but you must have the righteousness of Christ. Therefore, come unto the Lord Jesus Christ, and he will give it to you; he will not send you away without it." Idem, "Christ the Best Husband," in *TWRGW*, 5:76; idem, "Christ the Best Husband," in *SIS*, 86. To another group, the itinerant entreated, "Do not depend upon your-selves: say unto him; 'Save us, Lord, or we perish:' beseech him to be your guide, and your salvation; I beseech you by the tender mercies of God, which are in Christ Jesus, that you present yourselves to him as your reasonable service." Idem, "The Folly and Danger," in *TWRGW*, 5:325; idem, "The Folly and Danger," in *SIS*, 260. He encouraged listen-ers to "throw away your righteousness, and come to Christ, and be content to let Jesus Christ do all for you, and in you, then Christ is willing to be your Saviour." Idem, "Christ the Support of the Tempted," in *TWRGW*, 5:296; idem, "Christ the Support of the Tempted," in *SIS*, 241. For other examples in which the itinerant discouraged hearers from

relying upon themselves and encouraged them to rely fully upon Christ for their salvation, see Idem, "Christ the Support," in *TWRGW*, 5:292-93; idem, "Christ the Support," in *SIS*, 239; idem, "The Folly and Danger," in *TWRGW*, 5:325-26; idem, "The Folly and Danger," in *SIS*, 260-61; idem, "A Penitent Heart," in *TWRGW*, 6:10; idem, "A Penitent Heart," in *SIS*, 373; idem, "Soul Dejection," in *SIS*, 725.

506 See the sections in the previous chapter regarding the doctrine of total depravity and the doctrine of justification for a reminder of Whitefield's theological understanding of these matters.

507 Whitefield, "What Think Ye of Christ?," in *TWRGW*, 5:367; idem, "What Think Ye of Christ?," in *SIS*, 291.

508 In his sermon "Marks of a True Conversion", the itinerant preacher exhorted his hearers to "go home, and away to your closets, and down with your stubborn hearts before God; if ye have not done it before, let this be the night: or, do not stay till you go home; begin now, while standing here, pray to God, and let the language of thy heart be, Lord, convert me!" Whitefield, "Marks of a True Conversion," in *TWRGW*, 5:351; idem, "Marks of a True Conversion," in *SIS*, 279.

509 Whitefield, "The Wise and Foolish Virgins," in *TWRGW*, 5:376; idem, "The Wise and Foolish Virgins," in *SIS*, 297.

510 Whitefield, "The Folly and Danger," in *TWRGW*, 5:139; idem, "The Folly and Danger," in *SIS*, 130. The English evangelist also stated that "this is a faithful and true saying, and worthy of men to be received, 'that Jesus Christ came into the world to save sinners." Idem, "The Indwelling of the Spirit, the Privilege of All Believers," in *TWRGW*, 6:101; idem, "The Indwelling of the Spirit, the Privilege of All Believers," in *SIS*, 439.

511 Whitefield, "Christ the Only Preservative," in *TWRGW*, 6:290; idem, "Christ the Only Preservative," in *SIS*, 563.

512 Whitefield, "The Conversion of Zaccheus," in *TWRGW*, 6:59; idem, "The Conversion of Zaccheus," in *SIS*, 409.

513 Whitefield, "The Wise and Foolish Virgins," in *TWRGW*, 5:387; idem, "The Wise and Foolish Virgins," in *SIS*, 305-6. To another group of hearers, Whitefield described Christ hanging on a cross "with arms stretched and ready

to embrace them." Idem, "Of Justification By Christ," in *TWRGW*, 6:225; idem, "Of Justification By Christ," in *SIS*, 525.

514 Whitefield, "Christ the Only Preservative," in *TWRGW*, 6:294; idem, "Christ the Only Preservative," in *SIS*, 566. See also Whitefield, "Satan's Devices," in *TWRGW*, 6:246; idem, "Satan's Devices," in *SIS*, 537.

515 In his sermon "Walking with God," Whitefield preached, "The blood, even the precious blood of Jesus Christ, if you come to the Father in and through him, shall cleanse you from all sin." Whitefield, "Walking with God," in *TWRGW*, 5:36; idem, "Walking with God," in *SIS*, 57. See also Whitefield, "Saul's Conversion," in *TWRGW*, 6:159; idem, "Saul's Conversion," in *SIS*, 481; idem, "The Conversion of Zaccheus," in *TWRGW*, 6:61-62; idem, "The Conversion of Zaccheus," in *SIS*, 410-11.

516 Whitefield, "A Penitent Heart," in *TWRGW*, 6:3; idem, "A Penitent Heart," in *SIS*, 368.

517 Whitefield, "Christ's Transfiguration," in *TWRGW*, 5:455; idem, "Christ's Transfiguration," in *SIS*, 353.

518 Whitefield, "The Pharisee and Publican," in *TWRGW*, 6:46; idem, "The Pharisee and Publican," in *SIS*, 399. In another sermon, Whitefield addressed enemies of God, stating, "For you without repentance, is reserved the blackness of darkness forever. The Lord Jesus sits in heaven, ruling over all, and causing all things to work for his children's good; he laughs you to scorn; he hath you in the utmost derision, and therefore so will I." Idem, "The Seed of the Woman," in *TWRGW*, 5:20; idem, "The Seed of the Woman," in *SIS*, 45.

519 Regarding the issue of God's glory, Whitefield declared, "You are lost, undone, without him; and if he be not glorified in your salvation, he will be glorified in your destruction; if he does not come and make his abode in your hearts, you must take up an eternal abode with the devil and his angels. O that the Lord would be pleased to pass by some of you at this time! O that he may call you by his Spirit, and make you a willing people in this day of his power!" Whitefield, "The Conversion of Zaccheus," in *TWRGW*, 6:60-61; idem, "The Conversion of Zaccheus," in *SIS*, 410.

520 Whitefield, "The Marriage of Cana," in *TWRGW*, 6:76-77; idem, "The Marriage of Cana," in *SIS*, 421-22.

521 Whitefield, "The Gospel a Dying Saint's Triumph," in *SIS*, 660.

522 Whitefield, "God a Believer's Glory," in *SIS*, 767.

523 Whitefield, "The Good Shepherd," in *SIS*, 790.

524 Whitefield, "Jacob's Ladder," in *SIS*, 774.

525 Whitefield, *Journals*, 60.

526 Speaking of his efforts to share Christ with one recently incarcerated, the evangelist wrote, "Immediately I went to the prison, assuredly gathering that the Lord called me thither. I met with the person, and finding him and some others willing to hear the Word of God, and having gained leave of the keeper and two ordinaries, I constantly read to and prayed with them every day I was in town." Ibid., 63.

527 Ibid., 143.

528 Ibid., 110-11.

529 Regarding his evangelistic activity among the passengers, the itinerant wrote, "Expounded with more enlargement than usual; and gave my people notice that I intended speaking to them one by one; to see what account they could give of their faith." Ibid., 139.

530 Whitefield, "Letter CXXIX," in *TWRGW*, 1:122; idem, *Letters*, 122.

531 Whitefield, "Letter LXVI," in *TWRGW*, 1:64; idem, *Letters*, 64.

532 Whitefield, "Letter XCI," in *TWRGW*, 1:87; idem, *Letters*, 87.

533 Whitefield, "Letter CV," in *TWRGW*, 1:100; idem, *Letters*, 100.

534 Whitefield, "Letter CIX," in *TWRGW*, 1:104; idem, *Letters*, 104. In a thank you letter to a man who fed the evangelist during one of his evangelistic visits to a town, Whitefield warned that "it is but too notorious, that numbers rest in the outward form, and are strangers to the inward power of godliness in their hearts. Do not you so learn Christ. Beg of God that you may feel his spirit working mightily in your soul, and witnessing to your spirit that you are a child of God." Idem, "Letter CXXIV," in *TWRGW*, 1:118; idem, *Letters*, 118.

535 Whitefield, "Letter DCXXXV," in *TWRGW*, 2:139.

536 Whitefield, "Letter DCCCCXXVI," in *TWRGW*, 2:440. Benjamin Franklin and George Whitefield were friends from

the time they first met until the end of the itinerant's life. As mentioned in the first chapter of this book, regarding Whitefield, Franklin stated that he "never had the least suspicion of his integrity, but am to this day decidedly of the opinion that he was in all his conduct a perfectly honest man; and methinks my testimony in his favour ought to have the more weight, as we had no religious connection." Benjamin Franklin, *The Life of Benjamin Franklin* (Auburn and Buffalo, NY: Miller, Orton, & Mulligan, 1854), 118. Sadly, this quote from Franklin implies that he did not heed Whitefield's words regarding his need for new birth.

537 Whitefield, "Letter CCCLIV," in *TWRGW*, 1:321; idem, *Letters*, 321. For more examples of Whitefield witnessing to nobility through written correspondence, see Whitefield, "Letter DCCIV," in *TWRGW*, 2:198; idem, "Letter DCCIX," in *TWRGW*, 2:202-03.

538 For more of these letters used for witnessing, see Whitefield, "Letter XV," in *TWRGW*, 1:18; idem, "Letter XXXVI," in *TWRGW*, 1:39-40; idem, "Letter XLIV," in *TWRGW*, 1:47; idem, "Letter LXIII," in *TWRGW*, 1:61; idem, "Letter CXXXV," in *TWRGW*, 1:126; idem, "Letter CXLIII," in *TWRGW*, 1:133; idem, "Letter CXLVI," in *TWRGW*, 1:136-37; idem, "Letter CXCIII," in *TWRGW*, 1:183; idem, "Letter CCCXII," in *TWRGW*, 1:285; idem, "Letter CCCXCVII," in *TWRGW*, 1:369; idem, Letters, 18, 39-40, 47, 61, 126, 133, 136-37, 183, 285; idem, "Letter DCVIII," in *TWRGW*, 2:115; idem, "LetterMCCCXXIII," in *TWRGW*, 321.

539 For the remainder of this book, the term "follow up" will refer to Whitefield's efforts to disciple new believers and to respond to inquirers' questions. Follow up also involved the use of religious societies and local ministers in discipling new believers and in responding to inquirers.

540 Regarding such notes, Arnold Dallimore writes, "Many persons among his congregations came under such deep conviction of sin that, in their yearning for relief, they wrote notes (bills, Whitefield calls them) and passed them to him as he preached. These brought the individual to his attention by name, and implored a place in his prayers and often sought an opportunity to talk to him personally." Arnold A. Dallimore, *George Whitefield* (Carlisle, PA: The Banner of Truth Trust, 1980), 1:379.

541 Whitefield, *Journals*, 385. In another episode, as White-field was finishing one of his sermons, an unconverted minister under conviction passed him a note entreating the itinerant to pray for him and his salvation. Ibid., 470.

542 Whitefield, "Letter CCCCXI," in *TWRGW*, 1:386; idem, *Letters*, 386.

543 Describing his efforts to answer inquirers in Bristol, White-field wrote that he "was employed from seven in the morning till midnight, in talking and giving spiritual advice to awakened souls." Whitefield, *Journals*, 85.

544 Ibid., 455.

545 Ibid., 408.

546 Ibid., 196. For more examples of Whitefield's interaction with individual inquirers, see Whitefield, *Journals*, 92, 108, 201, 219, 227, 344, 346, 355, 357, 359, 408, 409, 413, 422, 423, 451, 469, 487, 488, 494; idem, "Letter DLXVI," in *TWRGW*, 2:75; idem, "Letter DCCLXXI," in *TWRGW*, 2:275.

547 Whitefield, *Journals*, 472. Describing a similar event that occurred the previous day, the itinerant wrote, "About four, we reached Boston, where I preached immediately, in Dr. Sewall's meeting house. I exhorted a great number afterwards at my lodgings; and then was employed, till near midnight, in settling my private affairs, answering letters, and speaking to those under conviction." Ibid. For other examples of the itinerant preaching to such crowds gathered around his lodgings, see Whitefield, *Journals*, 464, 471.

548 Ibid., 411.

549 To review the itinerant's sentiments regarding this issue, Whitefield stated, "I love now to wait a little, and see if people bring forth fruit; for there are so many blossoms which March winds you know blow away, that I cannot believe they are converts till I see fruit brought forth. It will do converts no harm to keep them a little back; it will never do a sincere soul any harm." Whitefield, "The Gospel a Dying Saint's Triumph," in *SIS*, 652-53.

550 Whitefield, *Journals*, 246.

551 Ibid., 179.

552 Ibid., 242.

553 Whitefield did present figures regarding "awakened" individuals. For example, in one of his letters, the itinerant stated that "three hundred and fifty awakened souls" responded to his preaching; however, he did not refer to these "awakened" individuals as distinctive converts. The English evangelist also did not present comprehensive figures regarding the overall number of conversions resulting from his preaching, but offered estimates related to local responses in a particular town.

Historians of the Great Awakening present helpful information regarding conversion estimates and the number of new churches resulting from that movement of God. Because George Whitefield was one of the key preachers of the Awakening, these figures must partly reflect the results of his evangelistic ministry. In his account of the Awakening, Joseph Tracy claimed that between 25,000 to 50,000 conversions occurred during this movement of the Holy Spirit. He pointed out that these numbers of conversions do not include the numerous church members who experienced conversion. Joseph Tracy, *The Great Awakening* (Boston: Tappan and Dennet, 1842; reprint, Edinburgh: The Banner of Truth Trust, 1997), 390-91. Ezra Stiles stated that 150 new Congregational churches were established as a result of the Great Awakening. Ezra Stiles, *A Discourse on the Christian Union* (Boston: Edes and Gill, 1761), 51. Regarding Whitefield's influence on conversions and increases in church membership during this era, Harry Stout stated that "Whitefield inspired a huge influx in many communities that threw the cycles out of rhythm and brought 'pools' of new converts into the church at once." Harry Stout, *The New England Soul: Preaching and Religious Culture in Colonial New England* (Oxford: Oxford University Press, 1986), 196. These historians give us an understanding of the impact of the itinerant's evangelistic efforts in eighteenth-century colonial America.

554 Whitefield, *Journals*, 402-03.

555 Ibid., 290. For other examples of Whitefield using the number of inquirers as a gauge for estimating numbers of conversions, see Whitefield, *Journals*, 358, 404, 411.

556 Whitefield, "Soul Dejection," in *SIS*, 725. For more examples of notes granting Whitefield an idea of the number of

conversions, see Whitefield, "All Men's Place," in *SIS*, 758; Idem, *Journals*, 148.

557 E. Pemberton quoted in Whitefield, *Journals*, 360.

558 Regarding such letters, Whitefield wrote, "Numbers of letters have been sent me from persons under convictions, and it is unknown what deep impressions have been wrought in the hearts of hundreds." Whitefield, *Journals*, 360-61.

559 Ibid., 406-08.

560 E. Gordon Rupp, *Religion in England 1688-1791* (Oxford: Clarendon Press, 1986), 327. This book is an excellent resource for information regarding Whitefield's use of societies as a follow up method. Rupp is the only biographer I encountered who offers a thorough treatment of this aspect of George Whitefield's evangelistic methodology.

561 Whitefield, "The Necessity and Benefits of Religious Society," in *TWRGW*, 5:107-22; idem, "The Necessity and Benefits of Religious Society," in *SIS*, 107-17.

562 Whitefield, *Journals*, 202.

563 Ibid., 230.

564 Ibid., 205, 214-15, 420, 422.

565 Whitefield, "The Necessity and Benefits," in *TWRGW*, 5:119; idem, "The Necessity and Benefits," in *SIS*, 116.

566 Whitefield, "Letter DCCLXXXVI," in *TWRGW*, 2:291.

567 Regarding the decision to leave these societies in the hands of John Wesley, Whitefield wrote, "What gives me the greater comfort is the consideration that my dear and honoured friend, Mr. Wesley, is left behind to confirm those who are awakened, so that, when I return from Georgia, I hope to see many bold soldiers of Jesus Christ." Whitefield, *Journals*, 243. The irony of this statement is that Whitefield would soon find that Wesley would preach against the doctrines of unconditional election and particular redemption within these societies that Whitefield entrusted to his friend.

568 In a letter to his brother, Whitefield wrote, "I had given over the immediate care of all my societies to Mr H____; so that now I am a preacher at large indeed." Whitefield, "Letter DCCLXXVIII," in *TWRGW*, 282.

569 Recounting one of his visits to Bristol, Whitefield wrote of preaching to two societies after having preached a sermon earlier that evening. Whitefield, *Journals*, 241. Whitefield

wrote that he preached an afternoon sermon in London and, later that evening, preached to three societies in that city. Ibid., 202. See also Whitefield, *Journals*, 201, 258-60.

570 Ibid., 193-94, 196-97, 200, 260-61, 271-72.

571 Whitefield, "Letter DXXVII," in *TWRGW*, 2:33.

572 Whitefield warned them, "Keeping company with God's people, does not give you a title to the privileges of God's children. It may increase, but not extenuate your condemnation, if you are not found in heart, and truly converted to our dear Lord Jesus Christ. I am persuaded you will not be offended at this plain dealing. God has been pleased to work upon you by my unworthy ministry. I would therefore watch over you for good, and warn you against those snares which await all true followers of the Lamb of God." Whitefield, "Letter CLXXXVIII," in *TWRGW*, 1:178; idem, *Letters*, 178.

573 Whitefield, "A Letter to the Religious Societies of England," in *TWRGW*, 2:26. For more examples of letters written to societies and their members, see Whitefield, "A Letter to the Religious Societies," in *TWRGW*, 2:24, 33; idem, "Letter XLVIII," in *TWRGW*, 1:50-51; idem, *Letters*, 50-51.

574 Whitefield, "Letter CLXXXVI," in *TWRGW*, 1:176; idem, *Letters*, 176.

575 Whitefield, "Letter CCCXCV," in *TWRGW*, 366; idem, *Letters*, 366.

576 Whitefield, "Letter CCCCIV," in *TWRGW*, 1:378; idem, *Letters*, 378.

577 Whitefield, "Letter DCCCCXVI," in *TWRGW*, 2:432.

578 Whitefield, "Letter DCI," in *TWRGW*, 2:108. For more examples of follow-up letters to pastors, see Whitefield, "Letter LXXVIII," in *TWRGW*, 1:74; idem, *Letters*, 74; idem, "Letter MCCCXXXIII," in *TWRGW*, 3:329; idem, "Letter MCCCLX," in *TWRGW*, 3:349-50.

579 Whitefield, "Letter CLXV," in *TWRGW*, 1:152; idem, *Letters*, 152. He also advised a man converted by his preaching in Savannah, Georgia, "Love not the world, neither the things that are in the world. No man can serve two masters." Idem, "Letter CCLIII," in *TWRGW*, 1:239; idem, *Letters*, 239.

580 Whitefield, "Letter DCXCI," in *TWRGW*, 2:188. For more examples of Whitefield's follow up correspondence with

believers, see Whitefield, "Letter DCCV," in *TWRGW*, 2:199; idem, "Letter DCCXLIV," in *TWRGW*, 2:245; idem, "Letter DCCLIII," in *TWRGW*, 2:254; idem, "Letter MXII," in *TWRGW*, 3:51.

581 Whitefield, *Journals*, 156.

582 Whitefield, *Letters*, 155.

583 Whitefield, "Letter DCCCLXXXVII," in *TWRGW*, 2:404-405.

584 Whitefield, "A Letter to the Inhabitants of Maryland, Virginia, North and South Carolina," in *TWRGW*, 4:37.

585 For a more comprehensive discussion of the orphan house and slavery as they relate to George Whitefield's ministry, see Thomas Kidd, *George Whitefield: America's Spiritual Founding Father*. New Haven: Yale University Press, 2014.

Chapter 4

586 In this section, I will reintroduce some quotes from previous chapters to remind readers of Whitefield's actual comments on his theology and methodology. These citations also add clarity to this discussion about the relationship between the itinerant's theology and methodology of evangelism.

587 George Whitefield, "The Seed of the Woman, and the Seed of the Serpent," in *TWRGW* (London: Printed for Edward and Charles Dilly, in the Poultry; and Messrs. Kincaid and Bell, at Edinburgh, 1771-1772) 5:13; idem, "The Seed of the Woman, and the Seed of the Serpent," in *SIS* (London: Henry Fisher, Son, & P. Jackson, 1828), 318.

588 George Whitefield, "Of Justification by Christ," in *TWRGW*, 6:218; idem, "Of Justification by Christ," in *SIS*, 520.

589 Whitefield, "The Resurrection of Lazarus," in *TWRGW*, 6:123-24; idem, "The Resurrection of Lazarus," in *SIS*, 456.

590 Whitefield, "The Potter and the Clay," in *TWRGW*, 5:199; idem, "The Potter and the Clay," in *SIS*, 172.

591 Whitefield, "Christ the Best Husband: Or an Earnest Invitation to Young Women to Come and See Christ," in *TWRGW*, 5:66; idem, "Christ the Best Husband," in *SIS*, 78.

592 Whitefield, "The Lord Our Righteousness," in *TWRGW*, 5:226; idem, "The Lord Our Righteousness," in *SIS*, 191.

593 Whitefield, "The Holy Spirit Convincing the World of Sin, Righteousness, and Judgment," in *TWRGW*, 6:140; idem, "The Holy Spirit Convincing the World of Sin, Righteousness, and Judgment," in *SIS*, 467-68.

594 Whitefield, "A Letter to the Reverend Mr. John Wesley: In Answer to his Sermon, Entituled, Free-Grace," in *TWRGW*, 4:71.

595 Whitefield, "The Beloved of God," in *SIS*, 680.

596 Whitefield, "The Righteousness of Christ," in *TWRGW*, 5:243; idem, "The Righteousness of Christ," in *SIS*, 203; Idem, "The Indwelling of the Spirit," in *TWRGW*, 6:92; idem, "The Indwelling of the Spirit," in *SIS*, 433.

597 Whitefield, "The Conversion of Zaccheus," in *TWRGW*, 6:62; idem, "The Conversion of Zaccheus," in *SIS*, 411.

598 Whitefield, "The Folly and Danger of Not Being Righteous Enough," in *TWRGW*, 5:139; idem, "The Folly and Danger of Not Being Righteous Enough," in *SIS*, 130; idem, "Christ the Only Preservative Against a Reprobate Spirit," in *TWRGW*, 6:290; idem, "Christ the Only Preservative Against a Reprobate Spirit," in *SIS*, 563; idem, "The Conversion of Zaccheus," in *TWRGW*, 6:59; idem, "The Conversion of Zaccheus," in *SIS*, 409.

599 Whitefield, "Christ the Only Preservative," in *TWRGW*, 6:294; idem, "Christ the Only Preservative," in *SIS*, 566.

600 Whitefield, "Christ the Believer's Wisdom, Righteousness, Sanctification, and Redemption," in *TWRGW*, 6:190; idem, "Christ the Believer's Wisdom, Righteousness, Sanctification, and Redemption," in *SIS*, 502; idem, "Christ the Best Husband," in *TWRGW*, 5:70; idem, "Christ the Best Husband," in SIS, 81; idem, "The Conversion of Zaccheus," in *TWRGW*, 6:54; idem, "The Conversion of Zaccheus," in *SIS*, 405.

601 Whitefield, "What Think Ye of Christ?," in *TWRGW*, 5:366; idem, "What Think Ye of Christ?," in *SIS*, 290; idem, "The Gospel Supper," in *TWRGW*, 6:31; idem, "The Gospel Supper," in *SIS*, 388

602 Whitefield, "Seed of the Woman," in *TWRGW*, 5:11; idem, "The Seed of the Woman," in *SIS*, 38.

603 Whitefield, "The Good Shepherd," in *SIS*, 788.

604 Whitefield, "Christ the Best Husband," in *TWRGW*, 5:71-72; idem, "Christ the Best Husband," in *SIS*, 82.

605 Whitefield, "The Righteousness of Christ, an Everlasting Righteousness," in *TWRGW*, 5:245; idem, "The Righteousness of Christ, an Everlasting Righteousness," in *SIS*, 205; idem, "The Seed of the Woman," in *TWRGW*, 1:19; idem, "The Seed of the Woman," in *SIS*, 44; idem, "Christ the Believer's Husband," in *TWRGW*, 1:190; idem, "Christ the Believer's Husband," in *SIS*, 166; idem, "The Folly and Danger," in *TWRGW*, 5:332; idem, "The Folly and Danger," in *SIS*, 265.

606 Whitefield, "A Letter to the Reverend the President, and Professors, Tutors, and Hebrew Instructor, of Harvard-College in Cambridge; in Answer to A Testimony Published by Them Against the Reverend Mr. George Whitefield, and His Conduct," in *TWRGW*, 4:218; idem, "Blind Bartimeus," in TWRGW, 5:411; idem, "Blind Bartimeus," in *SIS*, 322; idem, "The Gospel Supper," in *SIS*, 387.

607 Whitefield, "Letter CLXIX," in *TWRGW*, 1:156; idem, "Letter CLXIX," in *Letters*, 156.

608 Whitefield, "Christ the Only Preservative," in *TWRGW*, 6:295, 298-99; idem, "The Lord Our Righteousness," in *TWRGW*, 5:234; idem, "The Lord Our Righteousness," in *SIS*, 197.

609 Whitefield, "Christ the Only Preservative," in *TWRGW*, 6:298-99; idem, "Christ the Only Preservative," in *SIS*, 569. For more examples of Whitefield's universal invitations, see Whitefield, "Christ the Best Husband," in *TWRGW*, 5:70; idem, "Christ the Best Husband," in *SIS*, 81; idem, "What Think Ye of Christ?," in *TWRGW*, 5:371; idem, "What Think Ye of Christ?," in *SIS*, 293.

610 Whitefield, "The Marriage of Cana," in *TWRGW*, 6:75; idem, "The Marriage of Cana," in *SIS*, 420. See also Whitefield, "Christ the Best Husband," in *TWRGW*, 5:68, 74; idem, "Christ the Best Husband," in *SIS*, 79, 84.

611 Whitefield, "Self-Inquiry Concerning the Work of God," in *SIS*, 707; idem, "The Lord Our Righteousness," in *TWRGW*, 5:229; idem, "The Lord Our Righteousness," in *SIS*, 193; idem, "Marks of a True Conversion," in *TWRGW*, 5:346; idem, "Marks of a True Conversion," in *SIS*, 275; idem,

"The Potter and the Clay," in *TWRGW*, 5:213; idem, "The Potter and the Clay," in *SIS*, 182.

612 Whitefield, "A Penitent Heart, the Best New Year's Gift," in *TWRGW*, 6:6-8, 16; idem, "A Penitent Heart, the Best New Year's Gift," in *SIS*, 370-71, 378; idem, "Marks of a True Conversion," in *TWRGW*, 5:352; idem, "Marks of a True Conversion," in *SIS*, 280; Walking with God," in *TWRGW*, 5:35; idem, "Walking with God," in *SIS*, 56; idem, "Neglect of Christ the Killing Sin," in *SIS*, 745; idem, "The Potter and the Clay," in *TWRGW*, 5:214; idem, "The Potter and the Clay," in *SIS*, 637.

613 Whitefield, "The Folly and Danger," in *TWRGW*, 5:137; idem, "The Folly and Danger," in *SIS*, 128-29. See also Whitefield, "Christ the Only Preservative," in *TWRGW*, 6:294; idem, "The Folly and Danger," in *SIS*, 566; idem, "The Lord Our Light," in *SIS*, 704.

614 Whitefield, "The Extent and Reasonableness of Self-Denial," in *TWRGW*, 5:432; idem, "The Extent and Reasonableness of Self-Denial," in *SIS*, 337; idem, "The Pharisee and the Publican," in *TWRGW*, 6:46; idem, "The Pharisee and the Publican," in *SIS*, 399; idem, "Of Justification," in *TWRGW* 6:221; idem, "Of Justification," in *SIS*, 522.

615 Whitefield, "The Lord Our Righteousness," in *TWRGW*, 5:229; idem, "The Lord Our Righteousness," in *SIS*, 193; idem, "The Holy Spirit Convincing," in *TWRGW*, 6:132; idem, "The Holy Spirit Convincing," in *SIS*, 461.

616 Whitefield, "Christ the Only Rest," in *TWRGW*, 5:316; idem, "Christ the Only Rest," in *SIS*, 254. For more of Whitefield's instructions to forsake one's own attempts at righteousness and rely fully upon the righteousness of Christ, see Whitefield, "Christ the Best Husband," in *TWRGW*, 5:76; idem, "Christ the Best Husband," in *SIS*, 86; idem, "The Folly and Danger," in *TWRGW*, 5:325; idem, "The Folly and Danger," in *SIS*, 260; idem, "Christ the Support of the Tempted," in *TWRGW*, 5:296; idem, "Christ the Support of the Tempted," in *SIS*, 241.

617 Whitefield, "Spiritual Baptism," in *SIS*, 738; Christians, Temples of the Living God," in *TWRGW*, 6:284-85; idem, "Christians, Temples of the Living God," in *SIS*, 560-61; idem, "On Regeneration," in *TWRGW*, 6:266-67; Idem, "On Regeneration," in *SIS*, 549.

618 Whitefield, "Marks of a True Conversion," in *TWRGW*, 5:346; idem, "Marks of a True Conversion," in *SIS*, 275. For more examples of questions Whitefield asked pertaining to the new birth, see Whitefield, "Abraham's Offering," in *TWRGW*, 5:50; idem, "Abraham's Offering," in *SIS*, 67; idem, "On Regeneration," in *TWRGW*, 6:269; idem, "On Regeneration," in *SIS*, 551.

619 In addition to these questions regarding the new birth, one could also point to the numerous sermons the itinerant preached on the subject as evidence of the influence of this doctrine upon his methodology of evangelism. His sermons focused specifically upon the doctrine are: Whitefield, "The Resurrection of Lazarus," in *TWRGW*, 6:103-26; idem, "The Resurrection of Lazarus," in *SIS*, 440-57; idem, "On Regeneration," in *TWRGW*, 257-72; idem, "On Regeneration," in *SIS*, 543-51; idem, "Self- Inquiry Concerning the Work of God," in *SIS*, 704-12; idem, "Spiritual Baptism," in *SIS*, 730-38.

620 Remember that Whitefield preached the sermon "The Eternity of Hell-Torments," in which he expressed this doctrinal stance regarding hell. George Whitefield, "The Eternity of Hell-Torments," in *Sermons on Important Subjects* (London: Henry Fisher, Son, & P. Jackson, 1828), 308-16.

621 Whitefield, "Christ the Believer's Husband," in *TWRGW*, 5:192; idem, "Christ the Believer's Husband," in *SIS*, 252; idem, "The Care of the Soul Urged as the One Thing Needful," in *TWRGW*, 5:470- 71; idem, "The Care of the Soul Urged as the One Thing Needful," in *SIS*, 365.

622 Whitefield, "A Penitent Heart," in *TWRGW*, 6:3; idem, "A Penitent Heart," in *SIS*, 368; idem, "Christ's Transfiguration," in *TWRGW*, 5:455; idem, "Christ's Transfiguration," in *SIS*, 353.

623 Whitefield, "The Gospel a Dying Saint's Triumph," in *SIS*, 660; idem, "God a Believer's Glory," in *SIS*, 767; idem, "The Good Shepherd," in *SIS*, 790.

624 Whitefield, "What Think Ye of Christ?," in *TWRGW*, 5:367; idem, "What Think Ye of Christ?," in *SIS*, 291; Idem, "Marks of a True Conversion," in *TWRGW*, 5:351; idem, "Marks of a True Conversion," in *SIS*, 279.

625 Whitefield, "Jacob's Ladder," in *SIS*, 774.

626 Whitefield, *Journals*, 60, 62.

627 Ibid., 143.

628 The itinerant implored his mother to flee to Christ "by faith." Whitefield, "Letter CXXIX," in *TWRGW*, 1:122; idem, *Letters*, 122. To the owner of the coach, Whitefield wrote that he prayed she would possess a faith "that changes and renews the whole soul, takes it entirely off the world and fixes it wholly upon God." Whitefield, "Letter XCI," in *TWRGW*, 1:87; idem, *Letters*, 87.

629 Whitefield, "Letter LXVI," in *TWRGW*, 1:64; idem, Letters, 64; idem, "Letter DCXXXV," in *TWRGW*, 2:139.

630 Whitefield, "Letter DCCCCXXVI," in *TWRGW*, 2:440. For another example of the itinerant's treatment of the new birth in his evangelistic letters, see Whitefield, "Letter CIX," in *TWRGW*, 1:104; idem, *Letters*, 104.

631 Whitefield, *Journals*, 85.

632 Ibid., 455.

633 Whitefield, "The Gospel a Dying Saint's Triumph," in *SIS*, 652-53; idem, "A Letter to the Religious Societies of England," in *TWRGW*, 4:26.

634 Whitefield, "The Lord Our Righteousness," in *TWRGW*, 5:221; idem, "The Lord Our Righteousness," in *SIS*, 187-88.

635 Whitefield, *Journals*, 179, 242.

636 As mentioned in the chapter addressing Whitefield's theology of evangelism, the itinerant held that progressive sanctification is a synergistic process in which the Holy Spirit works within the heart of the believer, motivating and empowering him to perform acts of obedience that are conducive to his spiritual growth. Whitefield encouraged new believers to pray that God would "grant I may from henceforward work out my salvation with fear and trembling, since thou hast so graciously wrought in me to will and to do, after they good pleasure." Whitefield, "A Prayer for One Newly Awakened With a Sense of Divine Life," in *TWRGW*, 4:450. He intended the religious societies to serve as a catalyst for this process of spiritual growth.

637 Ibid., 230; Whitefield, "The Necessity and Benefits of Religious Society," in *TWRGW*, 5:119; idem, "The Necessity and Benefit of Religious Society," in *SIS*, 107-17.

638 Whitefield, "Letter DCCLXXXVI," in *TWRGW*, 2:291.

639 Whitefield understood that the Great Commission called him to preach the gospel to every person. One might ask

whether, by leaving the societies in the care of other ministers, the itinerant allowed this aspect of the Great Commission to overshadow the Commission's mandate to disciple or teach. Although he left the societies in the care of others, one must not forget that Whitefield wrote letters to society members and leaders and frequently preached to societies as he traveled. These practices were a means of teaching and discipling the members of these religious groups.

640 Whitefield, "Letter CLXXXVI," in *TWRGW*, 1:176; Idem, *Letters*, 176.

641 Ibid.

642 Whitefield, "Soul Prosperity," in *SIS*, 646.

643 Whitefield, "Letter CLXV," in *TWRGW*, 1:152; idem, Letters, 152; idem, "Letter DCXCI," in *TWRGW*, 2:188.

644 Whitefield, "Letter DCCCCXVI," in *TWRGW*, 2:432; idem, "Letter DCI," in *TWRGW*, 2:108

645 Dean R. Hoge, Benton Johnson, and Donald A. Luidens, *Vanishing Boundaries* (Louisville: Westminster/John Knox Press, 1994), 200, 201, 204, 205, 208.

646 Thom Rainer, *Effective Evangelistic Churches* (Nashville: Broadman & Holman Publishers, 1996), 56-57.

647 Ed Stetzer, "Why We Should Be Inviting Our Non-Christian Friends and Neighbors to Church at Easter," *Christianity Today*. http://www.christianitytoday.com/ edstetzer/2017/april/why-we-should-be-inviting-our-non-christian-friends-and-nei.html (accessed September 4, 2017).

648 Whitefield, "Letter CLXIX," in *TWRGW*, 1:156; idem, *Letters*, 156.

649 Whitefield, "Letter DCCXLVII," in *TWRGW*, 2:248.

BIBLIOGRAPHY

Primary Works

Books

Berkeley, George. *Alciphron*. London: Printed for J. Tonson, 1732.

Brine, John. *The Certain Efficacy of the Death of Christ*. London: Aaron Ward, 1743. Burnet, Gilbert. *Discourse of the Pastoral Care*. Lampeter, UK: The Edwin Mellen Press, 1997.

Bushman, Richard. *The Great Awakening: Documents on the Revival of Religion, 1740- 1745*. Chapel Hill: The University of North Carolina Press, 1969.

Butler, Joseph. *The Analogy of Religion to the Constitution and Course of Nature*. Philadelphia: J. B. Lippincott & Co., 1857.

Chauncy, Charles. *Seasonable Thoughts on the State of Religion in New England*. Hicksville, NY: The Regina Press, 1975.

Church of England, *The Thirty-Nine Articles of Religion, 1571*. In Christian Classics Etheral Library [on-line]. Accessed 6 July 2003. Available from http://www.ccel.org/c/cofe/39articles/39articles.lit; Internet.

Clarkson, David. *The Works of David Clarkson.* Vol. 1. Edinburgh: The Banner of Truth Trust, 1988.

Edwards, Jonathan. *The Works of Jonathan Edwards.* 2 vols. Edinburgh: The Banner of Truth Trust, 1995.

Flavel, John. *The Works of John Flavel.* Vol. 6. Edinburgh: The Banner of Truth Trust, 1968.

Franklin, Benjamin. *The Life of Benjamin Franklin.* Auburn and Buffalo, NY: Miller, Orton, & Mulligan, 1854.

Fuller, Andrew. *The Complete Works of the Rev. Andrew Fuller: With a Memoir of His Life, By Andrew Gunton Fuller.* 3 vols. Edited by Joseph Belcher. Harrisonburg, VA: Sprinkle Publications, 1988.

_____. *The Last Remains of the Rev. Andrew Fuller: Sermons, Essays, Letters, and Other Miscellaneous Papers, Not Included in His Published Works.* Philadelphia: American Baptist Publication Society, 1856.

_____. *The Work of Faith, the Labour of Love, and the Patience of Hope, Illustrated; in the Life and Death of the Rev. Andrew Fuller, Late Pastor of the Baptist Church of Kettering, and Secretary of the Baptist Missionary Society, From Its Commencement, In 1792.* Edited by John Ryland. Charlestown, UK: Samuel Etheridge, 1818.

Gillies, John. *Historical Collections Relating to Remarkable Periods of the Success of the Gospel Compiled by the Rev. John Gillies, D. D. Published Originally in 1754, and Now Reprinted With a Preface and Continuation to the Present Time by The Rev. Horatius Bonar, Kelso.* Kelso: John Rutherford, Market Place,

1845; reprinted as *Historical Collections of Accounts of Revival*, Fairfield: The Banner of Truth Trust, 1981.

_____. *Memoirs of Rev. George Whitefield*. New Haven: Whitmore & Buckingham and H. Mansfield, 1834.

Hartley, David. *Observations on Man, His Frame, His Duty, and His Expectations*. Bath: James Leake and Wm. Frederick, 1749; reprint, Gainesville: Scholar's Facsimiles & Reprints, 1966.

Heimert, Alan, and Perry Miller, eds. *The Great Awakening: Documents Illustrating the Crisis and Its Consequences*. Indianapolis: The Bobbs-Merrill Compancy, Inc., 1967.

Holyoke, Edward, *The Duty of Ministers of the Gospel to Guard Against the Pharisaism and Sudducism, of the Present Day. Shewed in a Sermon Preach'd to the Convention of Ministers in the Provence of the Massacusetts-Bay, N. E. at Boston, On Thursday, May 28, 1741*. Boston: T. Fleet, 1741.

Hussey, John. *God's Operations of Grace but No Offers of Grace*. Elon, NC: Primitive Publications, 1973.

Law, William. *The Case of Reason*. London: W. Innys, 1731.

Locke, John. *An Essay Concerning Human Understanding and a Treatise on the Conduct of the Understanding*. Philadelphia: Troutman & Hayes, 1852.

_____. *The Reasonableness of Christianity as Delivered in the Scriptures*. Bristol, UK: Thoemmes Press, 1997.

Schaff, Philip, ed. *A History of the Creeds of Christendom.* 3 vols. Grand Rapids: Baker Books, 1998.

Stiles, Ezra. *A Discourse on the Christian Union.* Boston: Edes and Gill, 1761. Tindal, Matthew. *Christianity as Old as the Creation.* London: n.p., 1730.

Wakeley, J. B. *Anecdotes of the Rev. George Whitefield.* London: Hodder and Stoughton, 1879.

Wesley, John. *A Sermon on the Death of the Rev. Mr. George Whitefield. Preached at the Chapel in Tottenham-Court-Road, and at the Tabernacle Near Moorfields, on Sunday, November 18, 1770.* London: J. and W. Oliver, 1770; reprint, Atlanta: The Library of Emory University, 1953.

Whitefield, George. *Doctrines of the Gospel Asserted and Indicated in Eighteen Genuine Sermons.* London: C. Davis, 1739.

_____. *Eighteen Sermons, Preached By the Late Rev. George Whitefield , A. M.* Lexington, KY: Thomas T. Skillman, 1825.

_____. *George Whitefield's Journals.* London: The Banner of Truth Trust, 1960.

_____. *George Whitefield's Letters.* Carlisle, PA: The Banner of Truth Trust, 1976.

_____. *A Letter From the Rev. Mr. George Whitefield From Georgia to a Friend in London, Shewing the Fundamental Error of a Book Entitled, "The Whole Duty of Man."* Philadelphia: B. Franklin, 1740.

_____. *A Letter to the Reverend Dr. Chauncy, On Account of Some Passages Relating to the Rev. Mr. Whitefield, In His Book Intitled Seasonable Thoughts on the State of Religion in New England.* Boston: S. Kneeland and T. Green, 1745.

_____. *A Letter to the Rev. President, and Professors, Tutors, and Hebrew Instructor, or Harvard-College in Cambridge; In Answer to A Testimony Publish'd by Them Against the Reverend Mr. George Whitefield, And His Conduct.* Boston: S. Kneeland and T. Green, 1745.

_____. *Select Sermons of George Whitefield.* Edited by J. C. Ryle. Carlisle, PA: The Banner of Truth Trust, 1997.

_____. *Sermons on Important Subjects.* London: Henry Fisher, Son, & P. Jackson, 1828.

_____. *The Works of George Whitefield* [CD-ROM]. Shropshire, UK: Quinta Press, 2000.

_____. *The Works of the Reverend George Whitefield, M. A. Late of Pembroke- College, Oxford, And Chaplain to the Rt. Hon. The Countess of Huntingdon. Containing All His Sermons and Tracts Which Have Been Already Published: With A Select Collection of Letters, Written to His Most Intimate Friends, and Persons of Distinction, in England, Scotland, Ireland, and America, from the Year 1734, to 1770, Including the Whole Period of His Ministry. Also, Some Other Pieces on Important Subjects, Never Before Printed; Prepared By Himself for the Press. To Which is Prefixed, An Account of His Life, Compiled From His Original Papers and Letters.* 6 vols. London: Printed for Edward and Charles Dilly, in the Poultry; and Messrs. Kincaid and Bell, at Edinburgh, 1771-1772.

Wigglesworth, Edward. *Dr. Wigglesworth's Two Discourses on the Ordinary and Extraordinary Ministers of the Church of Christ.* Boston: Thomas Fleet, 1754.

_____. *A Letter to the Reverend Mr. George Whitefield, by Way of Reply to His Answer to the College Testimony Against Him and His Conduct.* Boston: T. Fleet, 1745.

Woolston, Thomas. *A Discourse on the Miracles of Our Saviour, in View of the Present Controversy Between Infidels and Apostates.* London: n.p., 1729; reprint, London: Garland Publishing, 1979.

_____. *A Sixth Discourse on the Miracles of our Saviour, in View of the Present Controversy Between Infidels and Apostates.* London: n.p., 1729; reprint, London: Garland Publishing, 1979.

Articles

Drew, Samuel. "Memoir of the Rev. George Whitefield." In *Sermons on Important Subjects*, iii-x. London: Henry Fisher, Son, & P. Jackson, 1828.

Gill, John. "Answer to the Birmingham Dialogue-Writer, Part II." In *A Collection of Sermons and Tracts: In Two Volumes.* London: George Keith, 1773.

Smith, Joseph. "The Character, Preaching, &c. of the Rev. George Whitefield." In *Sermons on Important Subjects*, 791-99. London: Henry Fisher, Son, & P. Jackson, 1828.

Tillotson, John. "Sermon LVI." In *The Works of the Most Reverend Dr. John Tillotson, Lord Archbishop of Canterbury*. London: T. Birch, 1820.

Wesley, John. "Free Grace." In *The SAGE Digital Library* [CD ROM], 415-28. Albany, OR: Ages Software, 1996.

Whitefield, George. "Abraham's Offering Up His Son." In *Sermons on Important Subjects*, 58-67. London: Henry Fisher, Son, & P. Jackson, 1828.

_____. "All Men's Place." In *Sermons on Important Subjects*, 749-58. London: Henry Fisher, Son, & P. Jackson, 1828.

____. "The Almost Christian." In *Sermons on Important Subjects*, 491-99. London: Henry Fisher, Son, & P. Jackson, 1828.

_____. "An Abstract of a Letter from the Rev. Mr. Whitefield." *The Weekly History* 4 (1741): 1-4.

_____. "Answer to the Bishop of London's Last Pastoral Letter." In *The Works of the Reverend George Whitefield*, 4:4-19. London: Printed for Edward and Charles Dilly, in the Poultry; and Messrs. Kincaid and Creech, at Edinburgh, 1771.

_____. "An Answer to the First Part of an Anonymous Pamphlet, Entitled, 'Observations Upon the Conduct and Behaviour of a Certain Sect Distinguished by the Name of Methodists.' In a Letter to the Right Reverend the Bishop of London, and the Other Right Reverend the Bishops Concerned in the Publication Thereof." In *The Works of the Rev. George Whitefield*, 4:124-40. London: Printed for Edward and Charles Dilly, in the Poultry; and Messrs. Kincaid and Creech, at Edinburgh, 1771.

_____. "An Answer to the Second Part of an Anonymous Pamphlet, Entitled, "Observations Upon the Conduct and Behaviour of a Certain Sect, Usually Distinguished by the Name of Methodists." In a Second Letter to the Right Reverend the Bishop of London, and the Other Right Reverend the Bishops Concerned in the Publication Thereof." In *The Works of the Rev. George Whitefield*, 4:142-69. London: Printed for Edward and Charles Dilly, in the Poultry; and Messrs. Kincaid and Creech, at Edinburgh, 1771.

____. "The Beloved of God." In *Sermons on Important Subjects*, 678-86. London: Henry Fisher, Son, & P. Jackson, 1828.

____. "The Benefits of an Early Piety." In *Sermons on Important Subjects*, 143-50. London: Henry Fisher, Son, & P. Jackson, 1828.

_____. "Blind Bartimeus." In *Sermons on Important Subjects*, 317-26. London: Henry Fisher, Son, & P. Jackson, 1828.

_____. "A Brief Account of the Occasion, Process, and Issue, of a Late Trial at the Assize Held at Gloucester, March 3, 1743 Between Some of the People Called Methodists, Plantiffs, and Certain Persons of the Town of Minchin-Hampton, in the Said County, Defendants. In a Letter to a Friend." In *The Works of the Rev. George Whitefield*, 4:100-09. London: Printed for Edward and Charles Dilly, in the Poultry; and Messrs. Kincaid and Creech, at Edinburgh, 1771.

_____. "Britain's Mercies, and Britain's Duty." In *Sermons on Important Subjects*, 87-97. London: Henry Fisher, Son, & P. Jackson, 1828.

_____. "The Burning Bush." In *Sermons on Important Subjects*, 713-21. London: Henry Fisher, Son, & P. Jackson, 1828.

_____. "The Care of the Soul Urged as the One Thing Needful." In *Sermons on Important Subjects*, 354-67. London: Henry Fisher, Son, & P. Jackson, 1828.

_____. "A Caution Against Despising the Day of Small Things." In *Sermons on Important Subjects*, 607-19. London: Henry Fisher, Son, & P. Jackson, 1828.

____. "Christ the Believer's Husband." In *Sermons on Important Subjects*, 151-69. London: Henry Fisher, Son, & P. Jackson, 1828.

____. "Christ the Believer's Refuge." In *Sermons on Important Subjects*, 629-39. London: Henry Fisher, Son, & P. Jackson, 1828.

_____. "Christ the Believer's Wisdom, Righteousness, Sanctification, and Redemption." In *Sermons on Important Subjects*, 500-10. London: Henry Fisher, Son, & P. Jackson, 1828.

_____. "Christ the Best Husband: Or, An Earnest Invitation to Young Women to Come and See Christ." In *Sermons on Important Subjects*, 77-86. London: Henry Fisher, Son, & P. Jackson, 1828.

_____. "Christ the Only Preservative Against a Reprobate Spirit." In *Sermons on Important Subjects*, 561-69. London: Henry Fisher, Son, & P. Jackson, 1828.

_____. "Christ the Only Rest for the Weary and Heavy Laden." In *Sermons on Important Subjects*, 248-55. London: Henry Fisher, Son, & P. Jackson, 1828.

_____. "Christ the Support of the Tempted." In *Sermons on Important Subjects*, 234-41. London: Henry Fisher, Son, & P. Jackson, 1828.

_____. "Christians, Temples of the Living God." In *Sermons on Important Subjects*, 552-60. London: Henry Fisher, Son, & P. Jackson, 1828.

____. "Christ's Transfiguration." In *Sermons on Important Subjects*, 342-53. London: Henry Fisher, Son, & P. Jackson, 1828.

____. "The Conversion of Zaccheus." In *Sermons on Important Subjects*, 401-11. London: Henry Fisher, Son, & P. Jackson, 1828.

_____. "Directions on How to Hear Sermons." In *Sermons on Important Subjects*, 327-32. London: Henry Fisher, Son, & P. Jackson, 1828.

_____. "The Duty of Searching the Scriptures." In *Sermons on Important Subjects*, 423-29. London: Henry Fisher, Son, & P. Jackson, 1828.

____. "The Eternity of Hell-Torments." In *Sermons on Important Subjects*, 308-16. London: Henry Fisher, Son, & P. Jackson, 1828.

_____. "An Exhortation to the People of God Not to be Discouraged in Their Way, by the Scoffs and Contempt of Wicked Men." In *Sermons on Important Subjects*, 603-06. London: Henry Fisher, Son, & P. Jackson, 1828.

_____. "An Expostulatory Letter, Addressed to Nicholas Lewis, Count Zinzendorff, and Lord Advocate of the Unitas Fratum." In *The Works of the Rev. George Whitefield*, 4:252-61. London: Printed for Edward and Charles Dilly, in the Poultry; and Messrs. Kincaid and Creech, at Edinburgh, 1771.

_____. "The Extent and Reasonableness of Self-Denial." In *Sermons on Important Subjects*, 333-41. London: Henry Fisher, Son, & P. Jackson, 1828.

_____. "A Faithful Minister's Parting Blessing." In *Sermons on Important Subjects*, 620-28. London: Henry Fisher, Son, & P. Jackson, 1828.

_____. "The Folly and Danger of Not Being Righteous Enough." In *Sermons on Important Subjects*, 118-30. London: Henry Fisher, Son, & P. Jackson, 1828.

_____. "The Folly and Danger of Parting With Christ for the Pleasures and Profits of Life." In *Sermons on Important Subjects*, 256-67. London: Henry Fisher, Son, & P. Jackson, 1828.

____. "The Furnace of Affliction." In *Sermons on Important Subjects*, 687-44. London: Henry Fisher, Son, & P. Jackson, 1828.

_____. "Glorifying God in the Fire; or, the Right Improvement of Affliction." In *Sermons on Important Subjects*, 670-77. London: Henry Fisher, Son, & P. Jackson, 1828.

____. "God, a Believer's Glory." In *Sermons on Important Subjects*, 759-68. London: Henry Fisher, Son, & P. Jackson, 1828.

____. "The Good Shepherd." In *Sermons on Important Subjects*, 780-90. London: Henry Fisher, Son, & P. Jackson, 1828.

_____. "The Gospel, a Dying Saint's Triumph." In *Sermons on Important Subjects*, 649-59. London: Henry Fisher, Son, & P. Jackson, 1828.

_____. "The Gospel Supper." In *Sermons on Important Subjects*, 380-90. London: Henry Fisher, Son, & P. Jackson, 1828.

_____. "The Great Duty of Charity Recommended." In *Sermons on Important Subjects*, 526-33. London: Henry Fisher, Son, & P. Jackson, 1828.

_____. "The Great Duty of Family-Religion." In *Sermons on Important Subjects*, 68-76. London: Henry Fisher, Son, & P. Jackson, 1828.

_____. "The Heinous Sin of Drunkenness." In *Sermons on Important Subjects*, 570-77. London: Henry Fisher, Son, & P. Jackson, 1828.

_____. "The Heinous Sin of Profane Cursing and Swearing." In *Sermons on Important Subjects*, 226-33. London: Henry Fisher, Son, & P. Jackson, 1828.

_____. "The Holy Spirit Convincing the World of Sin, Righteousness, and Judgment." In *Sermons on Important Subjects*, 458-68. London: Henry Fisher, Son, & P. Jackson, 1828.

_____. "The Indwelling of the Spirit, the Common Privilege of All Believers." In *Sermons on Important Subjects*, 430-39. London: Henry Fisher, Son, & P. Jackson, 1828.

_____. "Intercession Every Christian's Duty." In *Sermons on Important Subjects*, 585-92. London: Henry Fisher, Son, & P. Jackson, 1828.

_____. "Jacob's Ladder." In *Sermons on Important Subjects*, 769-79. London: Henry Fisher, Son, & P. Jackson, 1828.

_____. "The Knowledge of Jesus Christ, the Best Knowledge." In *Sermons on Important Subjects*, 511-17. London: Henry Fisher, Son, & P. Jackson, 1828.

_____. "*Law* Gospelized; or an Address to All Christians Concerning Holiness of Heart and Life: Being an Attempt to Render Mr. Law's *Serious Call* More Useful to the Children of God, by Excluding Whatever is Not Truly Evangelical, and Illustrating the Subject More Fully From the Holy Scriptures." In *The Works of the Rev. George Whitefield*, 4:376-37. London: Printed for Edward and Charles Dilly, in the Poultry; and Messrs. Kincaid and Creech, at Edinburgh, 1771.

_____. "A Letter to the Inhabitants of Maryland, Virginia, North and South- Carolina." In *The Works of the Rev. George Whitefield*, 4:36-41. London: Printed for Edward and Charles Dilly, in the Poultry; and Messrs. Kincaid and Bell, at Edinburgh, 1771.

_____. "A Letter to the Religious Societies of England." In *The Works of the Rev. George Whitefield*, 4:22-34. London: Printed for Edward and Charles Dilly, in the Poultry; and Messrs. Kincaid and Bell, at Edinburgh, 1771.

_____. "A Letter to the Reverend Dr. Durell, Vice-Chancellor of the University of Oxford. Occasioned by a Late Expulsion of Six Students From Edmund-Hall."

In *the Works of the Rev. George Whitefield*, 4:310-41. London: Printed for Edward and Charles Dilly, in the Poultry; and Messrs. Kincaid and Creech, at Edinburgh, 1771.

_____. "A Letter to the Reverend Mr. John Wesley: in Answer to His Sermon, Entituled, *Free-Grace*." In *The Works of the Rev. George Whitefield*, 4:52-73. London: Printed for Edward and Charles Dilly, in the Poultry; and Messrs. Kincaid and Bell, at Edinburgh, 1771.

_____. "A Letter to the Rev. Thomas Church, M.A. Vicar of Battersea, and Prebendary of St. Paul's, in Answer to His Serious and Expostulatory Letter to the Rev. George Whitefield, On Occasion of His Late Letter to the Bishop of London, and Other Bishops." In *The Works of the Rev. George Whitefield*, 4:112-22. London: Printed for Edward and Charles Dilly, in the Poultry; and Messrs. Kincaid and Bell, at Edinburgh, 1771.

_____. "A Letter to Some Church-Members of the Presbyterian Persuasion, in Answer to Certain Scruples Lately Proposed, in Proper Queries Raised on Each Remark." In *The Works of the Rev. George Whitefield*, 4:44-49. London: Printed for Edward and Charles Dilly, in the Poultry; and Messrs. Kincaid and Bell, at Edinburgh, 1771.

_____. "Letters." In *The Works of the Rev. George Whitefield*, vols. 1-3. London: Printed for Edward and Charles Dilly, in the Poultry; and Messrs. Kincaid and Bell, at Edinburgh, 1771.

____. "The Lord Our Light." In *Sermons on Important Subjects*, 695-703. London: Henry Fisher, Son, & P. Jackson, 1828.

____. "The Lord Our Righteousness." In *Sermons on Important Subjects*, 184-96. London: Henry Fisher, Son, & P. Jackson, 1828.

____. "Marks of a True Conversion." In *Sermons on Important Subjects*, 268-79. London: Henry Fisher, Son, & P. Jackson, 1828.

_____. "Marks of Having Received the Holy Ghost." In *Sermons on Important Subjects*, 482-90. London: Henry Fisher, Son, & P. Jackson, 1828.

____. "The Marriage of Cana." In *Sermons on Important Subjects*, 412-22. London: Henry Fisher, Son, & P. Jackson, 1828.

_____. "The Method of Grace. A Sermon on Jeremiah 6:14; Thunder in the Pulpit." *Fundamentalist* 4, no. 10 (November 1985): 48-49.

_____. "The Necessity and Benefits of Religious Society." In *Sermons on Important Subjects*, 107-17. London: Henry Fisher, Son, & P. Jackson, 1828.

_____. "Neglect of Christ, the Killing Sin." In *Sermons on Important Subjects*, 739-48. London: Henry Fisher, Son, & P. Jackson, 1828.

_____. "The Observation of the Birth of Christ, the Duty of All Christians; or the True Way of Keeping Christmas." In *Sermons on Important Subjects*, 208-15. London: Henry Fisher, Son, & P. Jackson, 1828.

_____. "Observations on Select Passages of Scripture. Turned Into Catechetical Questions." In *The Works of the Rev. George Whitefield*, 4:344-73. London: Printed for Edward and Charles Dilly, in the Poultry; and Messrs. Kincaid and Creech, at Edinburgh, 1771.

_____. "Observations on Some Fatal Mistakes, in a Book Lately Published, and Intitled, 'The Doctrine of Grace, or, The Office and Operations of the Holy Spirit Vindicated From the Insults of Infidelity, and the Abuses of Fanaticism. By William Lord Bishop of Gloucester.' In a Letter to a Friend." In *The Works of the Rev. George Whitefield*, 4:284-302. London: Printed for Edward and Charles Dilly, in the Poultry; and Messrs. Kincaid and Creech, at Edinburgh, 1771.

_____. "Of Justification By Christ." In *Sermons on Important Subjects*, 518-25. London: Henry Fisher, Son, & P. Jackson, 1828.

_____. "On Regeneration." In *Sermons on Important Subjects*, 543-51. London: Henry Fisher, Son, & P. Jackson, 1828.

_____. "A Penitent Heart, The Best New Year's Gift." In *Sermons on Important Subjects*, 368-79. London: Henry Fisher, Son, & P. Jackson, 1828.

_____. "Persecution Every Christian's Lot." In *Sermons on Important Subjects*, 593-603. London: Henry Fisher, Son, & P. Jackson, 1828.

_____. "The Pharisee and Publican." In *Sermons on Important Subjects*, 391-400. London: Henry Fisher, Son, & P. Jackson, 1828.

____. "The Potter and the Clay." In *Sermons on Important Subjects*, 170-83. London: Henry Fisher, Son, & P. Jackson, 1828.

_____. "The Power of Christ's Resurrection." In *Sermons on Important Subjects*, 578-84. London: Henry Fisher, Son, & P. Jackson, 1828.

_____. "Prayers on Several Occasions." In *The Works of the Rev. George Whitefield*, 4:456-90. London: Printed for Edward and Charles Dilly, in the Poultry; and Messrs. Kincaid and Creech, at Edinburgh, 1771.

_____. "Preached Before the Governor and Council, and the House of Assembly, in Georgia, on January 28, 1770." In *The Works of the Rev. George Whitefield*, 6:369-87. London: Printed for Edward and Charles Dilly, in the Poultry; and Messrs. Kincaid and Creech at Edinburgh, 1771.

_____. "Preface to a New Edition of the Homilies; as Intended to Have Been Published by Mr. Whitefield." In *The Works of the Rev. George Whitefield*, 4:440-54. London: Printed for Edward and Charles Dilly, in the Poultry; and Messrs. Kincaid and Creech, at Edinburgh, 1771.

_____. "A Preface to the Serious Reader, on Behalf of the Rev. Samuel Clarke's Edition of the Bible." In *The Works of the Rev. George Whitefield*, 4:276-81. London: Printed for Edward and Charles Dilly, in the Poultry; and Messrs. Kincaid and Creech, at Edinburgh, 1771.

_____. "A Preservative Against Unsettled Notions, and Want of Principles, in Regard to Righteousness and Christian Perfection." In *Sermons on Important Sub-*

jects, 131-42. London: Henry Fisher, Son, & P. Jackson, 1828.

_____. "A Recommendatory Preface to the Works of Mr. John Bunyan." In *The Works of the Rev. George Whitefield*, 4:304-08. London: Printed for Edward and Charles Dilly, in the Poultry; and Messrs. Kincaid and Creech, at Edinburgh, 1771.

_____. "Remarks on a Pamphlet Entitled, The Enthusiasm of Methodists and Papists Compared; Wherein Several Mistakes in Some Parts of My Past Writings and Conduct Are Acknowledged, and My Present Sentiments Concerning the Methodists Explained. In a Letter to the Author." In *The Works of the Rev. George Whitefield*, 4:228-49. London: Printed for Edward and Charles Dilly, in the Poultry; and Messrs. Kincaid and Creech, at Edinburgh, 1771.

____. "Repentance and Conversion." In *Sermons on Important Subjects*, 660-69. London: Henry Fisher, Son, & P. Jackson, 1828.

____. "The Resurrection of Lazarus." In *Sermons on Important Subjects*, 440-57. London: Henry Fisher, Son, & P. Jackson, 1828.

_____. "The Righteousness of Christ an Everlasting Righteousness." In *Sermons on Important Subjects*, 197-207. London: Henry Fisher, Son, & P. Jackson, 1828.

_____. "Satan's Devices." In *Sermons on Important Subjects*, 534-42. London: Henry Fisher, Son, & P. Jackson, 1828.

_____. "Saul's Conversion." In *Sermons on Important Subjects*, 469-81. London: Henry Fisher, Son, & P. Jackson, 1828.

_____. "The Seed of the Woman, and the Seed of the Serpent." In *Sermons on Important Subjects*, 33-45. London: Henry Fisher, Son, & P. Jackson, 1828.

_____. "Self-Inquiry Concerning the Work of God." In *Sermons on Important Subjects*, 704-12. London: Henry Fisher, Son, & P. Jackson, 1828.

_____. "A Short Address to Persons of All Denominations, Occasioned By the Alarm of an Intended Invasion, in the Year 1756." In *The Works of the Rev. George Whitefield*, 4:264-74. London: Printed for Edward and Charles Dilly, in the Poultry; and Messrs. Kincaid and Creech, at Edinburgh, 1771.

_____. "Some Remarks Upon a Late Charge Against Enthusiasm, Delivered by the Right Reverend and Father in God, Richard, Lord Bishop of Litchfield and Coventry, to the Reverend and the Clergy in the Several Parts of the Diocess of Litchfield and Coventry, in a Triennial Visitation of the Same in 1741; and Published at Their Request in the Present Year 1744. In a Letter to the Rev. the Clergy of the Diocess." In *The Works of the Rev. George Whitefield*, 4:172-99.London: Printed for Edward and Charles Dilly, in the Poultry; and Messrs. Kincaid and Creech, at Edinburgh, 1771.

_____. "Soul Dejection." In *Sermons on Important Subjects*, 722-29. London: Henry Fisher, Son, & P. Jackson, 1828.

_____. "Soul Prosperity." In *Sermons on Important Subjects*, 640-48. London: Henry Fisher, Son, & P. Jackson, 1828.

_____. "Spiritual Baptism." In *Sermons on Important Subjects*, 730-38. London: Henry Fisher, Son, & P. Jackson, 1828.

_____. "The Temptation of Christ." In *Sermons on Important Subjects*, 216-25. London: Henry Fisher, Son, & P. Jackson, 1828.

_____. "Thankfulness for Mercies Received, A Necessary Duty." In *Sermons on Important Subjects*, 98-106. London: Henry Fisher, Son, & P. Jackson, 1828.

_____. "A Vindication and Confirmation of the Remarkable Work of God in New- England." In *The Works of the Rev. George Whitefield*, 4:76-98. London: Printed for Edward and Charles Dilly, in the Poultry; and Messrs. Kincaid and Creech, at Edinburgh, 1771.

_____. "Walking with God." In *Sermons on Important Subjects*, 46-57. London: Henry Fisher, Son, & P. Jackson, 1828.

_____. "What Think Ye of Christ?" In *Sermons on Important Subjects*, 280-94. London: Henry Fisher, Son, & P. Jackson, 1828.

_____. "The Wise and Foolish Virgins." In *Sermons on Important Subjects*, 295-307. London: Henry Fisher, Son, & P. Jackson, 1828.

_____. "Worldly Business No Plea for the Neglect of Religion." In *Sermons on Important Subjects*, 242-47. London: Henry Fisher, Son, & P. Jackson, 1828.

Secondary Works

Books

Abbey, Charles J., and John H. Overton. *The English Church in the 18th Century.* 2 vols. London: Longmans, Green, and Company, 1878.

Andrews, J. R. *George Whitefield, A Light Rising in Obscurity.* 2nd ed., rev. and enl. London: Morgan & Chase, 1930.

Ashton, T. S. *An Economic History of England: The 18th Century.* London: Methuen & Company, 1955.

Balleine, G. R. *A History of the Evangelical Party in the Church of England.* London: Longmans, 1908.

Barker, Esther T. *Lady Huntingdon, Whitefield and the Wesleys.* Maryville, TN: Esther S. Barker, 1984.

Bebbington, D. W. *Evangelicalism in Modern Britain: A history from the 1730s to the 1980s.* London: Routledge, 2002.

Belcher, Joseph. *George Whitefield: A Biography.* New York: American Tract Society, 1857.

Belden, Albert D. *George Whitefield, the Awakener: A Modern Study of the Evangelical Revival.* New York: Macmillan, 1953.

Bennett, Richard. *The Early Life of Howell Harris.* London: Banner of Truth Trust, 1962.

Berkhof, Louis. *Systematic Theology.* Grand Rapids: Wm. B. Eerdmans Publishing Co., 1941.

Boettner, Lorraine. *The Reformed Doctrine of Predestination.* Philadelphia: The Presbyterian and Reformed Publishing Company, 1965.

Bready, John Wesley. *England: Before and After Wesley: The Evangelical Revival and Social Reform.* London: Hodder and Stoughton, 1938.

Butler, Dugald. *John Wesley and George Whitefield in Scotland, or the Influence of the Oxford Methodist on Scottish Religion.* Edinburgh: W. Blackwood and Sons, 1898.

Caldwell, Mack M. *George Whitefield: Preacher to Millions.* Anderson, IN: The Warner Press, 1929.

Clarkson, George. *George Whitefield and Welsh Calvinistic Methodism.* Lewiston, NY: Edwin Mellen Press, 1996.

Clifford, James L. *Man Versus Society in Eighteenth-Century Britain.* Cambridge: The University Press, 1968.

Cragg, Gerald R. *The Church and the Age of Reason 1648-1789.* London: Penguin Books, 1970.

Crawford, Michael. *Seasons of Grace: Colonial New England's Revival Tradition in Its British Context.* Oxford: Oxford University Press, 1991.

Dallimore, Arnold A. *George Whitefield: The Life and Times of the Great Evanglelist of the Eighteenth-Century Revival.* 2 vols. Edinburgh: Banner of Truth Trust, 1970- 1980.

Dargan, Edwin C. *A History of Preaching*, vol. 2. Grand Rapids: Baker Book House, 1954.

Ferm, Robert L. *Issues in American Protestantism.* Gloucester: Peter Smith, 1976.

Finke, Roger, and Rodney Stark. *The Churching of America, 1776-1990: Winners and Losers in Our Religious Economy.* New Brunswick: Rutgers University Press, 1997.

Gaustad, Edwin Scott. *A Documentary History of Religion in America: To the Civil War.* 2nd ed. Grand Rapids: Eerdmans Publishing Company, 1993.

_____. *The Great Awakening in New England.* New York: Harper & Brothers, 1957.

George, Timothy. *Faithful Witness: The Life and Mission of William Carey.* Birmingham, AL: New Hope, 1991.

Gledstone, James Paterson. *George Whitefield M.A., Field-Preacher.* London: Hodder and Stoughton, 1900.

Grudem, Wayne. *Systematic Theology.* Grand Rapids: Zondervan Publishing House, 1994.

Hardman, Keith. *Seasons of Refreshing: Evangelism and Revivals in America.* Grand Rapids: Baker Books, 1994.

Hardy, Edwin Noah. *George Whitefield, the Matchless Soul Winner.* New York: American Tract Society, 1938.

Harlan, David. *The Clergy and the Great Awakening in New England.* Ann Arbor: UMI Research Press, 1980.

Harley, Timothy. *"George Whitefield," A Lecture, Delivered in Savannah, Georgia, On Monday Evening, December 16th, 1878, By the Rev. Timothy Harley, Pastor of the Baptist Church.* Savannah: Geo. N. Nichols, 1878?.

Henry, Stuart C. *George Whitefield: Wayfaring Witness.* New York: Abingdon Press, 1957.

Hoge, Dean R., Benton Johnson, and Donald A. Luidens. *Vanishing Boundaries.* Louisville: Westminster/John Knox Press, 1994.

Hulse, Erroll. *Give Him No Rest.* Durham, UK: Evangelical Press, 1991.

Kidd, Thomas S. *George Whitefield: America's Spiritual Founding Father.* Camden: Yale University Press, 2014.

_____. *The Great Awakening: A Brief History with Documents.* Boston: Bedford/St. Martin's, 2008.

Jarrett, Derek. *England in the Age of Hogarth.* New Haven: Yale University Press, 1992.

Lambert, Frank. *Inventing the "Great Awakening."* Princeton: Princeton University Press, 1999.

_____. *Pedlar in Divinity: George Whitefield and the Transatlantic Revivals.* Princeton: Princeton University Press, 1994.

Lloyd-Jones, D. M. *The Puritans: Their Origins and Successors.* Carlisle, PA: The Banner of Truth Trust, 1996.

Lovejoy, David. *Religious Enthusiasm and the Great Awakening.* Englewood Cliffs, NJ: Prentice Hall, 1969.

Lovett, Richard. *The History of the London Missionary Society 1795-1895.* Vol. 1. London: Oxford University Press, 1899.

Lumpkin, William Latane. *Baptist Confessions of Faith.* Chicago: Judson Press, 1959.

McConnell, Francis John. *Evangelicals, Revolutionists, and Idealists: Six English Contributors to American Thought and Action.* New York: Abingdon-Cokesbury Press, 1942.

McDow, Malcolm, and Alvin L. Reid. *Firefall: How God Has Shaped History through Revivals.* Nashville: Broadman & Holman Publishers, 1997.

Morden, Peter J. *Offering Christ to the World: Andrew Fuller (1754-1815) and the Revival of Eighteenth Century Particular Baptist Life.* Milton Keynes, UK: Paternoster, 2003.

Murray, Iain H. *Jonathan Edwards: A New Biography.* Edinburgh: The Banner of Truth Trust, 1996.

_____. *Revival and Revivalism: The Making and Marring of American Evangelicalism, 1750-1858.* Edinburgh: The Banner of Truth Trust, 1996.

Noll, Mark A. *A History of Christianity in the United States and Canada.* Grand Rapids: William B. Eerdmans Publishing Company, 1992.

_____. *The Rise of Evangelicalism: The Age of Edwards, Whitefield, and the Wesleys.* Downers Grove: InterVarsity Press, 2003.

Noll, Mark A., David W. Bebbington, and George A. Rawlyk, eds. *Evangelicalism: Comparative Studies of Popular Protestantism in North America, the British Isles, and Beyond, 1700-1990.* Oxford: Oxford University Press, 1994.

Nott, George Frederic. *Religious Enthusiasm Considered; in Eight Sermons, Preached Before the University of Oxford, in the Year MDCCCII. At the Lecture Founded By John Bampton, A. M. Canon of Salisbury.* Oxford: University Press, 1803.

Orr, J. Edwin. *The Event of the Century.* Wheaton, IL: International Awakening Press, 1989.

Overton, John Henry. *The Evangelical Revival in the Eighteenth Century.* London: Longmans, Green, and Co., 1907.

Packer, J. I. *A Quest for Godliness: The Puritan Vision of the Christian Life.* Wheaton, IL: Crossway Books, 1990.

Peirce, Benjamin. *A History of Harvard University: From Its Foundation, in the Year 1636, to the Period of the American Revolution.* Cambridge, MA: Brown, Shattruck, and Company, 1833.

Plummer, Alfred. *The Church of England in the Eighteenth Century.* London: Methuen & Company, 1910.

Pollock, John Charles. *George Whitefield and the Great Awakening.* Garden City: Doubleday, 1972.

Poole-Conner, E. J. *Evangelicalism in England*. Worthing, UK: Henry E. Walter Ltd., 1966.

Porter, Roy. *English Society in the Eighteenth Century*. London: Penguin Books, 1990.

Rainer, Thom. *Effective Evangelistic Churches*. Nashville: Broadman & Holman Publishers, 1996.

Roberts, Richard Owen. *Whitefield in Print*. Wheaton, IL: Richard Owen Roberts Publishers, 1988.

Rupp, E. Gordon. *Religion in England: 1688-1791*. Oxford: Clarendon Press, 1986.

Rutman, Darrett. *The Great Awakening: Event and Exegesis*. Huntington, NY: Robert E. Krieger Publishing Company, 1977.

Salter, Darius. *American Evangelism: Its Theology and Practice*. Grand Rapids: Baker Books, 1996.

Smith, Timothy L. *Whitefield and Wesley on the New Birth*. Grand Rapids: Francis Asbury Press, 1986.

Stearns, Monroe. *The Great Awakening 1720-1760*. New York: Franklin Watts, Inc., 1970.

Stout, Harry. *The Divine Dramatist: George Whitefield and the Rise of Modern Evangelicalism*. Grand Rapids: Eerdmans, 1991.

_____. *The New England Soul: Preaching Religious Culture in Colonial New England*. Oxford: Oxford University Press, 1986.

Sykes, Norman. *Church and State in England in the XVIIIth Century*. Hamden, CT: Archon Books, 1962.

Toon, Peter. *The Emergence of Hyper-Calvinism in English Nonconformity 1689-1765*. London: The Olive Tree, 1967.

Tracy, Joseph. *The Great Awakening*. Boston: Tappan and Dennet, 1842; reprint, Edinburgh: The Banner of Truth Trust, 1997.

Tyerman, Luke. *The Life of the Rev. George Whitefield*. 2 vols. London: Hodder and Stoughton, 1876-1877; reprint, Azle, TX: Need of the Times Publishers, 1995.

Articles

Aldridge, Marion D. "George Whitefield: The Necessary Interdependence of Preaching Style and Sermon Content to Effect Revival." *Journal of the Evangelical Theological Society* 23 (March 1980): 55-64.

Bartlett, Billy Vick. "George Whitefield—Gospel Rover." *Fundamentalist Journal* 4, no. 10 (November 1985): 45-47.

Belden, Albert D. "George Whitefield: His Influence on His Time." *London Quarterly and Holborn Review* 179 (1954): 217-22.

_____. "What America Owes to George Whitefield." *Religion in Life* 20, no. 3 (Summer 1951): 445-49.

Brauer, Jerald C. "Revivalism Revisited." *Journal of Religion* 77 (April 1997): 268-77.

Crump, David. "The Preaching of George Whitefield and His Use of Matthew Henry's Commentary." *Crux* 25 (September 1989): 19-28.

Dallimore, Arnold A. "A Bicentennial Remembrance of George Whitefield." *Methodist History* 9 (January 1971): 16-21.

_____. "The Man Who Loved His Critics." *Christianity Today*, 19 August 1957, 14-16.

Douglas, Walter B. T. "George Whitefield: The Man and His Mission." *Methodist History* 16 (October 1977): 46-53.

Estep, William R. "Doctrines Lead to 'Dunghill,' Prof Warns." *Baptist Standard,* 26 March 1997, 12.

Evans, Richard W. "The Relations of George Whitefield and Howell Harris, Fathers of Calvinistic Methodism." *Church History* 30 (June 1961): 179-90.

Goff, Phillip K. "Spiritual Enrichment and the Bull Market: Balancing the Books of American Religious History." *Religious Studies Review* 22 (April 1996): 106-12.

Harrington, Susan F. "Friendship Under Fire: George Whitefield and John Wesley, 1739-1741." *Andover Newton Quarterly* 15 (January 1975): 167-81.

Hatfield, James Taft. "A Letter From George Whitefield to Count Zinzendorf." *Methodist Review* 79 (November 1897): 913-19.

Houghton, S. M. "George Whitefield and Welsh Methodism." *Evangelical Quarterly* 22 (October 1950): 276-89.

"Humphreys: Calvinism Gaining Influence, Not Numbers." *Western Recorder*, 17 June 1997, 12.

Humphreys, Fisher. "Southern Baptists and Calvinism." *The Theological Educator* 55 (Spring 1997): 11-26.

Kelley, William Valentine. "The Real George Whitefield." *Methodist Review* 96 (September 1914): 779-97.

Lambert, Frank.   "The Great Awakening as Artifact: George Whitefield and the Construction of Intercolonial Revival, 1739-1745." *Church History* 60 (June 1991): 223-46.

_____. "'Pedlar in Divinity': George Whitefield and the Great Awakening, 1737-1745." *The Journal of American History* 77 (December 1990): 812-37.

Marsden, George M. "The Man Who Invented Evangelicalism." *Christianity Today*, 27 April 1992.

Miller, Kevin A. "Did You Know?" *Christian History* 38, no. 2 (1993): 2.

Nettles, Tom. "John Gill and the Evangelical Awakening. In *The Life and Thought of John Gill (1697-1771)*, ed. Michael A.G. Haykin. New York: Brill, 1997.

Nuttall, Geoffrey F. "George Whitefield: A Commemorative Address." *Churchman* 108, no. 4 (1994): 316-27.

Packer, J. I. "A Calvinist–and an Evangelist." In *Serving the People of God*, 2:205-10. Carlisle, PA: Paternoster Press, 1998.

_____. "Introductory Essay." In *The Death of Death in the Death of Christ*, by John Owen, 1-25. Carlisle, PA: The Banner of Truth Trust, 1995.

_____. "The Spirit with the Word: The Reformational Revivalism of George Whitefield." In *The Bible, the Reformation and the Church*, ed. W. P. Stephens. Sheffield, UK: Sheffield Academic Press, 1995.

Polk, Seth N. "The Theology and Methods of George Whitefield." *Journal of the American Society for Church Growth* 14 (Spring 2003): 3-16.

Reist, Irwin W. "John Wesley and George Whitefield: A Study in the Integrity of Two Theologies of Grace." *Evangelical Quarterly* 47 (January-March 1975): 26-40.

Rogal, Samuel J. "Toward a Mere Civil Friendship: Benjamin Franklin and George Whitefield." *Methodist History* 35, no. 4 (July 1997): 233-43.

Stetzer, Ed. "Why We Should Be Inviting Our Non-Christian Friends and Neighbors to Church at Easter," *Christianity Today.* http://www.christianitytoday.com/edstetzer/2017/april/why-we-should-be-inviting-our-non-christian-friends-and-nei.html (accessed September 4, 2017).

Stone, Lawrence. "Literacy and Education in England 1640-1900." *Past and Present* 42 (1969): 69-139.

Thompson, William Joseph. "George Whitefield: Educator and University Founder." *Methodist Review* 109 (May 1926): 340-55.

Tresch, John W., Jr. "The Reception Accorded George Whitefield in the Southern Colonies." *Methodist History* 6 (January 1968): 17-26.

Zehrer, Karl. "The Relationship Between Pietism in Halle and Early Methodism." *Methodist History* 17 (July 1979): 211-24.

Dissertations and Theses

Conrad, Flavius Leslie, Jr. "The Preaching of George Whitefield, with Special Reference to the American Colonies: A Study of His Published Sermons." Ph.D. diss., Temple University, 1959.

Houser, William G. "Identifying the Regenerate: the Homiletics of Conversion during the First Great Awakening." Ph.D. diss., University of Notre Dame, 1988.

Marsh, Roger A. "Diminishing Respect for the Clergy and the First Great Awakening: A Study in the Antecedents of Revival Among Massachusetts Congregationalists, 1630-1741." Ph.D. diss., Baylor University, 1990.

McCarty, Michael T. The Internal Congruity of George Whitefield's Letters, 1735-1742: A Word Frequency Analysis." M.A. thesis, Mississippi State University, 1990.

McVicker, W. Blaine. "A Study of the Contemplative Life of George Whitefield in the Context of the Eighteenth Century Society." D.Min. diss., Fuller Theological Seminary, 1999.

Olivas, J. Richard. "Great Awakenings: Time, Space, and the Varieties of Religious Revivalism in Massachusetts and Northern New England, 1740-1748." Ph.D. diss., University of California, 1997.

Pierce, Roderic Hall. "George Whitefield and His Critics." Ph.D. diss., Princeton University, 1962.

Schwenk, James Lee. "The Wesleyan/Whitefieldian Paradigm: The Quest For Evangelical Ecumenicity in Eighteenth Century British Methodism." Ph.D. diss., Drew University, 1999.

Smith, Lisa Herb. "The First Great Awakening in American Newspapers, 1739-48." Ph.D. diss., University of Delaware, 1998.

Thompson, William Oscar, Jr. "The Public Invitation as a Method of Evangelism: Its Origin and Development." Ph.D. diss., Southwestern Baptist Theological Seminary, 1979.

81424468R00185

Made in the USA
Columbia, SC
21 November 2017